CATHOLIC CONSCIENCE
FOUNDATION AND FORMATION

CATHOLIC CONSCIENCE FOUNDATION AND FORMATION

Proceedings of
The Tenth Bishops' Workshop
Dallas, Texas

Russell E. Smith
Editor

THE POPE JOHN CENTER

The Workshop for Bishops along with publication of the proceedings was made possible through a generous grant from

The Knights of Columbus.
New Haven, Connecticut

Nihil Obstat: Reverend James A. O'Donohoe, J.D.C.

Imprimatur: Bernard Cardinal Law   Date: November 22, 1991

The Nihil Obstat and Imprimatur are a declaration that a book or pamphlet is considered to be free from doctrinal or moral error. It is not implied that those who have granted the Nihil Obstat and Imprimatur agree with the contents, opinions or statements expressed.

Library of Congress Cataloging-in-Publication Data

Catholic conscience : foundation and formation : proceedings of the Tenth Bishops' Workshop, Dallas, Texas / Russell E. Smith, editor.
    p. cm.
    "The Pope John Center presented its tenth Workshop for Bishops from February 4–8, 1991"—Pref.
    Includes bibliographical references.
    ISBN 0–935372–32–6
    1. Conscience—Religious aspects—Catholic Church—Congresses. 2. Catholic Church—Doctrines—Congresses. 3. Christian ethics—Catholic authors—Congresses. I. Smith, Russell E. (Russell Edward) II. Pope John XXIII Medical-Moral Research and Education Center. III. Workshop for Bishops of the United States and Canada (10th : 1991 : Dallas, Tex.)
BJ1278.C66C38   1992
241'.1—dc20   91–39209
                                                                                CIP

CONTRIBUTORS TO THIS VOLUME

The Reverend Benedict Ashley, O.P., Ph.D.
Professor of Theology
Pope John Paul II Institute on Marriage and the Family
Washington, DC

The Reverend John Catoir, J.C.D.
Director, The Christophers
New York, NY

The Reverend Avery Dulles, S.J., S.T.D.
Laurence J. McGinley Professor of Theology
Fordham University
Bronx, NY

Mary Ellen Garvey-O'Brien
Family Counselling Service
Worcester, MA

Professor Robert George, Ph.D.
Professor Law and Politics
Princeton University
Princeton, NJ

The Reverend James Gill, S.J., M.D.
Senior Consultant in Psychiatry
Institute for Living, Hartford, CT
Associate Clinical Professor of Psychiatry
University of Connecticut School of Medicine
Founder, Editor-in-Chief, *Human Development*

The Reverend Richard Gula, S.S., Ph.D.
Professor of Moral Theology
St. Patrick's Seminary
Menlo Park, CA

Professor John Haas, Ph.D.
St. Charles Seminary
Overbrook, PA

Paul Lauer
Founder, Editor-in-Chief, *Veritàs Communications*
Los Angeles, CA

The Reverend James LeBar
Consultant on Cults
Archdiocese of New York

Sister Mary Louise Lyons, D.C.
President/CEO
St. Agnes Hospital
Baltimore, MD

The Reverend Monsignor James Mulligan
Director, Priestly Life and Formation
Diocese of Allentown

The Very Reverend Paul Philibert, O.P., Ph.D.
Provincial, Southern Dominican Province
New Orleans, LA

Bill Plante
White House/State Department Correspondent
CBS News
Washington, DC

Frank Shakespeare
Director, Heritage Foundation
Director, Bradley Foundation
Past President, CBS Television Services
Past President, RKO General, Inc.
Former US Ambassador to Portugal
Former US Ambassador to the Holy See

The Most Reverend Donald Wuerl, S.T.D.
Bishop of Pittsburgh

Contents

The Pope John Center presented its tenth Workshop for Bishops from February 4–8, 1991. This gathering was again made possible through a generous grant from the Knights of Columbus. Several hundred bishops from Canada, the United States of America, Mexico, the Caribbean and the Philippines gathered for a week of study, reflection and prayer.

The Pope John Center began these workshops in 1980. Workshops have occurred every year since, with the exceptions of 1982 and 1986. Each workshop concentrated on a specific topic or cluster of topics in the field of medical ethics. These proceedings are published in book form and are all still available from the Pope John Center. The titles are as follows:

New Technologies of Birth and Death (1980)

Human Sexuality and Personhood (1981) (now being revised for reprinting)

Technological Powers and the Person (1983)

Moral Theology Today: Certitudes and Doubts (1984)

The Family Today and Tomorrow: The Church Addresses Her Future (1985)

Scarce Medical Resources and Justice (1987)

Reproductive Technologies, Marriage and the Church (1988) (a detailed examination of the then recently published *Instruction* on Respect for Human Life in its Origin and on the Dignity of Procreation [*Donum vitae*])

Critical Issues in Contemporary Health Care (1989)

The Twenty-Fifth Anniversary of Vatican II: A Look Back and A Look Ahead

* * * * *

The theme of the 1991 Workshop was *Catholic Conscience: Foundation and Formation*. This theme is certainly broader than the specific arena of bioethics; however, "conscience" is a fundamental principle of ethics. As such, applied ethics presumes a clear understanding of conscience. But experience teaches that the notion of conscience is anything but clear at any level— whether in catechetics or in moral theology. It was therefore decided that an entire workshop should be devoted to this foundational reality.

Conscience is an organ intimately joined to the humanness of our humanity. It is the organ by which we engage in genuinely human activity, i.e., moral activity, freely chosen acts by which we assume a particular moral character. It is an organ like the eye, by which we see, not always clearly, the meaning of our world and our actions.

This moral sense grows and develops. It does not come to us like a pre-programmed hard disc. Conscience is a capacity to judge the moral value of actions through the knowledge it acquires from qualified teachers in the school of human nature, preeminently the Catholic Church. Its method of formation is more total than education. By means of conscience one relates to the world through knowledge of moral truth and love for that truth as a genuine good. For Christians, this love is the primary virtue that is cultivated by practice. This practice is rooted in and flowers forth from a spiritual life which is a sharing in the grace of Christ. His grace imparts motivation and strength in dealing with those one loves and with those one cannot love so well. In the end, everything is done for love of Him. This love also will enlighten compassion for oneself and others whose own love is either weak or side-tracked. By being living examples of the truth one professes, others will be encouraged in their own struggle to grow in virtue and will be attracted by the authenticity they experience by seeing genuine christian life in action. In this way, others' hearts will be warmed by the intensity of christians' love for Christ and desire to be like Him.

* * * * *

The year preceding this Workshop was an important one for the field of moral theology. The Congregation for the Doctrine of the Faith issued and *Instruction on the Ecclesial Vocation of the Theologian* on Ascension Thursday. The Synod of Bishops was convened on September 30 (the Feast of St. Jerome) to study Priestly Formation. The Feast of the Immaculate Conception was the twenty-fifth anniversary of the conclusion of the Second Vatican Council. A clear understanding of conscience is essential to appreciate the significance of the Church's message.

His Eminence, Joseph Cardinal Ratzinger delivered the keynote address, "Conscience and Truth." Father Benedict Ashley and Jesuit psychiatrist Father James Gill addressed the theological and psychological elements of the formation of conscience. A structured dialogue addressed the need for an adequate method in moral theology and in the formation of conscience. Father Philibert presented the major address with responses by Father Richard Gula and Professor John Haas.

Moral teaching in the formation of consciences as integral to the mission of the Church was the subject of the second structured dialogue. Bishop Donald Wuerl, of Pittsburgh, presented the major paper, with responses by Father Avery Dulles and Monsignor James Mulligan.

These major theoretical presentations were followed by examinations of several issues related to the conscience of various groups of individuals: the captive, the addicted, the Catholic health-care institution and the Catholic public person. Father James LeBar spoke about conscience vis-à-vis cult membership and demonic possession. Psychologist Mary Ellen Garvey-O'Brien spoke of addiction's affect on conscience. Sister Mary Louise Lyons spoke about maintaining the Catholic identity of our health-care institutions and the difficult decisions that face the administrators and boards in the present day. Professor Robert George addressed the issue of conscience and the public person, particularly the politician.

The Workshop concluded with a panel discussion on the relationship between the Church and the media. Various specialists spoke from their experience in various media industries. Archbishop John Foley, president of the Pontifical Council for Social Communications moderated the panel discussion. Father John Catoir, director of the Christophers, Paul Lauer, founder and editor of *YOU!* Magazine, Frank Shakespeare, former president of CBS television services (among many other things), and Bill Plante, State Department reporter for CBS News, comprised the panel.

The text of two plenary discussions with Cardinal Ratzinger round out the proceedings. The first plenary discussion occurred at the end of the keynote address. The other was an open forum which occurred on the last day of the Workshop.

We present this collection of essays to those who are engaged in the pastoral and health care ministries of the Church. We hope that this volume finds its way to seminary libraries and houses of religious formation to assist those who must know and communicate the message of the Church. For the same reason, we offer this volume to all the Catholic faithful, and to those beyond her borders who wish to know her teaching and understand its application. *"Tolle, lege . . . fruere!"*

* * * * *

Many people contributed generously to the successful execution of the 1990 Workshop for Bishops. The planning, content and hospitality necessary for an international event of this magnitude depend on many hard-working, self-sacrificing individuals who obviously love the Church very much. We are very grateful to everyone who made this Workshop such a success.

We are very grateful to the Supreme Knight, Mr. Virgil C. Dechant, and to the Knights of Columbus for their generous sponsorship of this workshop. We are also very grateful to the faculty of this year's workshop, for their patience with the many deadlines and for their scholarly competence and presentations.

Special thanks go to the Most Reverend Charles V. Grahmann, Bishop of Dallas, for his gracious hospitality. Thanks also to the staff and seminarians of Holy Trinity Seminary at the University of Dallas for serving the Masses, singing, and acting as sacristans. In this regard, special thanks go to Father Thomas Cloherty for overseeing all the liturgical arrangements. We are also very grateful to the local councils of the Knights of Columbus and the Catholic Women's Guilds of the Diocese of Dallas for their kind assistance. Thanks also to the Spanish translators—Father Rudy Vela, S.M. and Father Alberto F. Bueno, T.O.R. from San Antonio and Fort Worth.

We are also grateful to the staff of the Doubletree Hotel at Lincoln Centre in Dallas for their graciousness and service. A very special word of thanks goes to the Nuns of the Poor Clare Federation of Mary Immaculate who prayed for the success and for the participants of the conference. Finally, we are deeply grateful to Mrs. Jeanne Burke and Mr. Donald Powers for their indefatigable effort and diligent assistance from the beginning of this Workshop's conception to the moment this book was delivered to your hands.

The Reverend Russell E. Smith, S.T.D.
Editor

Feast of Sts. Peter and Paul, 1991
Boston, Massachusetts.

To My Brother Bishops
taking part in the Tenth Workshop organized by the
"Pope John XXIII Medical-Moral Research and
Education Center"

1. It is with great joy in Christ Jesus that I greet you as you gather in Dallas, Texas, for a time of study, reflection and prayer. As Pastors of the Christian faithful from many dioceses in Canada, the Caribbean, Central America, Mexico, the Philippines and the United States, you intend to reflect on important moral issues in the light of the teachings of the Gospel of our Lord Jesus Christ and of the Magisterium of his Church. This is the tenth such Workshop organized by the "Pope John XXIII Medical-Moral research and Education Center", and is therefore a fitting moment to express appreciation for the commitment and dedication of all who have had a part in the realization of this project. Again, I thank the Knights of Columbus who, by their generosity, provide the opportunity for you to come together in communion with one another and in union of spirit with the Successor of Peter.

2. The general theme of your Workshop, "Catholic Conscience: Foundation and Formation", embraces a wide range of topics that are basic to catechetical and pastoral activity at every level of Church life. The role of conscience in the Christian life was clearly addressed by the Second Vatican Council and has been constantly present in subsequent Papal teaching. It is all the more surprising therefore that in the years since the Council some Christian doctrine programs have not paid sufficient attention to this chapter of the Council's teaching, namely that in the depths of their conscience "individuals discover a law which

they do not make for themselves but which they are bound to obey, whose voice, ever summoning them to love and do what is good and to avoid what is evil, rings in their hearts when necessary with the command: Do this, keep away from that. For inscribed in their hearts by God, human beings have a law whose observance is their dignity and in accordance with which they are to be judged" (*Gaudium et spes,* 16).

In some cases, the character and attributes of this law have been questioned in such a way as to relativize completely the moral order. This is to disregard the Council's clear teaching that "the supreme rule of life is the divine law itself, the eternal, objective and universal law by which God, out of his wisdom and love, arranges directs and governs the whole world and the paths of the human community" (*Dignitatis humanae,* 3). In fidelity to the Council, I repeated this teaching in my Encyclical on the Holy Spirit: "The capacity to command what is good and to forbid evil, placed in man by the Creator, *is the main characteristic of the personal subject* . . . Conscience is the 'secret sanctuary' in which '*God's voice echoes*' " (*Dominum et Vivificantem,* 43; cf. *Gaudium et spes,* 16). I am convinced that a greater effort on the part of Pastors and teachers to present the Church's doctrine on conscience is a fundamental prerequisite of the duty to *defend and promote the dignity of the human person,* a dignity which comes from God who created man with the capacity to know his truth and to follow that truth with reverential love.

3. It is through the working of an upright conscience that an individual plays an active and responsible part in the universal drama that is the history of salvation. The fullness of truth is revealed in Jesus Christ who "fully reveals man to himself" (*Redemptor hominis,* 10). Although the Human heart is darkened by sin (cf. Rom 1: 18-25; *Gaudium et spes,* 13), God revealed his redemptive plan in the Paschal Mystery of the Incarnate Word. Man "must, so to speak, enter into Christ with all his own self, he must 'appropriate' and assimilate the whole of the reality of the Incarnation and Redemption in order to find himself" (*Redemptor Hominis,* 10).

Conscience reveals an inner call *from* and *towards* Love, and urges a loving response to that call. As I wrote in my Apostolic Exhortation *Reconciliatio et Paenitentia,* the "*mystery of God's infinite loving kindness towards us* is capable of penetrating to the hidden roots of our iniquity, in order to evoke in the soul a movement of conversion, in order to redeem it and set it on course towards reconciliation" (No. 20). The formation of a Christian conscience should ensure that "the *loving kindness of God* towards the Christian (is) matched by the *piety of the Christian* towards God . . . Piety means precisely the conduct of the Christian who responds to God's fatherly loving kindness with his own filial piety" (*ibid.,* 21), a peity that is not a merely subjective sentiment but an attitude of profound respect for the objective nature of all truth, including the truth of the moral law. A proper presentation of the doctrine on conscience is therefore integral to the Christian anthropology so clearly delineated by the Pastoral Constitution *Gaudium et spes,* and so succinctly summarized in these words: "man, who is the only creature on earth that God willed for its own sake, cannot fully find himself except through a sincere gift of self" (No. 24; cf. *Dominum et Vivificantem,* 59).

4. A positive development in the years since the Council can be noted in the attention given to the Council's call to transcend a narrow, individualistic morality through openness to the social dimension of Christian moral life (cf. *Gaudium et spes,* 30). In the formation of conscience there has been an increased general awareness that there are norms of social conduct and responsibility which one must observe, especially toward the "least of the Lord's brethren" (cf. Mt. 25:40). This trend must be consolidated through a more complete and incisive presentation of the Church's social doctrine. In this year dedicated to the Social Doctrine of the Church I appeal to you to make this a point of reference of your pastoral ministry.

May the Holy Spirit guide you, my dear brother Bishops, in the ways of wisdom and understanding as you reflect on the important issues of our human dignity in Christ and the nobility of conscience. May the Lord help you to explain the truths of faith and apply them with prudence and compassion, remembering that "it is an outstanding manifestation of charity towards souls to omit nothing from the saving doctrine of Christ" (*Humanae vitae,* 29). And may the intercession of the Blessed Virgin Mary,

Seat of Wisdom and Cause of our Joy, assist you in your service to the People of God. To all of you I joyfully impart my Apostolic Blessing.

From the Vatican, January 19, 1991

Joannes Paulus PP. II

GREETINGS FROM THE
KNIGHTS OF COLUMBUS

Virgil C. Dechant
Supreme Knight

Your Eminences, Your Excellencies, Reverend Monsignors and Fathers, Religious, Distinguished Presenters and guests:

Once again it is my privilege to present a few words of welcome at the beginning of this Tenth Workshop of Bishops. The Knights of Columbus are happy to renew our collaboration with the Pope John Center in affording this opportunity to our bishops. Experience has shown that this gathering has a multitude of benefits, first among which is educational. This Workshop allows Your Excellencies to update your knowledge of current moral, doctrinal, medical, and sociological thinking on the vital issues of life and death. Many bishops have pointed out to me that the information obtained in these few days in Dallas can only otherwise be had by weeks of intensive study and reading—time that they can ill afford.

Of course, we cannot forget the spiritual dimension. Not only do we work together we also pray together at the morning Liturgy and at afternoon prayer. Other bishops have told me that for them these days take on the atmosphere of a mini-retreat. Then there are the fellowship aspects enabling bishops of the many countries represented to form friendships, to get to know one another, to share experiences on a one to one basis. So, as this opening session begins, the Knights want to assure you of our prayers, that the week will be all that you want it to be and that the Holy Spirit will inspire you toward that end.

Please allow me to convey a personal welcome to our distinguished guest, His Eminence, Joseph Cardinal Ratzinger. We know that the burdens of his office may sometimes be heavy. But we also want him to know how much we appreciate his devotion to the Holy Father, to the Universal Church and to the Magisterium. We Knights are especially grateful for the personal interest he has taken in the progress of the Pope John Paul II Institute for Studies on Marriage and the Family in Washington, D.C., another initiative of the Order.

May I also welcome His Excellency Archbishop John Foley. We have collaborated over many years with him, and with his illustrious predecessor, in the satellite up-link program which brings the Holy Father's Christmas and Holy Week ceremonies and other special events to a world-wide television audience.

On behalf of the Knights—and I am indeed proud that many of you here are brother Knights—let me express a word of thanks to Archbishop Levada, to the Board, to Monsignor Roy Klister and to the staff of Pope John XXIII Center. In the final analysis they are the ones who put this Workshop together.

I close at this time of war in the Persian Gulf with the words of a message I wrote to my brother Knights and their families for the February issue of our publication *Knightline:* "I want to add my voice to those of our spiritual leaders, our parents, our fathers and mothers, urging us to pray for peace. Our Blessed Mother, Mary Queen of Peace, has assured us in her many apparitions that prayers for peace will be heard. If we can do nothing else, we can pray. And we can work together for a world order in which dictators and terrorists will never again be tempted to resort to arms. Let us pray together to a speedy end to this conflict and look to the day war will be recognized as the anachronism it is."

Thank you very much.

CONSCIENCE AND TRUTH

His Eminence
Joseph Cardinal Ratzinger

In the contemporary discussion on what constitutes the essence of morality and how it can be recognized, the question of conscience has become paramount, especially in the field of Catholic Moral Theology. This discussion centers on the concepts of freedom and norm, autonomy and heteronomy, self-determination and external determination by authority. Conscience appears here as the bulwark of freedom in contrast to encroachments of authority on existence. In the course of this, two notions of the Catholic are set in opposition to each other. One is a renewed understanding of the Catholic essence which expounds Christian faith from the basis of freedom and as the very principle of freedom itself. The other is a superseded, "pre-conciliar" model, which subjects Christian existence to authority, regulating life even into its most intimate preserves, and thereby attempts to maintain control over people's lives. Morality of conscience and morality of authority, as two opposing models, appear to be locked in struggle with each other. Accordingly, the freedom of the Christian would be rescued by appeal to the classical principle of moral tradition that conscience is the highest norm which man is to follow even in opposition to authority. Authority, in this case, the Magisterium, may well speak of matters moral, but only in the sense of presenting conscience with material for its own deliberation. Conscience would retain, however, the final word. Some authors reduce conscience in this its aspect of final arbiter to the formula: conscience is infallible.[1]

Nonetheless, at this point, a contradiction can arise. It is of course undisputed that one must follow a certain conscience, or at least not act against it. But whether the judgment of conscience, or what one takes to be such, is always right, indeed whether it is infallible, is another question. For if this were the case, it would mean that there is no truth—at least not in moral and religious matters, which is to say, in the areas which constitute the very pillars of our existence. For judgments of conscience can contradict each other. Thus there could be at best the subject's own truth, which would be reduced to the subject's sincerity. No door or window would lead from the subject into the broader world of being and human solidarity. Whoever thinks this through will come to the realization that no real freedom exists then and that the supposed pronouncements of conscience are but the reflection of social circumstances. This should necessarily lead to the conclusion that placing freedom in opposition to authority overlooks something. There must be something deeper, if freedom and, therefore, human existence are to have meaning.

1. A CONVERSATION ON THE ERRONEOUS CONSCIENCE AND FIRST INFERENCES

It has become apparent that the question of conscience leads in fact to the core of the moral problem and thus to the question of man's existence itself. I would now like to pursue this question, not in the form of a strictly conceptual and therefore unavoidably abstract presentation, but by way of narrative, as one might say today, by relating, to begin with, the story of my own encounter with this problem. I first became aware of the question with all its urgency in the beginning of my academic teaching. In the course of a dispute, a senior colleague, who was keenly aware of the plight to being Christian in our times, expressed the opinion that one should actually be grateful to God that He allows there to be so many unbelievers in good conscience. For if their eyes were opened and they became believers, they would not be capable, in this world of ours, of bearing the burden of faith with all its moral obligations. But as it is, since they can go another way in good conscience, they can still reach salvation. What shocked me about this assertion was not in the first place the idea of an erroneous conscience given by God Himself in order to save men by means of such artfulness—the idea, so to speak, of a blindness sent by God for the salvation of those in question. What disturbed me was the notion it harbored that faith is a burden which can hardly be borne and which no doubt was intended only for stronger natures—faith almost as a kind of punishment, in any case, an imposition not easily coped with. According to this view, faith would not make salvation easier but harder. Being happy would mean not being burdened with having to believe or having to submit to the moral yoke of the faith of the Catholic Church. The erroneous conscience, which makes life easier and marks a more human course, would then be the real grace, the normal way to salvation. Untruth, keeping truth at bay, would be better for man than truth. It would not be the truth that would set him free, but rather he would have to be freed from the truth. Man would be more at home in the dark than in the light. Faith would not be the good gift of the good God but instead an affliction. If this were the state of affairs, how could faith give rise to joy? Who would have the courage to pass faith on to others? Would it not be better to spare them the truth or even keep them from it? In the last few decades, notions of this sort have discernably crippled the disposition to evangelize. The one who sees the faith as a heavy burden or as a moral imposition is unable to invite others to believe. Rather he lets them be, in the putative freedom of their good consciences.

The one who spoke in this matter was a sincere believer, and, I would say, a strict Catholic who performed his moral duty with care and conviction. But he expressed a form of experience of faith which is disquieting. Its propagation could only be fatal to the faith. The almost traumatic aversion many have to what they hold to be "preconciliar" Catholicism is rooted, I am convinced, in the encounter with such a faith seen only as encumbrance. In this regard, to be sure, some very basic questions arise. Can such a faith actually be an encounter with truth? Is the truth about God and man so sad and difficult, or does truth not lie in the overcoming of such legalism? Does it not lie in freedom? But where does freedom lead? What course does it chart for us? At the conclusion, we shall come back to these fundamental problems of Christian existence today, but before we do that, we must return to the core of our topic, namely, the matter of conscience. As I said, what unsettled me in the argument just recounted was first of all the caricature of faith I perceived in it. In a second course of reflection, it occurred to me further that the concept of conscience which it implied must also be wrong. The erroneous conscience, by sheltering the person from the exacting demands of truth, saves him—thus went the argument. Conscience appeared here not as a window through which one can see outward to that common truth which founds and sustains us all, and so makes possible through the common recognition of truth the community of wants and responsibilities. Conscience here does not mean man's openness to the ground of his being, the power of perception for what is highest and most essential. Rather it appears as subjectivity's protective shell into which man can escape and there hide from reality. Liberalism's idea of conscience was in fact presupposed here. Conscience does not open the way to the redemptive road to truth which either does not exist or, if it does, is too demanding. It is the faculty which dispenses from truth. It thereby becomes the justification for subjectivity, which would not like to have itself called into question. Similarly, it becomes the justification for social conformity. As mediating value between the different subjectivities, social conformity is intended to make living together possible. The obligation to seek the truth terminates, as do any doubts about the general inclination of society and what it has become accustomed to. Being convinced of oneself, as well as conforming to others, are sufficient. Man is reduced to his superficial conviction, and the less depth he has, the better for him.

What I was only dimly aware of in this conversation became glaringly clear a little later in a dispute among colleagues about the justifying power of the erroneous conscience. Objecting to this thesis, someone countered that if this were so then the SS-people would be justified and we should seek them in heaven since they carried out all their atrocities with fanatic conviction and complete certainty of conscience. Another responded with utmost assurance that of course this was indeed the case. There is no doubting the fact that Hitler and his accomplices, who were deeply convinced of their cause, could not have acted otherwise. Therefore, the objective terribleness of their deeds notwithstanding, they acted morally, subjectively speaking. Since they followed their albeit mistaken consciences, one would have to recognize their conduct as moral and, as a result, should not doubt their eternal salvation. Since that conversation I knew with complete certainty that something was wrong with the theory of the justifying power of the subjective conscience, that, in other words, a concept of conscience which leads to such results must be false. Firm, subjective conviction and the lack of doubts and scruples which follow therefrom do not justify man. Some thirty years later, in the terse words of psychologist Albert Görres, I found summarized the perceptions I was trying to articulate. The elaboration of his insights forms the heart of this address. Görres shows that the feeling of guilt, the capacity to recognize guilt, belongs essentially to the spiritual make-up of man. This feeling of guilt disturbs the false calm of conscience and could be called conscience's complaint against my self-satisfied existence. It is as necessary for man as the physical pain which signifies disturbances of normal bodily functioning. Whoever is no longer capable of perceiving guilt is spiritually ill, "a living corpse, a dramatic character's mask," as Görres says.[2] "Monsters, among other brutes, are the ones without guilt feelings. Perhaps Hitler did not have any, or Himmler, or Stalin. Maybe Mafia bosses do not have any guilt feelings either, or maybe their remains are just well hidden in the cellar. Even aborted guilt feelings . . . All men need guilt feelings."[3]

By the way, a look into Sacred Scripture should have precluded such diagnoses and such a theory of justification by the errant conscience. In Psalm 19: 12–13, we find the ever worth pondering passage: "But who can discern his errors? Clear thou me from my unknown faults." That is not Old Testament objectivism, but profoundest human wisdom. No longer seeing one's guilt, the falling silent of conscience in so many areas, is an even more dangerous sickness of the soul than the guilt which one still recognizes as such. He who no longer notices that killing is a sin has fallen further than the one who still recognizes the shamefulness of his actions, because the former is further removed from the truth and conversion. Not without reason does the self-righteous man in the encounter with Jesus appear as the one who is really lost. If the tax collector with all his undisputed sins stands more justified before God than the pharisee with all his undeniably good works (Luke 18: 9–14), this is not because the sins of the tax collector were not sins or the good deeds of the pharisee, not good deeds. Nor does it mean that the good that man does is not good before God, or the evil, not evil or at least not particularly important. The reason for this paradoxical judgment of God is shown precisely from our question. The pharisee no longer knows that he too has guilt. He has a completely clear conscience. But this silence of conscience makes him impenetrable to God and men, while the cry of conscience which plagues the tax collector makes him capable of truth and love. Jesus can move sinners. Not hiding behind the screen of their erroneous consciences, they have not become unreachable for the change which God expects of them—of us. He is ineffective with the "righteous," because they are not aware of any need for forgiveness and conversion. Their consciences no longer accuse them but justify them.

We find something similar in Saint Paul, who tells us, that the pagans, even without the law, knew quite well what God expected of them (Romans 2: 1–16). The whole theory of salvation through ignorance breaks apart with this verse: There is present in man the truth, that is not to be repulsed, that one truth of the creator which in the revelation of salvation history has also been put in writing. Man can see the truth of God from the fact of his creaturehood. Not to see it is guilt. It is not seen because man does not want to see it. The "no" of the will which hinders recognition is guilt. The fact that the signal lamp does not shine is the consequence of a deliberate looking away from that which we do not wish to see.[4]

At this point of our reflections, it is possible to draw some initial conclusions with a view toward answering the question regarding the essence of conscience. We can now say: it will not do to identify man's conscience with the self-consciousness if the I, with its subjective certainty about itself and its moral behavior. On the one hand, this consciousness may be a mere reflection of the social surroundings and the opinions in circulation. On the other hand, it might also derive from a lack of self-criticism, a deficiency in listening to the depths of one's own soul. This diagnosis is confirmed by what has come to light since the fall of Marxist systems in Eastern Europe. The noblest and keenest minds of the liberated peoples speak of an enormous spiritual devastation which appeared in the years of the intellectual deformation. They speak of a blunting of the moral sense which is a more significant loss and danger than the economic damage which was done. The new patriarch of Moscow stressed this poignantly in the summer of 1990. The power of perception of people who lived in a system of deception was darkened. The society lost the capacity for mercy, and human feelings were forsaken. A whole generation was lost for the good, lost for humane deeds. "We must lead society back to the eternal moral values," that is to say, open ears almost gone deaf, so that once again the promptings of God might be heard in human hearts. Error, the "erring" conscience, is only at first convenient. But then the silencing of conscience leads to the dehumanization of the world and to moral danger, if one does not work against it.

To put it differently, the identification of conscience with superficial consciousness, the reduction of man to his subjectivity, does not liberate but enslaves. It makes us totally dependent on the prevailing opinions and debases these with every passing day. Whoever equates conscience with superficial conviction, identifies conscience with a pseudo-rational certainty, a certainty which in fact has been woven from self-righteousness, conformity, and lethargy. Conscience is degraded to a mechanism for rationalization, while it should represent the transparency of the subject for the divine and thus constitute the very dignity and greatness of man. Conscience's reduction to subjective certitude betokens at the same time a retreat from truth. When the psalmist in anticipation of Jesus' view of sin and justice pleads for liberation from unconscious guilt, he points to the following relation. Certainly, one must follow an erroneous conscience. But the departure from truth which took place beforehand and now takes its revenge is the actual guilt which first lulls man into false security and then abandons him in the trackless waste.

2. NEWMAN AND SOCRATES: GUIDES TO CONSCIENCE

At this juncture, I would like to make a temporary digression. Before we attempt to formulate reasonable answers to the questions regarding the essence of conscience, we must first widen the basis of our considerations somewhat, going beyond the personal which has thus far constituted our point of departure. To be sure, my purpose is not to try to develop a scholarly study on the history of theories of conscience, a subject on which different contributions have appeared just recently in fact.[5] I would prefer rather to stay with our approach thus far of example and narrative. A first glance should be directed to Cardinal Newman, whose life and work could be designated a single great commentary on the question of conscience. Nor should Newman be treated in a technical way. The given framework does not permit us to weigh the particulars of Newman's concept of conscience. I would simply like to try to indicate the place of conscience in the whole of Newman's life and thought. The insights gained from this will hopefully sharpen our view of present problems and establish the link to history, that is, both to the great witnesses of conscience and to the origin of the Christian doctrine of living according to conscience. When the subject of Newman and conscience is raised, the famous sentence from his letter to the Duke of Norfolk immediately comes to mind: "Certainly, if I am obliged to bring religion into afterdinner toasts, (which indeed does not seem quite the thing), I shall drink—to the Pope, if you please,—still, to conscience first, and to the Pope afterwards."[6] In contrast to the statements of

Gladstone, Newman sought to make a clear avowal of the papacy. And in contrast to mistaken forms of ultramontanism, Newman embraced an interpretation of the papacy, which is only then correctly conceived when it is viewed together with the primacy of conscience—a papacy not put in opposition to the primacy of conscience but based on it and guaranteeing it. Modern man, who presupposes the opposition of authority to subjectivity, has difficulty understanding this. For him, conscience stands on the side of subjectivity and is the expression of the freedom of the subject. Authority, on the other hand, appears to him as the constraint on, threat to, and even negation of freedom. So then we must go deeper to recover a vision in which this kind of opposition does not obtain.

For Newman the middle term which establishes the connection between authority and subjectivity is truth. I do not hesitate to say that truth is the central thought of Newman's intellectual grappling. Conscience is central for him because truth stands in the middle. To put it differently, the centrality of the concept conscience for Newman is linked to the prior centrality of the concept truth and can only be understood from this vantage point. The dominance of the idea of conscience in Newman does not signify that he, in the nineteenth century, and in contrast to "objectivistic" neoscholasticism, espoused a philosophy or theology of subjectivity. Certainly, the subject finds in Newman an attention which it had not received in Catholic theology perhaps since Saint Augustine. But it is an attention in the line of Augustine and not in that of the subjectivist philosophy of the modern age. On the occasion of his elevation to Cardinal, Newman declared that most of his life was a struggle against the spirit of liberalism in religion; we might add, also against Christian subjectivism, as he found it in the Evangelical movement of his time and which admittedly had provided him the first step on his lifelong road to conversion.[7] Conscience for Newman does not mean that the subject is the standard vis-à-vis the claims of authority in a truthless world, a world which lives from the compromise between the claims of the subject and the claims of the social order. Much more than that, conscience signifies the perceptible and demanding presence of the voice of truth in the subject himself. It is the overcoming of mere subjectivity in the encounter of the interiority of man with the truth from God. The verse Newman composed in 1833 in Sicily is characteristic: "I loved to choose and see my path; but now Lead thou me on!"[8] Newman's conversion to Catholicism was not for him a matter of personal taste or of subjective, spiritual need. He expressed himself on this even in 1844, on the threshhold, so to speak, of his conversion: "No one can have a more unfavorable view than I of the present state of the Roman Catholics."[9] Newman was much more taken by the necessity to obey recognized truth than his own preferences, that is to say, even against his own sensitivity and bonds of friendship and ties due to similar backgrounds. It seems to me characteristic of Newman that he emphasized truth's priority over goodness in the order of virtues. Or, to put it in a way which is more understandable for us, he emphasized truth's priority over consensus, over the accommodation of groups. I would say, when we are speaking of a man of conscience, we mean one who looks at things this way. A man of conscience, is one who never acquires tolerance, well-being, success, public standing, and approval on the part of prevailing opinion, at the expense of truth. In this regard Newman is related to Britain's other great witness of conscience, Thomas More, for whom conscience was not at all an expression of subjective stubborness or obstinate heroism. He numbered himself, in fact, among those fainthearted martyrs who only after faltering and much questioning succeed in mustering up obedience to conscience, mustering up obedience to the truth which must stand higher than any human tribunal or any type of personal taste.[10] Thus two standards become apparent for ascertaining the presence of a real voice of conscience. First, conscience is not identical to personal wishes and taste. Secondly, conscience cannot be reduced to social advantage, to group consensus, or to the demands of political and social power.

Let us take a sidelook now at the situation of our day. The individual may not achieve his advancement or well-being at the cost of betraying what he recognizes to be true; nor may humanity. Here we come in contact with the really critical issue of the modern age. The concept of truth has been virtually given up and replaced by the concept of progress. Progress itself "is" the truth. But through this seeming exaltation, progress loses its direction and becomes nullified. For if no direction exists, everything can just as well be regress as progress. Einstein's relativity theory properly concerns the physical cosmos. But it seems to me to describe exactly the situation of the intellectual/spiritual world of our time. Relativity theory states there are no fixed systems of reference in the universe. When we declare a system to be a reference point from which we try to measure the whole, it is we who do the determining. Only in such a way can we attain any results at all. But the determination could always have been done differently. What we said about the physical cosmos is reflected in the second "Copernican revolution" regarding our basic relationship to reality. The truth as such, the absolute, the very reference point of thinking, is no longer visible. For this reason, precisely in the spiritual sense, there is no longer "up or down." There are no directions in a world without fixed measuring points. What we view to be direction is not based on a standard which is true in itself, but on our decision, and finally on considerations of expediency. In such a "relativistic" context, so-called teleological or consequentialist ethics ultimately becomes nihilistic, even if it fails to see this. And what is called conscience in such a worldview is, on deeper reflection, but a euphemistic way of saying that there is no such thing as an actual conscience, conscience understood as a "co-knowing" with the truth. Each person determines his own standards. And needless to say, in general relativity, no one can be of much help to the other, much less prescribe behavior to him.

At this point, the whole radicality of today's dispute over ethics and conscience, its center, becomes plain. It seems to me that the parallel in the history of thought is the quarrel between Socrates-Plato and the sophists in which the fateful decision between two fundamental positions has been rehearsed. There is, on the one hand, the position of confidence in man's capacity for truth. On the other, there is a worldview in which man alone sets the standards for himself.[11] The fact that Socrates, the pagan, could become in a certain respect the prophet of Jesus Christ has its roots in this fundamental question. Socrates' taking up of this question bestowed on the way of philosophizing inspired by him a kind of salvation-historical privilege and made it an appropriate vessel for the Christian Logos. For the Christian Logos we are dealing with liberation through truth and to truth. If you isolate Socrates' dispute from the accidents of the time and take into account his use of other arguments and terminology, you begin to see how much his is the same dilemma we face today. Giving up the idea of man's capacity for truth leads first to pure formalism in the use of words and concepts. Again, the loss of content, then and now, leads to a pure formalism of judgment. In many places today, for example, no one bothers any longer to ask what a person thinks. The verdict on someone's thinking is ready at hand as long as you can assign it to its corresponding, formal category: conservative, reactionary, fundamentalist, progressive, revolutionary. Assignment to a formal scheme suffices to render unnecessary coming to terms with the content. The same thing can be seen in more concentrated form in art. What a work of art says is indifferent. It can glorify God or the devil. The sole standard is that of formal, technical mastery.

We have now arrived at the heart of the matter. Where contents no longer count, where pure praxeology takes over, technique becomes the highest criterion. This means, though, that power becomes the preeminent category, whether revolutionary or reactionary. This is precisely the distorted form of being like God of which the account of the fall speaks. The way of mere technical skill, the way of sheer power, is imitation of an idol and not expression of one's being made in the image and likeness of God. What characterizes man as man is not that he asks about the "can" but about the "should" and that he opens himself to the voice and demands of truth. It seems to me, this was the final meaning of the Socratic search, and it is the profoundest element in the witness of all martyrs. They attest to the fact that man's capacity for truth is a limit on all power and a guarantee of man's likeness to God. It is precisely in this way that the martyrs are the great witnesses of conscience, of that capability given to man to perceive the "should" beyond the "can" and thereby render possible real progress, real ascent.

3. Systematic Consequences: The Two Levels of Conscience

a) Anamnesis

After all these ramblings through intellectual history, it is finally time to arrive at some conclusions, that is, to formulate a concept of conscience. The medieval tradition was right, I believe, in according two levels to the concept of conscience. These levels, though they can be well distinguished, must be continually referred to each other.[12] It seems to me, many unacceptable theses regarding conscience are the result of neglecting either the difference or the connection between the two. Mainstream scholasticism expressed these two levels in the concepts *synderesis* and *conscientia.* The word *synderesis (synteresis)* came into the medieval tradition of conscience from the stoic doctrine of the microcosm.[13] It remained unclear in its exact meaning and for this reason became a hindrance to a careful development of this essential aspect of the whole question of conscience. I would like, therefore, without entering into philosophical disputes, to replace this probematic word with the much more clearly defined Platonic concept of anamnesis. It is not only linguistically clearer and philosophically deeper and purer, but anamnesis above all also harmonizes with key motifs of biblical thought and the anthropology derived therefrom. The word anamnesis should be taken to mean exactly that which Paul expressed in the second chapter of his Letter to the Romans: "When Gentiles who have not the law do by nature what the law requires, they are a law to themselves, even though they do not have the law. They show that what the law requires is written on their hearts, while their conscience also bears witness . . . (2:14f.)." The same thought is strikingly amplified in the great monastic rule of Saint Basil. Here we read: "The love of God is not founded on a discipline imposed on us from outside, but is constitutively established in us as the capacity and necessity of our rational nature." Basil speaks in terms of "the spark of divine love which has been hidden in us," an expression which was to become important in medieval mysticism.[14] In the spirit of Johannine theology Basil knows that love consists in keeping the commandments. For this reason, the spark of love, which has been put into us by the Creator, means this: "We have received interiorly beforehand the capacity and disposition for observing all divine commandments . . . These are not something imposed from without." Referring everything back to its simple core, Augustine adds: "We could never judge that one thing is better than another, if a basic understanding of the good had not already been instilled in us."[15]

19

This means that the first so-called ontological level of the phenomenon conscience consists in the fact that something like an original memory of the good and true (both are identical) has been implanted in us, that there is an inner ontological tendency within man, who is created in the likeness of God, toward the divine. From its origin, man's being resonates with some things and clashes with others. This anamnesis or the origin, which results from the godlike constitution of our being is not a conceptually articulated knowing, a store of retrievable contents. It is so to speak an inner sense, a capacity to recall, so that the one whom it addresses, if he is not turned in on himself, hears its echo from within. He sees: That's it! That is what my nature points to and seeks.

The possibility for and right to mission rest on this anamnesis of the creator which is identical to the ground of our existence. The gospel may, indeed, must be proclaimed to the pagans because they themselves are yearning for it in the hidden recesses of their souls (cf. Isaiah 42:4). Mission is vindicated then when those addressed recognize in the encounter with the word of the gospel that this indeed is what they have been waiting for. In this sense, Paul can say: the gentiles are a law to themselves—not in the sense of the modern liberal notions of autonomy which preclude transcendence of the subject, but in the much deeper sense that nothing belongs less to me than I myself. My own I is the site of the profoundest surpassing of self and contact with him from whom I came and toward whom I am going. In these sentences, Paul expresses the experience which he had had as missionary to the gentiles and which Israel may have experienced before him in dealings with the "god-fearing." Israel could have experienced among the gentiles what the ambassadors of Jesus Christ found reconfirmed. Their proclamation answered an expectation. Their proclamation encountered an antecedent basic knowledge of the essential constants of the will of God which came to be written down in the commandments, which can be found in all cultures, and which can be all the more clearly elucidated the less an overbearing cultural bias distorts this primordial knowledge. The more man lives in "fear of the Lord"—consider the story of Cornelius (especially, Acts 10: 34–35)—the more concretely and clearly effective this anamnesis becomes.

Again let us take a formulation of St. Basil. The love of God, which is concrete in the commandments, is not imposed on us from without, the Church Father emphasizes, but has been implanted in us beforehand. The sense of the good has been stamped upon us, Augustine puts it. We can now appreciate Newman's toast first to conscience and then to the pope. The pope cannot impose commandments on faithful Catholics because he wants to or finds it expedient. Such a modern, voluntaristic concept of authority can only distort the true theological meaning of the papacy. The true nature of the Petrine office has become so incomprehensible in the modern age no doubt because we only think of authority in terms which do not allow for bridges between subject and object. Accordingly, everything which does not come from the subject is thought to be externally imposed. But the situation is really quite different according to the anthropology of conscience which we have tried to come to an appreciation of in these relections. The anamnesis instilled in our being needs, one might say, assistance from without so that it can become aware of itself. But this "from without" is not something set in opposition to anamnesis but ordered to it. It has maieutic function, imposes nothing foreign, but brings to fruition what is proper to anamnesis, namely, its interior openness to the truth. When we are dealing with the question of faith and Church whose radius extends from the redeeming Logos over the gift of creation, we must, however, take into account yet another dimension which is especially developed in the Johannine writings. John is familiar with the anamnesis of the new "we" which is granted to us in the incorporation into Christ (one body, that is, one I with him). In remembering they knew him, the gospel has it in a number of places. The original encounter with Jesus gave the disciples what all generations thereafter receive in their foundational encounter with the Lord in Baptism and the Eucharist, namely, the new anamnesis of faith which unfolds, similarly to the anamnesis of creation, in constant dialogue between within and without. In contrast to the presumption of gnostic teachers who wanted to convince the faithful that their naive faith must be understood and applied much differently, John could say: you do not need such instruction, as anointed ones (baptized ones) you know everything (cf. 1 John 2: 20). This does not mean a factual omniscience on the part of the faithful. It does signify however, the sureness of the Christian memory. This Christian memory, to be sure is always learning, but proceeding from its sacramental identity, it also distinguishes from within between what is a genuine unfolding of its recollection and what is its destruction or falsification. In the crisis of the Church today, the power of this recollection and the truth of the apostolic word is experienced in an entirely new way, where much more so than hierarchical direction, it is the power of memory of the simple faith which leads to the discernment of spirits. One can only comprehend the primacy of the pope and its correlation to Christian conscience in this connection. The true sense of the teaching authority of the pope consists in his being the advocate of the Christian memory. The pope does not impose from without. Rather he elucidates the Christian memory and defends it. For this reason the toast to conscience indeed must precede the toast to the Pope because without conscience there would not be a papacy. All power that the papacy has is power of conscience. It is service to the double memory upon which the faith is based and which again and again must be purified, expanded, and defended against the destruction of memory which is threatened by a subjectivity forgetful of its own foundation as well as by the pressures of social and cultural conformity.

b) Conscientia

Having considered this first, essentially ontological, level of the concept of conscience, we must now turn to its second level, that of judgment and decision which the medieval tradition designates with the single word *conscientia,* conscience. Presumably this terminological tradition has not insignificantly contributed to the diminution of the concept of conscience. Thomas, for example, only designates this second level as *conscientia.* For him it stands to reason that conscience is not a *habitus,* that is a lasting ontic quality of man, but *actus,* an event in execution. Thomas of course assumes as given the ontological foundation of anamnesis *(synderesis).* He describes anamnesis as an inner repugnance to evil and an attraction to the good. The act of conscience applies this basic knowledge to the particular situation. It is divided according to Thomas into three elements: recognizing *(recognoscere)*, bearing witness *(testificari)*, and finally judging *(iudicare)*. One might speak of an interaction between a function of control and a function of decision.[16] Thomas sees this sequence according to the Aristotelian tradition's model of deductive reasoning. But he is careful to emphasize what is peculiar to this knowledge of moral actions whose conclusions do not come from mere knowing or thinking.[17] Whether something is recognized or not, depends too on the will which can block the way to recognition or lead to it. It is dependent, that is to say, on an already formed moral character which can either continue to deform or be further purified.[18] On this level, the level of judgment (*conscientia* in the narrower sense), it can be said that even the erroneous conscience binds. This statement is completely intelligible from the rational tradition of scholasticism. No one may act against his convictions, as St. Paul had already said (Romans 14:23). But the fact that the conviction a person has come to certainly binds in the moment of acting, does not signify a canonization of subjectivity. It is never wrong to follow the convictions one has arrived at—in fact, one must do so. But it can very well be wrong to have come to such askew convictions in the first place by having stifled the protest of the anamnesis of being. The guilt lies then in a different place, much deeper—not in the present act, not in the present judgment of conscience, but in the neglect of my being which made me deaf to the internal promptings of truth.[19] For this reason, criminals of conviction like Hitler and Stalin are guilty. These crass examples should not serve to put us at ease but should rouse us to take seriously the earnestness of the plea: "Free me from my unknown guilt" (Psalm 19: 13).

Epilogue: Conscience and Grace

At the end there remains the question with which we began. Is not he truth, at least as the faith of the Church shows it to us, too lofty and difficult for man? Taking into consideration everything we have said, we can respond as follows. Certainly, the high road to truth and goodness is not a comfortable one. It challenges man. Nevertheless, retreat into self, however comfortable, does not redeem. The self withers away and becomes lost. But in ascending the heights of the good, man discovers more and more the beauty which lies in the arduousness of truth which constitues redemption for him. But not everything has yet been said. We would dissolve Christianity into moralism if no message which surpasses our own actions became discernible. Without many words an image from the Greek world can show us this. In it we can observe simultaneously both how the anamnesis of the creator extends from within us outward toward the redeemer, and how everyone may see him as redeemer, because he answers our own innermost expectations. I am speaking of the story of the expiation of the sin of the matricide of Orestes. He had committed the murder as an act of conscience. This is designated by the mythological language of obedience to the command of the god Apollo. But now he finds himself hounded by the furies or *erinyes,* who are to be seen as mythological personifications of conscience which, from a deeper wellspring of recollection, reproach Orestes, declaring that his decision of conscience, his obedience to the "saying of the gods" was in reality guilt. The whole tragedy of man comes to light in this dispute of the "gods," that is to say, in this conflict of conscience. In the holy court, the white stone of Athena leads to Orestes' acquittal, his sanctification of the power of which the *erinyes* are transformed into *eumenides,* the spirits of reconciliation. Atonement has transformed the world. The myth, while representing the transition from a system of blood vengeance to the right order of community, signifies much more than just that. Hans Urs von Balthasar expressed this "more" as follows: ". . . Calming grace always assists in the establishing of justice, not the old graceless justice of the Erinyes period, but that which is full of grace . . ."[20] This myth speaks to us of the human longing that conscience's objectively just indictment and the attendant destructive, interior distress it causes in man, not be the last word. It thus speaks of an authority of grace, a power of expiation which allows the guilt to vanish and makes truth at last truly redemptive. It is the longing for a truth which does not just make demands of us but also transforms us through expiation and pardon. Through these, as Aeschylus puts it, "guilt is washed away"[21] and our being is transformed from within, beyond our own capability. This is the real innovation of Christianity. The Logos, the truth in person, is also the atonement, the transforming forgiveness above and beyond our capability and incapability. Therein lies the real novelty upon which the larger Christian memory is founded and which indeed, at the same time, constitutes the deeper answer to what the anamnesis of the creator expects of us. Where this center of the Christian message is not sufficiently expressed and appreciated, truth becomes a yoke which is too heavy for our shoulders and from which we must seek to free ourselves. But the freedom gained thereby is empty. It leads into the desolate land of nothingness and disintegrates of itself. Yet the yoke of truth in fact became "easy" (Matthew 11: 30) when the truth came, loved us, and consumed our guilt in the fire of his love. Only when we know and experience this from within, will we be free to hear the message of conscience with joy and without fear.

* * * * * * * * * * * * * * * * *
* * * * * * * * * * * * * *

NOTES

1. This thesis was apparently first proposed by J.G. Fichte; "Conscience does and cannot err," because it is "itself judge of all conviction," which "recognizes no higher judge over itself. It is the ultimate authority and cannot be appealed" (*System der Sittenlehre*, 1798, III, 15; Werke Bd. 4, Berlin 1971, p. 174). Cf. H. Reiner, *Gewissen*, in: J. Ritter (ed.), *Historisches Wörterbuch der Philosophie III*, p. 574–592, here p. 586. Kant had already previously formulated the counterarguments. They appear in more depth in Hegel for whom conscience "as formal subjectivity . . . (is) always on the verge of changing into evil:" Cf. H. Reiner, *Ibid.* Nevertheless, the thesis of the infallibility of conscience is at present again in the ascendancy in popular theological literature. I find an—in a certain respect—mediating position in E. Schockenhoff *Das umstrittene Gewissen* (Mainz, 1990), which expressly reckons with the possibility that conscience can miss its mark by going astray of the other requirement of the moral law, the mutual recognition of the free rational being" (p. 139). Schockenhoff, however,—relying on Linsenmann—rejects talk of an erring conscience: "In view of the quality of conscience as such, there is no sense in speaking of error because there is no higher observation point from which error could be ascertained" (p. 136). Why not? Is there no truth concerning the good accessible to all of us in common? To be sure, the point is then so significantly nuanced that finally in the end it is even less clear to me why the concept of the erring conscience should be untenable. Helpful here is M. Honecker's *Einführung in die theologische Ethik*. Berlin, 1990. pp. 138ff.

2. A. Görres, "Schuld und Schuldgefühle," in *Internationale katholische Zeitschrift 'Communio'* 13 (1984), p. 434.

3. Ibid., p. 442.

4. Cf. M. Honecker, op. cit. (cf. Note 1), p. 130.

5. Besides the important article already cited of H. Reiner and the work of Schockenhoff on new studies, cf. A. Laun, *Das Gewissen: Oberste Norm sittlichen Handelns* (Innsbruck, 1984) and his *Aktuelle Probleme der Moraltheologie* (Vienna, 1991), pp. 31–64; J. Gründel (ed.), *Das Gewissen: Subjektive Willkür oder oberste Norm?* (Düsseldorf, 1990); summary overview: K. Golser, "Gewissen," in H. Rotter, G. Virt, *Neues Lexikon der christlichen Moral* (Innsbruck, Vienna, 1990), pp. 278–286.

6. Letter of Norfolk, in *Works of Cardinal Newman: Difficulties of Anglicans II* (Westminster, Maryland: Christian Classics, 1969), p. 261; cf. J. Honoré, Newman; *Sa Vie et sa Pensée* (Paris, 1988), p. 65; I. Ker. J. H. *Newman, A Biography* (Oxford, 1990), pp. 688ff.

7. Cf. Ch. St. Dessian, *J. H. Newman* (Oxford Univ. Press, 3rd ed., 1980); G. Biemer, *J. H. Newman: Leben und Werk (Mainz, 1989)*.

8. *From the famous poem "Lead Kindly Light" in Versus on Various Occasions* (London, 1888); cf. Ker, op. cit., p. 79; cf. Dessain, *op. cit.,* pp. 33–34.

9. Letter to J. Keble of Dec. 29, 1844 in *Correspondence of J. H. Newman with J. Keble and Others: 1839–1845* (London 1917), p. 364, cf. also p. 351; cf. Dessain, *op. cit.,* p. 79.

10. Cf. P. Berglar, *Die Stunde des Thomas Morus* (Olten and Freiburg, 3rd ed., 1981), pp. 155ff.

11. Regarding the debate between Socrates and the Sophists, cf. J. Pieper, "Missbrauch der Sprache—Missbrauch der Macht," In *Über die Schwierigkeit zu glauben* (Munich, 1974), pp. 255–282 and *Kümmert euch nicht um Sokrates* (Munich, 1966). A penetrating treatment of the question of the truth as the center of Socratic searching is found in R. Guardini, *The Death of Socrates*.

12. A short summary of the medieval doctrine of conscience can be found in H. Reiner, op. cit., (cf. Note 1), pp. 582f.

13. Cf. E. von Ivánka, *Plato christianus* (Einsiedeln, 1964), pp. 315–351, esp. pp. 320f.

14. *Regulae fusius tractatae* Resp 2, 1 PG 31, 908.

15. *De trin VIII* 3, 4 PL 42, 949.

16. Cf. H. Reiner, *op. cit.,* p. 582: S. *theol I* q 79 a 13; De ver. q 17 a 1.

17. Cf. the careful study of L. Melina, *La conoscenza morale: Linee di riflessione sul Commento di san Tommaso all 'Etica Nicomachea* (Rome: Città Nuova Editrice, 1987), pp. 69ff.

18. In reflecting on his own inner experience in the decades following his conversion, St. Augustine elaborated fundamental insights into the essence of freedom and morality concerning the relationships between knowledge, will, emotion, and inclination through habit. Cf. the excellent presentation of P. Brown, *Augustine of Hippo: A Biography* (New York: Dorset, 1986), pp. 146–157.

19. That this precisely is also the position of St. Thomas Aquinas is shown by I. G. Belmans in his extremely enlightening study "Le paradoxe de la conscience erronée d 'Abélard à Karl Rahner in *Rev Thom 90* (1990), pp. 570–586. He shows how with the publication of Sertillanges' book on St. Thomas in 1942 a then widely adopted distortion of Thomas' Doctrine of conscience takes hold which—to put it simply—consists in the fact that only the *Summa theologica* I–II q 19 a 5 ("Must one follow an erroneous conscience?")

is cited and the following article 6 ("Is it sufficient to follow one's conscience in order to act properly?") is simply ignored. That means imputing the doctrine of Abelard to Thomas whose goal was in fact to overcome Abelard. Abelard had taught that the crucifiers of Christ would not have sinned if they had acted from ignorance. The only way to sin consists in acting against conscience. The modern theories of the autonomy of conscience can appeal to Abelard but not to Thomas.

20. H. U. v. Balthasar, *Glory of the Lord: A Theological Aesthetics IV: The Realm of Metaphysics in Antiquity* (San Francisco: Ignatius Press, 1989), p. 121.

21. Aeschylus, *Eumenides* 280–281, (Oxford edition by G. Murray, 2nd ed. 21 1955); Balthasar, *op. cit.,* p. 121.

Chapter 2

Dialogue with Cardinal Ratzinger

BISHOP: In 1969, you wrote a book, *The New People of God*. Although the expression "People of God" is in the Bible and in Vatican Council texts it indicates there a small part of the humanity. All human beings are people of God. Can we avoid this expression or else extend it to the whole of humanity?

CARDINAL RATZINGER: I would distinguish the terminological problem and the theological problem. We have first the terminological problem, and here I think it's important to respect the Biblical terminology in which "people of God" is the designation of Israel, first, and with the Christ event, the pagans begin also to be people of God in continuity with Israel.

So, we can see that in the terminology of the Holy Scripture "people of God" designates the special election made by God, this special history which begins with Abraham and is continuing in the Church.

I would say it's not good to extend the word to all humanity because the Biblical idea is universal, yes, but the universality of

God is reached by His action through a determinate group whose destination is to be the message for all. This is my first point. To respect Biblical terminology, which is also the terminology of tradition we see people of God as God acts between the one and the other brother, and we designate only this one determined history with His word.

The other point is not terminological but theological. On this level it is clear that the love of God is directed to all His creatures, to all human beings, and all are seen in the eyes of the love of God. The ways whereby God comes to His people are different and the Church is an instrument for His coming to this people, but not the unique instrument. Conscience is the other instrument.

In this sense, we can say God acts for all and not for a part. We must find a way to reconcile the specificity of the action of God with Israel and the Church with the intentional universality He also has. If we continue to apply the Biblical terminology "people of God" to this determined part of humanity we must take into account that this is not only for this group, but always includes a universal destination.

BISHOP: You said that erroneous conscience does not justify all persons. And you applied that to Hitler, Himmler, Stalin, Mafia chieftains, and abortionists. I agree fully with that.

But, it raises a question for me when does erroneous conscience justify a person? The Belgian bishops in their response to *Humanae Vitae* wrote only about erroneous conscience and the fact that people who continue to practice birth control on the basis of erroneous conscience would be all right.

How would this apply, for instance, to theologians who dissent from clear-cut practical teaching of the Church, like *Humanae Vitae?* Would you think this is possibly good conscience, probably not good conscience, or should we simply leave that in God's hands? And how would it apply to people who continue to practice birth control in the face of *Humanae Vitae?*

CARDINAL RATZINGER: Yes, the problem is a general problem. In a sense, erroneous conscience is an old problem discussed in the 12th and 13th Century because Abelard had formulated the theory that the murderers of Christ had acted morally because in good conscience they saw it was necessary for the people. Their intention alone and their good conscience would be sufficient for justification.

Thomas Aquinas and other theologians were not in agreement with his thesis and they said, yes, one must act following conscience, but the conscience must follow the inner light of our anamnesis as creatures. At this moment I do not have present all the details of this discussion, but I think we must read it and find also the answers to our present struggle, because he says that there are things about which the anamnesis is not sufficient if we do not have teaching from outside.

But there are fundamental elements of truth which are identical with our human nature, identical with our being made in the image of God, and he identifies this essential remembering of truth with the Ten Commandments, more or less.

If these great indications are present in our heart and man can see it, this is also the foundation of salvation for non-Christians, this presence of truth in the heart.

But concrete applications and elucidations are not so clearly present in our fundamental memory of being. We need illumination and instruction and so pagans, and also perhaps not well informed Christians, can not know this and in this sense erroneous conscience is a saving conscience for them.

I think it's very important to distinguish in these Christians between their essential memory of good and truth which are really open to our hearts and the concrete developments which must be explicated from authority, and are not so easily accessible. So, I could say that for *Humanae Vitae* the problem is much more difficult than the problem of the activity of the murderers of Christ or the problem of Hitler and Stalin and Mafia bosses.

Especially in our contemporary circumstances the truth is not so accessible and here erroneous conscience is almost understandable. In this sense I can agree with the Belgian bishops and other Episcopates. But perhaps an oversight in the declarations of some bishops' conferences was that they do not emphasize that this erroneous conscience is always a lack of light, and so of truth, and so of good in our existence and so also in our social existence, and in the existence of humanity. A conscience must be educated. It must be illuminated.

The impression could exist in the Christian people that all we have are erroneous consciences and perhaps they are erroneous. It must be clearer that, even if in this moment you can not understand this and you are fixed in your erroneous conscience, you must go on living with the Church to arrive at more light, more truth and more goodness for humanity.

BISHOP: You would lay more stress on the need for human redemption than many other people do, even if you apply it to Hitler, Stalin, Himmler, and the Mafia chieftains. But I am still not clear on how big a problem you see it to be of people being responsible for erroneous conscience? I think it may have a great deal to do with the force or the thrust of our evangelization.

We have lost a great deal of thrust in our work of evangelization. I think that part of the reason is that there is virtually nobody that we believe is going to go to hell, or is in serious risk of going to hell, with the result that there isn't any great urgency in bringing the message. And part of the reason for that is a general notion that everybody is sincerely doing what they believe they are supposed to do. So, it doesn't make much difference if we get to them with the message of Jesus or not.

I must confess I don't find any kind of an expressed real need to escape hell, or not to risk salvation, even in the documents from the Holy See. It almost never is mentioned on any level of the Church at the present time. This seems to me to convey the impression that we really do believe that erroneous conscience has practically excused almost everybody and that they aren't obliged in practice to the stronger faith that you had mentioned.

CARDINAL RATZINGER: Yes, I spoke about the problem of society and of conscience in the Communist world, and what in consequence was the deterioration of all the people, and of their history. But, we could say that this also applies to our rich world that even in our western world we have a certain silence of conscience.

If so many people can not understand, for example, the teaching of *Humanae Vitae*, this supposes a silence of conscience in many areas. Even if we can say that the poor people in the eastern world are victims of this silence of conscience created from the political powers, and so personally we hope that many are saved, there remains a great evil that this silence of conscience was imposed and destroyed part of humanity and of history.

The same thing, *mutatis mutandis,* is valid also for us. We have the silence of conscience which, can save individual persons, but there remains ever that silence, that social silence, the historical silence of conscience in so many areas destroying society, and the heart of man.

And so we can see the necessity of reevangelization that God can begin to speak in our hearts and can change our hearts, can change society, and can change history. If we begin to study the effects of the historical silence of conscience created by certain powers of history, we can better understand how it's necessary to have the presence and strong presence of the word of God, of the word of the gospel in our history, to liberate us from this silence of conscience.

BISHOP: It seems to me that conscience is something dynamic, continually growing and depending on it's identification with truth. But truth is a person, Christ. Could we say that when we neglect this personal dimension in the formation of conscience, we gradually are getting away from a right conscience?

CARDINAL RATZINGER: I agree, absolutely. I think this is a very good complement to what I have said. Really this absence of the word of Christ, this disappearance of the incarnate truth is also the loss of conscience and the formation of conscience.

BISHOP: A preoccupation, I think, with many of us is the question of how to interpret or explain to our young people this question of conscience as they apply it in the society that they have to grow up in today. I think you helped us very much in explaining the notion of how the Holy Father teaches using the concept of calling forth the memory of the Church and our history. Have you seen any practical developments in working with youth in helping them to grasp this notion?

CARDINAL RATZINGER: I do not have so frequent contact with youth at the present time. But, generally, in my academic experiences when I was a teacher in a very secularized world, it was my impression that if you begin to explain it with the contrast in the world, they begin to understand the silence, a collective silence of conscience which is the destruction of man.

If you say that our society is not good perhaps they accept it, but in the time when I was an academic teacher many were convinced that Marxism would make the very best world, and they could not see there a silence of conscience and so the destruction of the human being.

But they could see that in other parts of the world, or in other parts of history as in the Hitler history, the collective silence was a destruction of men. If we can find the elements where our youth are sensible and have the capacity to understand they will see that a silent social conscience at the same time causes a destruction of man.

They will also begin to think and to reflect that even in their own life they are blind, because they are part of the silent conscience. It is possible with a certain analysis of our circumstances, our situation, to renew the sense of conscience that is the voice Christ within our conscience.

BISHOP: What would be the role and the responsibility of the normal Christian to help in the formation of the conscience of others through the exercise of fraternal correction?

CARDINAL RATZINGER: I think your question is an answer! I think the normal Christian can be part of the evangelization work for the presence of Christ, especially with fraternal correction given with understanding of the brother, but also with love for Christ. He can help the brother in his own circumstances to see more light, to understand more fully the message of Christ.

BISHOP: The Islamic conscience is all but impenetrable to the message of Christ. And it seems to be totally informed by the Koran. How do we meet that challenge? The Christian conscience seems to be flabby and infinitely flexible in comparison with the rigidity of the Islamic conscience. Is dialogue possible and is there any possible meeting of minds with the people of Islamic faith?

CARDINAL RATZINGER: This is a very difficult question. You know that the Council for Interreligious Dialogue has some dialogue with Islamic world. The first difficulty is that the Islamic world is very divided. They have common emotions, as we see, but in their ideas and their convictions they are very divided, and do not have a common religious authority. If you speak with one group you can not hope to have agreement from others. You have always only a partial dialogue. This is one of the problems.

The other problems is a lack of formation ranging from the fanaticism that we see, for example, in Iran, to the simple lack of formation and simple adhesion to their guidance.

But even if we see here our limits and our incapacity to make any great work of evangelizing in this situation for a collective alteration of conscience, we must do the possible and have dialogue with the persons and groups that are open.

And something is possible. For example, it was interesting for me that the King of Morocco last Christmas said after an Islamic congress, that he was very anguished about the problem of the political interpretation of Islamic doctrines. He said that "I read the Old and the New Testament and reading the Bible I understood better also the message of the Koran. I am now a better Moslem because I have seen the message of the Bible." It is my suggestion to all Islamic people, read the Bible and you will be a better Moslem.

It's not our intention to have better Moslems, but Moslems who are nearer to the real voice of God. I think we must find the persons and the groups who are able to understand a more Islamic position and so more open to the one voice of the one God, and the one Truth.

BISHOP: My comments are simply an invitation to you to perhaps share some reflection that you may have had while preparing your paper regarding the forces that are pervasive and influencing of conscience today. I particularly am concerned about the mass media. It is so extensive and it's continuous. It's a continuous bombardment in their war to either destroy or to form, or to win people to their way of thinking, and as we know, they are not proposing the Christian concept of values. Did you have some reflections when you were preparing your paper that you might share with us?

CARDINAL RATZINGER: I do not have answers. I see the problem of collective deformation of conscience with the collective powers present in our world. I think we all must reflect what we can do to help to liberate conscience from these pressures.

PART ONE

FOUNDATION OF CHRISTIAN LIFE AND MORAL THEOLOGY

Chapter 3

ELEMENTS OF A CATHOLIC CONSCIENCE

The Reverend Benedict Ashley, O.P., Ph.D., S.T.M.

I: CONSCIENCE IN BIBLE AND TRADITION

The formation of the Christian conscience must always be a primary concern of the pastoral office. Yet oddly, in the Gospels the chief Shepherd, Jesus Christ, never uses the term *syneidēsis* which Latin exactly renders as *conscientia,* from which come both the English "consciousness" and "conscience." *Syneidēsis* means "knowing together with", that is , "knowing shared with another" and hence "with one's self"—"knowing that I know," to which "conscience" adds the specification of "knowing myself precisely as a free and morally responsible being."

Perhaps Jesus did not use the term "conscience" because the Hebrew Scriptures had no equivalent word.[1] Yet they often speak of feelings of *shame* before God, the community, or oneself for sin. Adam and Eve hid their nakedness from the Creator (Gn 3:1–14) and David's "heart struck him" with remorse (1 Sm 24:6; 2 Sm 24:10) and he prayed, "A clean heart create for me, O God, and a steadfast spirit renew within me" (Ps 51:12). These writers were less interested in psychological analysis than in showing that we stand always before God our sole judge. "Against you alone have I sinned." (Ps. 51:6).[2]

Yet Jesus, as the very Wisdom of God (1 Cor 1: 24) and our "only teacher" (Mt 23:10), formed the Christian conscience both by example and by *Torah,* instruction.[3] The early Church Fathers saw in the Sermon on the Mount (Mt 5–7) the New Law, the *summa* of Jesus' moral teaching on which we, as the Jews on the Old Law, are to "mediate the day and night" (Ps 1:2; cf. Ps 119).[4] In it and in many of his parables (e.g. Mt 13:44–46), Jesus insisted that "Remember, where your treasure is, there your heart is also . . . No man can serve two masters" (Mt 6:21–24).

Thus for Jesus the foundation of morality is total commitment to a single goal in life, to enter into God's Reign, the communion of God's own life, God's "glory." In the Fourth Gospel Jesus prays, "I have given them [my disciples] the glory you gave me that they may be one, as we are one—I living in them, you living in me, that their unity may be complete." (Jn 17:22).

Meta-ethics, therefore, should classify Jesus' moral teaching as *teleological,* since he measured the morality of acts as *means* to one *goal* (*telos*), the "one thing necessary" (Lk 10:42).[5] As he declared in the Sermon of the Mount, "Seek first the kingdom of God, his way of holiness, and all these things will be given you besides." (Mt 6:33). Hence on the commandment to "love" God and neighbor "the whole law is based, and the prophets as well" (Mt 22:34–36; cf 7:12; Mk 12:13–17; Lk 20:20–26), since "love" is precisely the realization of God's Reign.

Nevertheless, I cannot agree with some recent authors that in summing up morality as "love", Jesus showed little interest in concrete moral norms.[6] Because Jesus denounced the Pharisees for clinging to the letter of the Law, these authors contend the concrete norms in the New Testament are too time-conditioned to be permanently valid. Hence some moral theologians take the Bible simply as *parenesis,* exhortation to do good and avoid evil, and rely almost exclusively on philosophical reasoning to determine what is right and wrong in our world today.[7]

In the Matthaean Sermon on the Mount, however, Jesus says plainly, "Do not think that I have come to abolish the law and the prophets. I have come not to abolish, but to fulfill them" (Mt 5:17).[8] He repeats the Mosaic Commandments but frees them from rabbinic misinterpretation and certain concessions which he attributes to "the hardness of your hearts" (Mk 10:2–12; Mt 19:3–9). Thus he reestablishes God's original plan of creation (Mt 19:4) to which he requires total conformity. "You must be perfect as your heavenly Father is perfect." (Mt 19:4) 5:48). While this seems impossible for us sinners, yet "with God all things are possible" (Mt 19:16–26). We must even forgive our enemies (Mt 6:14–15), because what we cannot do ourselves, we can obtain the grace to do by prayer (Mt 6:12, 14–15; 7:7:11).[9]

Thus, although Jesus' ethics is teleological, it includes a *deontology,* in the sense of concrete moral norms, such as the Old Testament commandments against murder, adultery, revenge, lying, etc. and positive precepts of fasting, prayer, almsgiving, etc. But it is not, as some say, a "mixed" deonto-telelogical system, because its deontological aspect is totally subordinated to the teleological by the supreme commandment of love.

Jesus rebuked the Pharisees for scrupling about the letter of the law while neglecting its "weighter provisions" (Mt 23:23), and he looked with compassion on the poor and the outcast whom the learned rabbis despised for their ignorance of these legal minutiae. This shows that Jesus recognized there can be a gap between a person's *subjective* conscience and *objective* morality, and therefore warned us "Do not judge lest you be judged" (Mt 7:1). Thereby he completed the prophets' warnings that God is not pleased by external works unless they flow from the interior service of the heart, of the whole person (Am 6:21–25; Hos 6:6, 8:13: Is 1:11–16: Mi 6:6–8).[10] The Pharisees, who knew the Law's objective truth yet from hypocrisy or self-deception failed to keep it, were far worse than the poor who were excused (Lk 18:9–14) by their involuntary ignorance.

Yet Jesus did not leave the poor in their ignorance. After healing and feeding them, he taught them in simple stories they could ponder (Mt 13:1–53).[11] The Pharisees he warned that a proud conscience will grow blind and hardened to sin (Mt 15:14; 23: 24–26) and blind teachers who mislead others risk damnation (Mt 18:6). Once he had instructed his apostles, Jesus gave them authority to instruct others and "to bind and to loose on earth as in heaven" (Mt 16:19). He also obliged those who hear apostolic preaching to listen and follow. "He who hears you, hears me. He who rejects you, rejects me." (Lk 10: 16). But they were *not* to listen to "false prophets" (Mt 7:15–23; cf 1 Jn 4: 1–6).

In the Fourth Gospel Jesus also promises to *all* Christians the interior guidance of the Holy Spirit (Jn 16:12–13 cf. 1 Jn 2:20–21, as the prophet Joel had predicted (Jl 3:1). This interior guidance does not replace the need of the faithful for the teaching of their pastors, but frees Christians to apply this teaching intelligently to the circumstances of their own lives.

According to *Acts* 15, the apostles were soon faced with a difficult question on which they had no instructions from the Lord: "Must gentile converts observe the ceremonial precepts of the Old Law?". They gathered in Jerusalem, and relying on the Holy Spirit, decided that gentile Christians were obliged only to the so-called Law of Noah (Gn 9: 3–7) thought by the rabbis to apply to all humanity. Thus the apostles recognized that even the Gentiles knew something of the moral law through the evidence of God's creation (Jb 31; Ws 13:1).[12]

Confronted with such pastoral problems, St. Paul for the first time in literature used the term *syneidésis* (and its corresponding verb) in its full and rich meaning, some 14 times in his authentic writings. His influence probably accounts for its use 18 times elsewhere in the New Testament.[13] For Paul not only Jews under the revealed Law, but all peoples bear responsibility before God (Rm 1:18–2:16).[14] In 1 Cor. (8:1–13; 10:25–30), we have the paradigmatic example of the pastoral use of this notion of conscience. Here Paul explains how the Gospel frees well-instructed Christians from the ceremonial provisions of the Old Law, but not from moral accountability to God. They must not only obey the great command of love of God and neighbor, but also all it implies, including the duty to respect the misinformed consciences of their neighbors, even at the expense of some restriction of their own Christian freedom.

The other New Testament writers recognize that conscience must be in harmony with faith, yet this is possible only through the transforming work of the Holy Spirit.

> Baptism is not removal of physical stain, but the pledge of God of an irreproachable conscience through the resurrection of Jesus Christ. He went to heaven and is at God's right hand, with angelic rulers and powers subjected to him (1 Pt 3:21).

But the human conscience can become corrupted, "seared" (1 Tm 4:16; cf. Pt 2; Jd 5–19).

> To the clean all things are clean, but to those defiled unbelievers nothing is clean. Their very minds and consciences are tainted. They claim to "know God" but by their actions they deny he exists. They are disgusting— intractable and thoroughly incapable of any decent action. (Titus 1:15–16).

Thus, while teaching the Corinthians their duty to respect the consciences of the scrupulous, St. Paul saw the deeper implication of Jesus' teaching, namely, that the "law of Christ" (Gal 6:2) is a universal law freeing us from historical conditioning. The Law of Moses, although uniquely approved by God, was only a particular law for a particular people, local and temporary. Nevertheless, Paul repudiated those who claimed Christian freedom was a licence to do as they pleased.[15]

No, the "law of Christ," that "faith which expresses itself through love" (Gal 5:6) is, as Jesus had insisted, a law of perfection, imitating God the Father, no longer written on tablets of stone (2 Cor 3:3), but in the human heart by the Holy Spirit (Rm 8:2), a law of the virtues of faith, hope, and charity, and all the other virtues these imply (1 Cor 13:13). This law abides always and everywhere because the Holy Spirit is ever-living. It is not a mere attitude of benevolence, but a sure guide for Christians in all life's circumstances. It unites Christians of every time and place into one community, the body of Christ (Rm 12:4–5), which lives according to the mind of Christ (Rm 3: 10–16).

Hence, while the Spirit guides each of us in the depths of our hearts, it completes this guidance through the pastors of the Church invested with apostolic authority to interpret the moral law according to God's true intentions (compare 1 Cor 7:10, 12–15, 25). As a pastor, St. Paul gave such direction firmly and insisted on its enforcement in the communities he had founded, even when his authority met with resistance (1 Cor 1–13).[16]

Relying on Paul's teaching and example, the Church Fathers often wrote about the formation of conscience.[17] Thus the *Didache* (4:14) warned that a good conscience is a condition of effective prayer. Clement of Rome spoke of "a clean conscience" (*IClement,* 45, 7) and St. Ignatius of Antioch warned that without harmony with the bishops and presbyters there could be no "clean conscience" (Tr. 7, 2; Mg., 4). The great Greek moralists St. Basil and John Chrysostom dwelt on the sense of shame and remorse and how sin blinds the conscience. Among the Latin Fathers, Tertullian made the Latin term "conscience" common Christian usage. St. Ambrose related it to the Stoic account of the virtues. And St. Augustine argued Platonically that moral principles are innate to our intellects and intimately linked to good will. Yet a puzzle remained which the Church Fathers never clearly resolved: If God has made the natural law accessible to the conscience of all humanity then why do Jews and Christians need to have their consciences instructed by revelation and Church teaching?[18]

While the scriptural and patristic tradition always gave primary emphasis to conscience as objective responsibility to God, the scholastic theology of the Middle Ages began to see more problems about the subjective or psychological aspect of conscience.[19] Abelard even argued that a good intention makes an act morally good and that acts are sinful only when contemptuous of God, an error that is still very much with us. Generally, however, the scholastic theologians followed the tradition of St. Augustine. Yet the Aristotelian concern for exact definitions of the virtues led them to ask whether *conscientia* (or what they called *synderesis*)[20] is a special virtue, in what respect it is a gift of grace, and in what human faculty it resides.

To these questions St. Thomas Aquinas gave precise answers. *Synderesis* or conscience in a broad sense is the natural *habitus* of the intelligence supplying the first principles of practical reason, that is, of the natural law.[21] Conscience in the strict sense, however, is not a district faculty but only an act of intelligence, namely practical judgement about what ought to be done in concrete situations. While rejecting Platonic innate knowledge, Aquinas saved St. Augustine's opinion by saying that the first principles of natural law are "natural" in that they are known to all from common experience.[22] He admits, however, these first principles excepted, humans can be ignorant or mistaken about the rest of the natural law.[23] Since we cannot be blamed for involuntary ignorance, this means that the gap between a *subjectively* good conscience and the *objective* moral truth can be very wide. Nevertheless, he insists that an objectively bad action, which is not culpable because of invincible ignorance, is not morally good *per se,* but only *per accidens.* Hence, the true maxim is not "Act according to your conscience," but "Inform your conscience objectively, and then act according to it."[24]

At the end of the Middle Ages a marked change came over moral theology under the influence of Duns Scotus and William of Ockham who so stressed the sovereign freedom of God that they reduced morality deontologically to conformity to the inscrutable Divine Will and positive civil and canon law. Until the neo-scholastic revival at the end of last century this legalism dominated moral theology and spawned interminable controversies over probabilism. Since in this positivistic perspective a good conscience is conformity to the will of the legislator, all the virtues become the one virtue of obedience and the formation of conscience is reduced to knowing the law. There is no need to understand the intrinsic character of human acts in relation to the human person's goal in life and Catholic moral theology verges on "pharasaic" scruplosity.

With Leo XIII's Thomistic revival moral theology slowly began to reorient itself to the teleology accepted, nominally at least, by almost all moral theologians since Vatican II.[25] Nevertheless, certain other tendencies have been widely adopted, without magisterial approval. These stem from theologians' efforts to assimilate the ethical system of Immanel Kant which has so deeply shaped the whole culture of modernity.

Kant's ethics, the center-piece of his effort to replace Christianity with a Humanism based on reason without revelation, is a radical deontology, based not on a heteronomous law of God, but on the autonomous human reason. It is also a purely "formal" ethics, that is, it states the *a priori* form of the laws which reason legislates, without supplying any concrete content to these norms. This content must be derived from *affectivity,* or "feeling" as Rousseau, whom Kant much admired, had argued. This dichotomy between the *a priori* or transcendental and the concrete, affective field of actual moral decisions haunts many current efforts to revise moral theology.

The most influential of these methodologies is *proportionalism* developed in Europe by Louis Janssens, Josef Fuchs, Peter Knauer and Bruno Schüller and in the U.S.A. by Richard A. McCormick.[26] It derives from the phenomenology and trancendentalism of Edmund Husserl, Max Scheler, Martin Heidegger and Karl Rahner. As formulated by its chief ethicist, Scheler, proportionalist methodology retains Kant's *a priorism* but seeks to avoid his formalism by positing a transcendental affective intuition of values. These values, however, remain abstract, and cannot be realized categorially by conforming to concrete norms. Instead moral decisions must be *creative* acts guided by a single principle, the *principle of proportionate reason,* which balances the positive and negative premoral (ontic) values involved in the act and its consequences. What the many varieties of proportionalism have in common is that they collapse the classical teleological distinction between the moral object of an act as primary determinant of morality and its circumstances as secondary determinants. Hence, they deny the possibility of *exceptionless* concrete negative moral norms, such as "Never assert a falsehood."

Other attempts at revision which have significantly influenced American pastoral practice have been made by Bernard Häring and his student Charles E. Curran. On the grounds of Christian love and compassion Häring makes extensive use of *epicheia* to soften what he regards as the rigorism of recent magisterial pronouncements.[27] Traditionally, however, *epicheia* never permitted dissent from law, but only tried to determine what the legislator would reasonably have provided if he had foreseen the circumstances of the case.

Curran even more openly dissents from the Magisterium and grounds this dissent in a "responsibility-relationality" model of ethics more comprehensive than deontology or teleology. In this model, moral life is viewed "primarily in terms of the person's multiple relationships with God, neighbor, world and self and the subject's actions in this context." He also proposes a "theology of compromise" by which what would be objectively wrong in ideal circumstances can become objectively right in the actual conditions of a sin-distorted world. Hence he denies that morality is primarily determined by the intrinsic nature of acts, including their physical structures. Thus, his ethics of responsibility-relationality turns out to be an Abelardian morality of intentionality.[28]

Such trends have many critics, among whom the most prominent are Germain Grisez and John Finnis, who stoutly defend magisterial teaching on absolute moral norms, yet also seek to find a new way to ground these norms. They no longer rely, as Aquinas did, on the contemplative goal of human life as the measure of the morality of acts, but appeal to certain incommensurable values which can be known without direct reference to a theory of human nature or to its transformation by the virtues.[29]

None of these attempts at revising the Catholic moral tradition seem to me wholly successful or to do full justice to its richness. What the Magisterium should encourage theologians to develop for the service of the Church is a moral theology that will be: (1) rooted in the concrete moral teaching and example of Christ as found in the Scriptures read in the light of Tradition;[30] (2) scholarly and critical, yet conformed to the teaching of the Magisterium as normative; (3) consistently teleological, free of voluntarism and legalism; (4) free of the idealistic dichotomy between the transcendental and the categorial; (5) not merely a theology of decision-making but also one of transformation by the virtues; (6) critically assimilative of the great resources of modern history and the sciences, and finally, (7) especially sensitive to the problem of the "morality gap" between subjective and objective morality.

47

II: FORMATION OF CONSCIENCE

The aim of conscience formation is to bring the subjective conscience into accordance with the objective one, i.e. with moral reality. The immense obstacles raised by the historical burden of original sin must be overcome through the flowering of the baptismal gifts of the virtues and gifts of the Holy Spirit, specifically of the supernatural virtue of prudence perfected by the gift of *counsel.* All the baptized in the state of grace possess this prudence for their personal guidance. If he is to be a Christian father, a man needs the additional domestic prudence (proportionately shared by his wife) to head his family, which is supplied by the Sacrament of Matrimony.[31] Still other forms of prudence needed to govern larger communities is given by graces of office and by the Sacrament of Holy Orders.

These kinds of supernatural prudence will be frustrated in their full operation if the corresponding natural virtues are not also acquired by active practice supported by the supernatural virtues.[32] Moreover, the perfect exercise of natural prudence presupposes all the other virtues. First of all, it presupposes control by the virtue of *temperance* over the bodily drives for pleasure, since immoderate indulgence makes fools of the most intelligent, as it did wise Solomon (Sir 47:19–20). Hence Jesus chose to be celibate to teach us that such temperance is both possible and beautiful. Second, it presupposes the virtue of courage or *fortitude,* like that of the Crucified, to control the fear of suffering and hard work, since fear and weakness make impossible fidelity to conscience. Morality, therefore, is not only a matter of right reason but of affectivity moderated by the virtues of temperance and fortitude. Chaste, courageous Christians have the freedom necessary to judge moral matters rightly, realistically. Their emotions support, not hinder prudence.

Freed of emotional blindness, the judgment of conscience concerns itself with matters of *justice,* the rights of others and one's own duties and responsibilities as expressed in the Ten Commandments.[33] This is the element of truth in deontological ethics, since in matters of justice law plays a large, though not exclusive part. Law by its universality enables us to rise above our own subjectivity and self-interest to consider what is fair to all.

The Mosaic Law was a law of justice, or righteousness, which Jesus faithfully observed, to teach us to respect the rights of all and be advocates of the poor and powerless.[34] Christian morality, however, transcends justice, because it is supremely a morality of loving God and neighbor through the action of the Holy Spirit in our hearts. By this *charity* we are incorporated in Christ and the Church in a life which will endure as the Reign of God in the Triune Community. This love extends even to our enemies as long as their conversion in this life remains open, and it seeks for all the same promises of eternal life that we hope to share.

Christian love, therefore, presupposes *faith*'s true vision of reality rendered docile to the Holy Spirit by the intellectual gifts of understanding, knowledge, and wisdom, and also firm *hope* for the total fulfillment of God's plan.[35] Faith enlightens us to grasp the principles of conscience by enabling us to accept the teaching of Jesus through his Church. Hope gives us confidence that this teaching need not remain a mere ideal but can be practically realized even for us poor, ignorant, sinners.

To form consciences, therefore, is not simply to convey information, but is to form the Christian community in all the virtues, since without these prudence falters, and without prudence conscience fails. The basic community in which conscience is formed is the family. God designed it to provide children with that emotional climate, network of relationships, and impressive models required to nurture the virtues. Here the roots of faith, hope, and love are implanted, and especially the passions are moderated so that children begin to be chaste and courageous. Hence to strengthen family life, today so disrupted by social change and even attacked as outmoded or harmful is a primary pastoral goal.[36] In this task our model for the family should not be some mythical ideal, nor the "traditional family" (often very sick as its present collapse proves), but the Holy Family, where the father both as head and priest of the home was no tyrant but a loving, self-sacrificing servant, and where the mother by the constancy of her wise and courageous love made their home a temple (Eph 5:22–23).[37]

Modern psychology has helped us understand the difference between the conscience of childhood, the "super-ego" constituted of emotionally charged images of right and wrong absorbed largely in the family, and the adult conscience which is a realistic judgement of reason. The childhood conscience lays the necessary groundwork for the mature conscience, but if too punitive and perfectionist or too permissive and chaotic it breeds neuroses that undermine mature judgment. We just recognize that today many Catholics suffer neurotic guilt, or rebel against all moral restrictions, because their childhood training was unsound.

Such family defects ought to be corrected when children enter the wider society, which should supply them with schools in which civic virtues are inculcated both through instruction and by living with peers and teachers representative of the social order and its culture. Even if our country were united in the faith of Christ this task would require the society's best resources, but in fact its is pluralistic and the task is overwhelming. Yet Vatican II taught us not to look back nostalgically to a Christendom when the state was truly Christian—it never was. The civic order and the religious order remain distinct and autonomous in history, because the state cannot require of its citizens any standard of conduct beyond the natural law, since it should not coerce the faith of its citizenry.[38]

Thus, if the state is to be truly neutral in religion, it ought to leave the control of the lower education of children in the hands of their parents and schools of their choice, provided young people are taught the principles of natural law required for citizenship.[39] Yet the state ought also to foster higher forms of education and culture, including the social media and entertainment through which we receive so much of our moral formation, thus encouraging the dialogue of values necessary for a healthy society. Hence the state cannot evade its duty to check the commercial and political exploitation of sex, violence, racism, sexism, and greed in entertainment and the public media.[40]

For its part the Church must have its own organs of evangelization, catechization, and preaching. On the one hand it has to carry on a counter-cultural critique of the social order and of the errors pluralism tolerates, and on the other hand it has to incarnate and enculturate the Gospel in the sound traditions of the society.[41] How poorly and distortedly the life-giving, unifying proclamation of the Gospel by Vatican II has been communicated to the Church and the world! Nor can we forget that along with preaching, the liturgy well celebrated is the Church's most powerful instrument in forming character.

How then is this formation to be carried out? When the reformer Ezra had the Law read to the people on their return from the Exile with its pagan influences, it caused them to weep and moan with terror (Neh 8:9). Jesus chose a better way, and it is his pattern that the Church must follow. First of all, Jesus gave a living example of what his law requires. The lives of the saints and the example of clergy, religious, and parents continue that example. Without its existential reality, efforts to form a Christian conscience are empty ideals.

Second, the much discussed principle of "the hierarchy of truths" must be applied correctly. That principle does not mean we should select only our favorite truths to teach.[42] We must not do like Pharisees who "strained at a gnat and swallowed a camel", neglecting the "weightier things of the law" (Mt 23:23–24). We must teach the whole moral law of the Gospel down to the least letter of the law, but with the right accent (Mt 5:18–19). Only in the light of the first principles of the Gospel, do lesser doctrines become meaningful and obvious, when in isolation they indeed seem "hard sayings" (Jn 6:60; cf. Mk 10:23–27). How foolish is today's debate between those who cry for social justice yet are ashamed of the Church "outmoded" teaching on sexuality and those who argue for just the reverse!

In the hierarchy of moral truths *first* comes the love of God and neighbor which informs all the other virtues. *Second* comes righteousness or justice, the respect for others demanded by the Ten Commandments, without which love is a sham. Thus the theological virtue of love and the moral virtue of justice are intimately linked. *Third* comes asceticism or control of the passions by temperance and fortitude, without which we are not free to keep the commandments. The moral virtues of temperance and fortitude are closely related to the theological virtue of hope, since it is hope for eternal life that frees us from enslavement to the pleasures and power of this life.

At all three levels the moral virtue of prudence is our wise guide—not a worldly prudence but one rooted in the supernatural virtue of Christian faith. Such prudence always requires docility to the teaching of the Magisterium and of civil authority when not contrary to divine law (Rm 13:1–7; Ti 3:1; 1 Pt 2:13–17; cf. Acts 5:29). Yet as Christians advance in maturity and the range of responsibilities they must also learn to apply this teaching intelligently to the situations they meet as members of the laity and citizenry. Genuine creativity and ingenuity in one's practical affairs in service of the common good is a true form of obedience to law.[43]

Note that although the virtues of temperance and fortitude which control the personal appetites are lowest in the threefold heirarchy, nevertheless they are necessary for the freedom which is demanded by the higher virtues. Hence in actual pedagogy emphasis on the practice of these virtues come first. Teen-agers who are drug addicts or unmarried mothers are not free for lessons in justice or prudence.

To sum up: *First,* the Church has pastoral responsibility to form Christian consciences by preaching the whole moral law without any ambiguity, a task itself requiring the highest prudence. The clergy cannot do their part if they do not understand this moral law, the heirarchy of its truths, and their interrelations. Today priests are confused and polarized by the deadlocked debates among the theologians to whom they have looked for help. Both they and the laity must come to see that while such debates can help develop the moral insight of the Christian community, the final judgment on moral truth remains the prerogative of the Magisterium. Hence, dissenting theological opinions, however "probable," cannot be the proximate norms for Christian conscience.[44] The bishops, with all love and prudence, must also have the courage of St. Paul when he said and repeated, "If anyone preaches a gospel to you other than the one you received, let a curse be upon him" (Gal 1:9).

Second, to denounce is not enough, we must also strengthen in Christian values those institutions—family, school, the government, the public media, entertainment, the Church itself—in which are formed the virtues which make sound moral judgment possible. We cannot form consciences so as to close the gap between subjective and objective morality unless we also strive to reform our society and culture.

NOTES

1. On the use of this word see C. Maurer, *Theological Dictionary of the New Testament,* ed. by Gerhard Friedrich, translated and edited by Geoffrey W. Bromiley (Grand Rapids, MI: Wm. B. Eerdmans, 1971), vol. 7, 898–919 and the bibliograph on pp. 898 f. *Syneidesis* occurs only three times in the Septuagint and in books showing Hellenistic influences (Eccl. 10:20; Wis 17:11; Sir 42:18); cf. also Michael Darton, ed., *Modern Concordance to the New Testament* (London: Darton Longman & Todd, 1976), pp. 330–331.

2. Maurer, p. 908.

3. See Ceslaus Spicq, "La conscience dans le Nouveau Testament, " *Revue Biblique,* 47 (1958): 50–80 and *Théologie Morale du Nouveau Testament,* (Paris: J. Gabalda, 1965), II, c. VIII, pp. 567–622.

4. See Edouard Massaux, L'influence de l'Évangile de Saint Matthieu sur la literature chrétienne avant saint Irenée (University of Louvain, Gembloux: Duculot, 1950).

5. Current writers often distinguish "deontological" ethics from "teleological" ethics by saying the former maintains absolute (i.e. exceptionless) norms, while the latter does not. This does not correspond to the etymology of the terms and in fact both types of ethics may or may not have absolute norms. A better usage is to distinguish the terms by saying that in a deontological ethics morality rests on a law expressing the will of the legislator, while a teleological ethics rests on the conformity of an act as a means to the true goal of life, and its moral laws are derived from this relation and simply express it. On this see Bruno Schuller, S. J., "Various Types of Grounding for Ethical Norms," in Charles E. Curran and Richard A. McCormick, ed., *Moral Norms and Catholic Tradition,* Readings in Moral Theology, No. 1 (New York: Paulist, 1979), pp. 184–187. The terminology seems to have been made popular by C. D. Broad, *Five Types of Ethical Theory* (London: Routledge, Kegan Paul, 1930), pp. 162–166, who however, adds a third type, "logical" (i.e. self-consistent), and has different definitions.

6. Thus in a well-known (and in some ways excellent) essay by Sean Freyne, "The Bible and Christian Morality," in Ronald P. Hamel and Kenneth R. Himes, OFM, *Introduction to Christian Ethics: A Reader* (New York: Paulist, 1989), pp. 9–32, we find that, "Jesus' basic request to men was to 'follow me', to imitate the selfless pattern of his life; this rather than spell out a detailed moral code for them. Hence the Johannine writings are correct when they put forward Jesus' moral teaching chiefly in terms of the command to love, spelled out mainly in concrete terms of forgiveness, practical caring and unlimited self-sacrifice. As far as codified law is concerned, Jesus inherited and refined rather than innovated" (p. 18). A range of opinions on this subject, many of the same tenor, can be found in Charles E. Curran and Richard A. McCormick, *The Use of Scripture in Moral Theology,* Readings in Moral Theology, No. 4 (New York: Paulist, 1984). Curran's own view in "The Function of the Scripture in Moral Theology", *ibid.,* pp. 178–212 are much the same as Freyne's. An extreme example of this position by a Protestant author is Jack T. Sanders, *Ethics in the New Testament* (Philadelphia: Fortress, 1975) who thinks that the only substantive ethical teaching in the New Testament is in the *Epistle of St. James!*

7. Richard A. McCormick, *The Critical Calling* (Washington, DC: Georgetown University Press, 1989), pp. 58–59 thinks that "probably the most common error in contemporary Christian ethics" is the "Confusion of parenetic discourse with normative discourse." Is it not even a worse error to fail to ground arguments in moral theology in revelation, thus rendering them *extrinsic* to theology? For a survey of views on this topic see Richard M. Gula, SS, *What They are Saying About Moral Norms,* (New York: Paulist, 1982), pp. 29–34 and selection of essays in Charles E. Curran and Richard A. McCormick,

The Use of Scripture In Moral Theology, Readings in Moral Theology, No. 4, (New York: Paulist, 1984).

8. Freyne neutralizes this test by commenting, "Matthew paints a conservative picture of Jesus's attitude to Jewish law (Mt 5:17–19), yet it must be recognized that in all probability this gospel was written within a polemical situation in the Jewish Christian wing of the early Church, and may therefore be more conservative than Jesus in regard to this law. At all events we would do well to cross-check our conclusions from the other sources for the teaching of Jesus, Mark and Q.", *op. cit.,* p. 17. He does not tell us what this "cross-check" yields.

9. For ample evidence of the thoroughly Jewish character of Christian ethics, see E. P. Sanders, *Paul, the Law, and the Jewish People* (Philadelphia: Fortress, 1983) and *Jesus and Judaism* (Philadelphia: Fortress Press, 1985).

10. For a defense of rabbinic ethics against the charge of mere legalism, see Louis Jacobs, "Sin", *Encyclopedia Judaica,* 14:1587–1593.

11. In an excellent summary of the results of recent parable studies, Madeleine I. Boucher, *The Parable,* New Testament Message, vol. 7, (Wilmington, DL: Michael Glazier, 1981) the author defines a parable as "A topical [metaphor, simile, synecdoche, etc.] narrative which functions as religious or ethical rhetorical speech" (p. 39) and says that "the purpose of a parable is to move to decision or action" (p. 46). Yet she also says that a parable is "more rhetorical than scientific (the kind of speech to which teaching or instruction belongs" (p. 35). This can be misunderstood because biblical teaching and instruction (Torah) is generally couched in rhetorical forms, because it has a practical purpose: it instructs us how to act and moves us to make a decision to act. Therefore it would be an error to conclude, as some do, that because it is rhetorical (parenetic) that it moves us to act, but does not instruct us concretely how to act, i.e., does not lay down concrete moral norms. For a very thorough analysis of the performative character of the parable see Mogens Stiller Kjargaard, *Metaphor and Parable* (Leiden: E. J. brill, 1986), particularly the summary on pp. 238–239.

12. See Jean Daniélou, *Holy Pagans of the Old Testament* (Baltimore: Helicon, 1956).

13. It occurs 6 times in the *Pastoral Epistles,* 5 in Hebrews, 3 in *1 Peter* and 2 in *Acts* (Maurer, p. 917).

14. Maurer, pp. 914–917.

15. On this still very controversial topic see Joseph A. Fitzmeyer, SJ, *Paul and His Theology,* (Englewood Clifts, NJ: Prentice-Hall, 1989). Also E. P. Sanders, "On the Question of Fulfilling the Law in Paul and Rabbinic Judaism", in *Donum Gentilicum: New Testament Studies in Honour of David Daube,* ed. by E. Bammel, C. K. Barrett, and W. D. Davies (Oxford: Clarendon Press, 1978), pp. 103–126 and *Paul, the Law, and the Jewish People* (Philadelphia: Fortress, 1985); also Heim Raisanen, *Paul and the Law* (Philadelphia: Fortress, 1983) who maintains that Paul was simply inconsistent.

16. See Pierre Grelot, *Église et ministerès: pour un dialogue critique avec Edward Schillebeeckx* (Paris: Editions du Cerf, 1983) for a detailed analysis of the New Testament teaching on the transmission of apostolic authority in the Church.

17. See Erich Osborn, *Ethical Patterns in Early Christian Thought,* (Cambridge: Cambridge University Press, 1976); LThK 4: 859–867; PL, Index CXLIII, 220:351–355; and Gregorio Armas, ORSA, *La Moral de San Agustin* (Madrid: 1954), pp. 135–144.

18. See Osborn, pp. 183–191.

19. On the scholastic treatment of conscience see Odon Lottin, *Psychologie et morale aux XII et XIII siécles,* pp. 103–349 and M. B. Crowe, "The term synderesis and the scholastics," *Irish Theological Quarterly,* 1956, 151–164, 228–245.

20. As M. B. Crowe, *op. cit.* shows that this term attributed to St. Jerome by the scholactics was the result of a scribal error.

21. For Aquinas on synderesis and conscience see 2 *Sent.*, d. 24, q. 1–3; q. 39, q. 3; *De Veritate*, q. 16–17; *S. Th.*, I, q. 79, a. 12–13; I–II, q.94, a. 1, ad 2.

22. IV *Sent.*, dist. 33, q. a.1 ; *S. Th.*, I–II, q. 94, a.2.

23. *Ibid.*, a.4.

24. On this point see T. G. Belmans, "Le paradoxe de la conscience erronée d'Abelard a Karl Rahner," *Revue Thomiste*, 90 (1990): 570–586 and also his "Au croisement des chemins en morale fondamentale", *Revue Thomiste*, 89 (1989): 246–278.

25. My view of this transition is different than that of John A. Gallagher in his useful, *Time Past, Time Future: A Historical Study of Catholic Moral Theology* (New York: Paulist, 1990) chiefly because he seems to ignore the fundamental shift toward voluntarism in the late Middle Ages and the philosophical roots of proportionalism in Kantian *a priorism*.

26. See Gallager, pp. 245–268 and Bernard Hoose, *Proportionalism: The American Debate and its European Roots* (Georgetown, MD: Georgetown University Press, 1987) for sympathetic accounts of proportionalism. Gallagher stresses the variety of views which the term includes. For my critique see B. M. Ashley and K. D. O'Rourke, *Health Care Ethics* (St. Louis: Catholic Health Association, 3rd. ed., 1989) pp. 164–171.

27. See Bernard Häring, "Does God Condemn Contraception: A Question for the Whole Church", *Commonweal*, Feb. 10, 1989, pp. 69–71 and the unsigned commentary "The Moral Norms of 'Humanae Vitae' ", *Osservatore Romano, Origins,* vol. 18, no. 38, pp. 629–632. Haring exemplifies his method by arguing that when married people find Natural Family Planning impractical as a means of legitimate birth regulation, *epicheia* permits them to use contraception.

28. See his essay, "Method in Moral Theology: An Overview from an American Perspective," *Studia Moralia* 18 (1980): 107–128. Curran further explains his view by contrasting it to a teleological method which would define lying as acting contrary to the teleology of the faculty of speech, or sexual sin as acting contrary to the "innate teleology inscribed in the sexual faculty." But any adequate description of the teleology of the faculty of speech must show that speech is essentially ordered to communicate with (*relate to*) another person, often in *response to*.questions from that person; or of the teleology of the sexual faculty that it is essentially ordered to the covenantal and physical union of a male and female person and to the procreation of children to whom these parents become intimately related and for whom they are responsible. "Teleology" is a relational concept, and moral teleology primarily concerns relationship between and for persons.

29. See Germain Grisez, *The Way of the Lord Jesus*, vol 1., *Christian Moral Principles* (Chicago: Franciscan Herald Press, 1983) and John Finnis, *Natural Law and Natural Rights* (Oxford: Clarendon Press, 1980). For my friendly criticism of Grisez's work see "Christian Moral Principles: A review Discussion," *The Thomist*, 48 (1984): 450–460.

30. On suggestions as to how this revision might be done see my article, "Scriptural Grounding of Concrete Moral Norms", *Persona Verità et Morale*, Atti del Congressio Internazionale di Teologia Morale (Roma, 7–12 aprile 1986), (Roma: Citta Nuova Editrice, 1987), pp. 637–652; also in the *The Thomist*, 52 (1988), pp. 1–22.

31. Whatever is to be said for feminist complaints about "patriarchy" we cannot explain away the Biblical teaching of Eph 5:23, "For the husband is head of his wife just as Christ is head of the church" (Eph 5:23; cf. Col 4:18–19; 1 Tm 2: 9–15; Ti 2:4–5; 1 Pt 3:1. It should be noted, however, that this headship is not one of domination but service in a relationship that requires mutual responsibilities and respect (Eph 5: 21–23). See Stephen

B. Clark, *Man and Woman in Christ* (Ann Arbor, MI: Servant Books, 1980) for extensive discussion of these texts.

32. In the current debate on whether there is a specifically Christian ethics, the nay-sayers often cite Aquinas's view (S.Th. I–II q. 100, a.1) that the Ten Commandments (except the Sabbath law) are simply matters of natural law. They ignore S.Th I–II, q.63, a.1–4 and *De Virtutibus, q.1, a.10* which argue that Christians are obliged to keep the Commandments in a supernatural mode which requires infused virtue imposing concrete moral norms beyond those demanded by natural law. Aquinas' example is the rules of asceticism practiced by St. Paul (I Cor 9:24–27) in view of his supernatural goal. Thus it is not strange that mandatory priestly celibacy is not easy to justify by purely natural law arguments.

33. St. Thomas Aquinas, S.Th, I–II, q. 100, a.2, shows that the Ten Commandments directly concern only matters of *justice,* and only indirectly those of the other virtues. For example while adultery is directly a sin against temperance, it is forbidden by the Sixth Commandment not as a sexual sin but as a breach of contract.

34. On the relation of Jesus to the Mosaic Law, E. P. Sanders, *Jesus and Judaism* (Philadelphia: Fortress, 1985) writes, "We have found one instance in which Jesus, in effect, demanded transgression of the law: the demand to the man whose father had died. [Mt 8:21 f.; Lk 9:59 f.] Otherwise the material in the Gospels reveals no transgression by Jesus." (p. 267; cf. the whole discussion, pp. 245–269). This very shocking exception was justified by Jesus' need to demonstrate the authority and urgency of his mission.

35. The English work "love" overworked by today's preachers and catechists is so broad as to be completely misunderstood if we do not often point out that the New Testament Writers faced with the same problems in Greek, developed the term *agape* as a kind of technical term to distinguish Christian love, the love motivated by faith and hope and participation in God's own divine love for us, from erotic and sentimental love. Latin used the term *caritas* to make the same distinction so that formerly Catholics used the term "charity" but this is unfortunately now largely restricted to mean alms-giving.

36. Paul Taylor, *New York Times,* Jan 22, 1991, A3, reports that 25.7% of all children born in the United States are illegitimate (in comparison with 5% in Italy and 48% in Sweden), and between 70 and 90% of these end up sometime in their lives on welfare. Only 30 percent of blacks and 51 percent of whites of ages 15 to 44 are now married. Since these rates are increasing rapidly (only 4% of children in the U.S. were illegitimate in 1950), it seems obvious that we are headed to a situation in which at least half of our population will have been raised in poverty and never known a two-parent family.

37. On this topic see the essays in *The Family Today and Tomorrow* (Braintree, MA: The Pope John Center, 1985), including my paper, "The Family in Church and Society", pp. 101–112 with its reference to Edward Shorter, *The Making of the Modern Family* (New York: Basic Books/ Harper Torchbooks, 1977) who shows that the fundamental "sexual revolution" took place not in the 1960's but with the Enlightenment (secular Humanism) about 1800. The Victorian Family was not the "traditional Christian family" but only a flawed, ultimately unsuccessful effort to stem the advance of the war on the family, which secular humanists have always wanted to replace with sexual "liberation" and the rearing of children by "experts."

38. Vatican II, *Declaration on Religious Liberty (Dignitatis Humanae),* Dec. 7, 1965, 1–6.

39. Vatican II, *Declaration on Christian Education (Gravissmum educationis),* Oct. 28, 1965.

40. Vatican II, *Decree on the Means of Social Communication, December 4, 1963 (Inter mirifica),* n.12, and the subsequent *Pastoral Instruction on the Means of Social*

Communication (Communio et Progressio), January 29, 1971, n. 48–62. The criticisms this conciliar document received, which made necessary the subsequent more positive supplementary instruction, was in part a reflection of the power of media persons to counter all criticism of their activities, and do not prove it valueless or obsolete.

41. These are themes developed in the apostolic exhortation *Evangelii nuntiandi,* December 8, 1975; and the encyclical *Redemptoris missio,* December 7, 1990.

42. Cardinal Josef Ratzinger, "Update on the Universal Cetechism" *Origins,* vol. 20. no. 22 (1990): 356–359 defines this hierarchy as the "connection of all truths with the nucleus of revelation", not, he remarks, to be confused with the "theological notes" which classify magisterial teachings according to the mode in which they are authenticated.

43. The influence of Karl Rahner has led many recent moralists to treat moral decisions on the analogy of artistic decisions which are characterized by a creative response to a situation in which many values have to be uniquely selected and synthesized. This is a useful analogy, but it should not be pressed to the point of eliminating at least some absolute negative concrete moral norms. Artistic skill can be demonstrated even by its abuse, but moral virtue cannot.

44. Congregation for the Doctrine of the Faith, *Instruction on the Ecclesial Vocation of the Theologian,* May 24, 1990, n. 34.

Chapter 4

PSYCHOLOGY AND CONSCIENCE

The Reverend James Gill, S.J., M.D.

I was delighted to be invited to come here today to speak to you about the way or ways psychologists are currently thinking and writing about conscience. But, like most of you, I'm looking at the scene as an outsider, not being a psychologist myself. As a psychiatrist, and as a priest, I have found myself intrigued by this assignment. And what I'm going to try to do right now is share with you some of the interesting fruits of my homework.

Some psychologists today, influenced by the psychoanalytic manner of thinking, talk about conscience as an essential component of the so-called "structural theory" that Sigmund Freud devised. You may recall that he divided the psyche's functioning into three distinct types of operations, the id, the ego, the superego. The conscience is traditionally viewed by psychoanalysts as being incorporated within the superego, that is, the psychic structure responsible for self-criticism and censorship. It is also the source of a person's sense of self-esteem.

The superego has three elements: (1) a conscious part called "conscience," (2) the unconscious self-critical part, and (3) the partly conscious and partly unconscious component that has to do with self-love and self-esteem. The superego, according to Freud, is principally the origin of prohibition. When telling us what not to do, it is called conscience. But when the superego is serving as the source of idealization, i.e., telling us what we ought to become, it is labelled as the "ego ideal." It can be looked upon as a collection of abiding beliefs that tell us what we would be doing if we were acting as our best possible selves.

I want to speak briefly about the development of the superego. Freud made three important observations regarding this process. (1) Parents communicate to their children their own values and social norms which are provided to the parents by the culture in which they are living. (2) The superego is initially developed as a result of the resolution of the child's oedipal conflict, somewhere near the end of the sixth year of life. (3) What the child experiences when the conscience is operating is guilt feelings. These are produced automatically whenever the individual transgresses, i.e., engages in behavior (interior or exterior) which falls short of the person's ideal.

The superego is irrational, rigid, unreflective and often fierce. Ultimately it is activated by the child's fear of his or her parents. The child fears being punished, rejected, abandoned, or even annihilated by them. As the child grows up, the parental prohibitions tend to remain in force. Even in our adult years we, as it were, hear their voices within us. Just try to put your feet up on an expensive piece of furniture, or try to use a spoon to eat peas or a piece of meat while dining in a good restaurant and see how you feel. And many a spouse feels irrationally guilty when he or she disrobes in front of the person they have married either months or years before.

As psychologist Charles Shelton has pointed out in his excellent pastoral book, *Morality and the Adolescent*, recent psychologists in the psychoanalytic school describe a source for morality that is present well before the emergence of the superego. They see the nurturing presence of care givers, especially the mother, as an origin for conscience and early moral development. Shelton explains, "the positive experiences displayed in such a supportive relationship elicit a secure attachment bond that fosters the child's internalization of moral values (dos and don'ts). Further, early child development—even as early as the first few years of life—shows children's readiness to display "early moral emotions." These emotions (hurt feelings, positive feelings of sharing, shame, and so on) point to an inchoative moral sense that is prior to the forming of the superego."

Psychologists also observe that the child—even during the very early childhood years—manifests a capacity for empathy, i.e., vicarious emotional arousal to another person's experience. This finding too suggests that the child possesses an elementary moral self that is by its very nature inclined to manifest sensitivity and care towards others.

Just one more thought about the superego. As many of you bishops know, I have the opportunity to work at The Institute of Living in Hartford, Connecticut, where we treat in a specialized, in-patient unit of the hospital, professional persons including physicians, nurses, lawyers, teachers, clergy and religious. One of the major sources of emotional pain, we find, even among the most highly educated priests and religious women and men, is the guilt (not the moral guilt, but the psychological guilt) that arises from their superego and that plagues even their adult years. These are persons who failed to develop a true moral conscience during their adolescence. That is to say, their educators (including teachers, parents and preachers) were unable to help them learn to sense their own unique value as persons, to recognize their bonding with and responsibility to others, and to discern value in their concrete life situations. In their moral life they still operate mainly at the level of the superego—fearful of offending authority figures, feeling guilty and depressed when they think they have displeased or disappointed them, and incapable of responsible moral decision making which requires, as Shelton has described, "personal reflection and the adoption of a personal value system that is consciously articulated and continually evaluated." In other words, they operate more like children than adults in their morality, not having done the work in adolescence that prepares people to function autonomously as adults.

Aside from psychoanalytically oriented theorists, most contemporary psychologists who are involved in the domain of moral psychology refrain from discussing conscience as such. They address themselves to what they call "morality" and define it variously as (1) behavior that helps another human being, (2) behavior in conformity with societal norms, (3) the internalization of social norms, (4) the arousal of empathy or guilt, or both, (5) reasoning about justice, and (6) putting another's interest ahead of one's own.

Psychologists generally subdivide the area of morality into three elements—thoughts, emotions and behavior. Cognitive developmentalists (such as Jean Piaget and Lawrence Kohlberg) study moral thought. Psychoanalytic psychologists study emotions. Behaviorists study, of course, behavior. Rather than attempt to summarize all that has been reported regarding these studies— an impossible task in these few minutes—I simply want to remind you that the best known (at least in North America) of contemporary moral psychologists, Kohlberg, focuses on basic cognitive structures that are believed to underlie and organize moral reasoning, and not upon learning specific moral rules. He describes stages of development that include a series of transformations in the way thinking is organized. The central concept in Kohlberg's system is justice, and he does not regard didactic teaching by adults as especially important in the child's moral development. One of his professional colleagues, James Rest, of the University of Minnesota, in criticizing Kohlberg's work has observed, "We have no direct assurance that the schemes that a person verbalizes in a hypothetical situation are those operative in actual decision making in real situations."

Rest himself is probably one of the most interesting and helpful to us among the contemporary moral psychologists. He writes, in Handbook of Child Psychology, "Morality concerns how people determine rights and responsibilities in their social interactions, how people arrange the terms of cooperation and promotion of their mutual welfare." Rest's research shows that a person's moral behavior in a particular situation involves an ensemble of psychological processes. He identifies four major components:

(I) sensitivity—interpreting the situation to identify how one's actions will affect the welfare of others,

(II) judgement—figuring out what the ideally moral course of action would be,

(III) planning—selecting from among multiple values what one actually intends to do, and

(IV) executing—implementing the moral plan of action. Rest is most interested in the second of these elements. He writes, "Development in component II is not just stamping in more rules by the ministrations of socializing agents or even learning subtleties in how to apply the rules or in learning more complex rules (although progress in these regards might go along with development) but rather development is the progressive understanding of why people have rights and responsibilities—understanding what kinds of social arrangements are possible and what it takes to create and sustain them."

Rest finds in his studies that "fairly strong evidence supports the general claim that over time people generally change in the direction of making moral judgments on the basis of a better understanding of social arrangements." He believes that these shifts in moral judgement reflect new cognitive capacities. He insists, however, that it is not possible to reduce moral thinking to general cognitive and linguistic development. Rest argues, "Concepts about bargaining, sustaining loyalty in relationships, doing one's share of the duties in social organizations, participating in consensus government, taking account of ameliorating circumstances in judgements of blameworthiness—such ideas involve more than just formal logic, propositional thinking, or the learning of special jargon." He concludes, "Moral discussion with peers and parents seems to facilitate development, as does formal education, social interaction, and involvement in complex social organizations."

It should be noted that Rest's studies focus on social morality, i.e., questions of duties to others, justice, and the conditions of social cooperation. Little psychological research has been done regarding duties to oneself that involve no one else, and regarding other sorts of values.

In relation to Rest's four components of morality, Charles Shelton at Regis University in Denver has developed a contemporary theory of conscience. He names its four components with the same labels Rest gives them. The first, "sensitivity", Shelton describes as the ability to be aware that a situation exists which calls forth a moral response—realizing that the welfare of someone is at stake and that one's own actions influence the other's welfare.

The second component, "judging", says Shelton, involves looking at the problem in terms of one's personal moral ideals and then attempting to decide what action is appropriate. One asks oneself: "What ideal is central to the moral concern at hand?"

The third component, "planning" Shelton sees as the choosing of an action that reflects one's valued ideals. The essence of this step is an act of the will. Recognizing various aspects of the situation the person decides to act in a specific way according to his or her ideals.

The fourth component, "executing" involves acting to implement one's goals despite the various obstacles. Perseverance is involved here; the response must be sustained over time.

Shelton, as a psychologist, acknowledges that he is attempting to translate the insights of psychological science into "the faith perspective of the Christian moral tradition." In doing so, commenting on Rest's "sensitivity" component, Shelton writes, "Empathy represents a human foundational response for the emergence of Christian behaviors. Empathic experiences orient the person to be aware of the hurt and plight of those in need." Empathy fosters social bondedness and community; it provides the impetus (together with grace) for making real the gospel's command to love. Shelton observes: "It is the human capacity to empathize which allows us to feel and to understand the needs, concerns and cares of another." He shows how Jesus' own ministry was based on empathy, and how an empathic sensitivity to one's brothers and sisters has nourished and sustained faith communities of believers from apostolic times to the present.

Looking at the "judging component", Shelton says: "The traditions of the faith community must be ideals to which one can appeal. Aspects of this tradition include the history of the faith community, the authority given the faith community in the Spirit, and the life themes that have nourished the community (e.g., the Exodus in the Old Testament and the challenge of conversion in the New Testament). The Ten Commandments, the Sermon on the Mount, Paul's exhortation on the fruits of the Spirit, as well as personal experience of Jesus Christ furnish the ideals we cherish as Christians."

Regarding the "planning" component, Shelton points out that we need the virtue of prudence to choose one ideal from among many. We also need the ability to discern the better among several competing goods, and the lesser of two evils. Also, any decision to act in a particular way must accept the part suffering plays in human life. As a Christian, one should not make decisions which avoid the inevitable suffering entailed in the laying down of one's life for the well-being of others.

Finally, in relation to the "execution" component, Shelton cites St. Paul bemoaning the fact that "the good that I would, I do not; but the evil which I would not, that I do." He observes, "Obviously, more than intentions are needed for an act to be moral. A firm character, resolute goals, and perseverance are essential to a moral course of action. It is the community that sustains the Christian who commits his or her life to the cultivation of habits oriented toward living out the fruits of the Spirit.

But where does *conscience* fit into this scheme? Moral theologian Timothy O'Connell has described conscience in three ways that stem from traditional moral theology, and I see these corresponding to Rest's components I, II, and III. Corresponding to component I, O'Connell writes about *conscience,* in *Principles for a Catholic Morality,* "We are called to goodness and responsibility. We experience ourselves as accountable, as challenged by ourselves and our world, as worthy of praise or blame depending on how we respond." This element, as I understand it, seems to matches Rest's concept of "sensitivity" as an essential element in moral behavior.

Matching Rest's component II, "judgement", O'Connell explains: "Conscience deals with the specific perception of values, concrete individual values. It emerges in the ongoing process of reflection, discussion and analysis . . . We seek to find and understand the concrete moral values in our situation, but we may fail. We are capable of blindness . . . distraction . . . misunderstanding . . . (Conscience) needs to be educated. (Morally sincere) persons will turn to their friends, their colleagues, their peers, and seek to benefit from their insights. They will listen to the larger culture, to the wisdom of previous generations, and they will listen to voices from other situations, more objective voices, as these help them to interpret their situation." Conscience, says O'Connell, needs to be formed, guided, directed and illuminated. This is where the church fits in, as a teacher of moral values. The prudent person will listen to its declarations. It is a source of moral wisdom. Common sense and faith say: "Consult the Christian community."

In parallel with Rest's component III, "planning" O'Connell writes: "(Conscience) constitutes the final norm by which a person's action must be guided . . . If I genuinely *believe* that I should do something, it is not only accurate to say that I may do it. More than that, I should do it. Indeed, I *must* do it . . . one must surely follow conscience. For in the last analysis that is the only possible guide for action by a free and knowing person." O'Connell supports contemporary moralist Josef Fuchs' statement, in *Theologia Moralis Generalis,* "The dictate of conscience . . . enjoys absolute certainty. For it dictates that the person acting ought to act according to the personal judgement which he has concerning the act. In a word, the judgement (of conscience) . . . is not only infallibly true but is also absolutely certain."

If our time here permitted, I would talk a little about the way psychologists are finding in their research that very young children are pro-social (i.e., inclined to be self-sacrificing) as well as altruistic, (i.e., ready to invest in the well being of others). I would also point out that Kohlberg, Piaget, Rest, and other cognitive developmental psychologists have shown that as a person develops, he or she goes through progressive stages of thinking about justice and other values. This would suggest that conscience operates differently in different persons, according to the level of psychosexual and social maturity that an individual has mastered. But I'm sure these issues will be taken up in other talks these days, particularly in relation to the way moral education is accomplished.

In closing, I would offer for your discussion the following description of conscience as a summary of what I have said up to this point. I would say that conscience is a complex operation of the person which involves thinking, imagining, and feeling as well as making choices affecting behavior. It is not just a moral syllogizing about the specific good thing that ought to be done, or the evil thing that ought to be avoided. It is not merely a feeling or simply moral knowledge. It is the developing individual striving to do the will of God, to glorify God, and to actualize one's self fully as a created, socially responsible and accountable, loving and caring human person. Thank you.

Chapter 5

PASTORAL CONCERNS PSYCHOLOGY AND CONSCIENCE

BISHOP: Is it difficult for you as a priest and as a psychologist when you have these various theories offered out to you to bridge between that which has been our theological thought on the one hand and, on the other hand, a world view offered out by persons through an anthropology much different from ours in many cases? How do you reconcile all that?

FATHER GILL: I find it's like there are two different worlds, two different languages, two different ways of perceiving reality, two different beliefs about what reality consists in.

The value I see in learning psychology is not that it gives so much of an interpretation to what theologians are seeking as it gives some categories to think in. A theologian obviously is concerned about a person having general principles of morality and seeing the moral aspect of reality.

But, I certainly don't see the psychologist coming anywhere near saying what these moral principles should be. All they're studying is quantifiable behaviors.

It's the same way that a psychiatrist shifts from moment to moment. At one moment, when somebody is telling you he or she is guilty and wants to go to confession, you have to somewhere straddle those two worlds that I implied were there.

One of them is the possibility and the goodness there is in experiencing really felt guilt if one has consciously, deliberately transgressed the divine law.

On the other hand, it's useful to have another category to think in that psychology suggests wherein the feelings of guilt could also be proceeding from an entirely different source, which is understood in terms of the super-ego and the unconscious elements in the conscience.

So, they really are two useful ways of moving back and forth so that there is some illumination. I wear two hats and take one off and put the other one on.

BISHOP: The two hat thing is the thing we would like to address. When you talk of Shelton's components of moral behavior, and that first element of sensitivity, the empathy that you need to respond morally, what is the basis of that morality? Is it just human experience, or is it revelation?

FATHER GILL: I think if I understand Shelton and these psychologists who believe that empathy and feelings have to play a part in the complete moral act, I think what they are trying to say is there is evidence that even from shortly after infancy we, in fact, behave in a way that reveals a sensitivity or a responsiveness to others who are in need.

On top of that primitive inclination to respond, then, education comes along and says there are things you have to keep consciously in mind. This is the intellectual part of that sensitivity. And there are principles that you have to keep in mind.

On the other hand, there are people who will never get that education or that instruction, or aren't capable of benefitting from it like people who are mentally defective. But they can still have the inclination to be empathic.

At another stage you can also come to the point where you begin to be manipulative and to use people around you for your own purposes because of the kind of understanding that you have of what a human person is.

There is always going to be in the term psychology an emphasis on what's it to do to or for me. On the other hand, our whole purpose in theology, in religion, in spirituality, is to ask if we are going to follow what God has revealed, namely, the fact that love is the quintessence of life. Shelton's starting point as a psychologist is just that we respond to others according to how we perceive their condition. The starting point of theology and one's spiritual life is far beyond that. That is both in age and as far as the content, the comprehension in theology.

FATHER GILL: I don't want to forget to mention the fact that Charles Shelton has written an excellent volume on adolescence and the development of the morality of adolescence with many good principles and applications and fine ways of dealing with young people at different stages of development, early adolescence, later adolescence, young childhood. I'd certainly recommend that book.

I think that the task of any educator is to help the individual, starting at the point where he is, how he understands God, what he has experienced in relation to Jesus Christ, what his concepts are with regard to morality and salvation. They need to start where they are and to begin to do the tasks that every adolescent needs to do. Namely, to make the principles and the ideals, the convictions, the values their own.

In other words, they ought to believe things not because somebody says you have to believe them, or somebody taught it and you have to memorize an answer, or you have to please them by regurgitating it, but to ask, what do I believe? This entails the examination of one's own experience.

I only know what Maslow said about growth. The reason people don't grow, 99 out of 100 people don't reach anything like a full development spiritually, socially, culturally, affectively, is that they lack two things. The first is challenge, or invitation to keep growing, to keep striving to make progress in development. But the other is models.

I don't think that there is any better gift for anyone whether it's a bishop or a priest or teacher or sister, or parent to offer to young people trying to grow than to keep exemplifying Christian behavior that's ethical and moral. But, we also need to be able to talk about why we do what we do, how *we* think about God, how *we* think about actions, how *we* think about values.

BISHOP: We have been told a confessor should demand obedience. You become the conscience for the poor sick person. Is that still valid?

FATHER GILL: I think it is still valid in certain cases, but I certainly wouldn't recommend it as a general form of treatment or dealing with a scrupulous person.

I think it depends upon whether a person has enough background to understand what usually goes on in the scrupulous person's psyche. What generally is happening, as I understand it, is that the impulses, the inclinations, the wishes that come out of, if you want to talk Freudian language, the id, are not well held in check by the super-ego.

In other words, the policeman isn't working quite well enough to squelch these inclinations, these thoughts, fantasies, feelings, and so forth.

But, if a person has aggressive impulses or aggressive wishes, or aggressive fantasies, there is going to be anxiety and often that's what interpreted as guilt feelings by the individual. Then the person feels that he can get that taken away by going to Confession.

Now, the problem is that what the person thinks is causing the guilt feeling is often not what's causing it at all.

I had a parent, for example, who was anxious because he thought about the fact that he might pick up a knife and slice the body of his infant child. This would sound like anxiety about a very aggressive inclination, in fact, he was feeling anxious and guilty because of sexual inclinations toward that child. It gets pretty deceptive, pretty sophisticated, pretty difficult at times. And that's when one should refer the person for clinical help.

ARCHBISHOP: Father, you had mentioned a definition of conscience of Father Fuchs in regard to conscience as infallible. I don't know whether I understood it correctly, because conscience may be certain, but it may be wrong. If you say conscience is infallible, the implications of that seem to be somewhat enormous.

FATHER GILL: I relied on O'Connell to teach me about the three different concepts of conscience: conscience one, conscience two, conscience three. In conscience three, at least as I understand O'Connell, you can't go wrong by following the conscience, which is the decision you have made if you have gotten in touch with the sources of a rightly formed conscience. It's right for you and it can't be wrong for you if you act in virtue of whatever decision you have actually made. I think that's what he means by infallible, meaning you can't do wrong if you have actually sought to be correctly informed and made the best decision you can.

BISHOP: Is conscience a relatively unimportant topic to most psychologists?

FATHER GILL: Yes. Most psychologists are not concerned about doing research, and if you are not doing research in it, most psychologists don't care how a child of ten compared with a person of thirteen draws a conclusion about what should be done or what should not be done.

Structured Dialogue:

Methods in Moral Theology

Chapter 6

THE SEARCH FOR AN ADEQUATE THEOLOGICAL METHOD IN THE FORMATION OF CONSCIENCE

The Very Reverend Paul Philibert, O.P., Ph.D.

Conscience is the mature person in action. Conscience requires the dynamic coordination of intelligence and desire in a way that effectively integrates the light of reason with the commanding force of moral deliberation. An adequate theory of conscience formation cannot deal with information alone nor with moral reasoning alone to the exclusion of educating sensibilities and appetites. Yet, as I will show, too often conscience is conceived in purely rational terms.

Let me begin with a description of the idea of conscience that appears to be dominant in our popular culture and with the influence this culture has upon our Roman Catholic ethos at this time. One hundred years ago, our church was an immigrant phenomenon, generally marginalized, and cautiously set apart from the mainstream of the developing culture. The Catholic Church's high ritual profile—tied closely to ethnic expressions of Catholic piety imported from abroad—and its attachment to Roman approbation and direction made the church a fearful or untrustworthy phenomenon for many in this "new world" where so much was conceived "in reaction" against old world traditions.

Today, far from being a suspect newcomer, the Roman Catholic Church is the largest single denomination here and Roman Catholics are the most prosperous and influential religious group in the country as a whole. This gives Catholics great moral authority, a fact which our bishops have repeatedly used as a platform for pastoral reflection to their credit. Yet the social dynamics of Catholicism have changed dramatically. Most educated Catholics are no longer instinctively dependent upon the moral decisions of their bishops or pastors. Further the bishops have urged Catholics to become agents of social change out of the convictions of their moral and political experience. Catholics in America—and generally throughout the world—are less passive than before and more willing to stand up for their own account of how things accord with the demands of the Gospel.

Two dynamics may be cited here. One is the growing assimilation of Catholics to the prevailing attitudes toward authority in the dominant culture. We have systematically eradicated taboos from our moral life. That is not to say that there are no longer any limits to moral acceptance (although that is not far from the case). Rather, what is unacceptable in the popular culture is any placing of moral limits or taboos on the basis of authority alone. This has become coupled with a very dubious use of the idea of "rights," employed to justify the interests of special groups in society in fairly arbitrary fashion.

Those of us who were raised in the 20s, 30s, and 40s lived Catholicism in our youth vividly aware of the distinctiveness of our moral community. We had Catholic dietary laws of fasting and Friday abstinence, national guidelines for movie censorship, and sometimes outspoken advice in the local church about how and for whom to vote in elections. The removal of some of these ecclesiastical constraints as well as a growing independence of spirit among adult Catholics have changed the nature of the rapport between lay Catholics and church authorities.

Another dynamic that has had great importance for Catholics has been the renewed emphasis upon autonomy of conscience that has been the fruit of both the ecclesiology and the moral teaching of the Council Documents of Vatican II. As I will discuss later in this paper, classical Catholic moral teaching does hold for "autonomy" of conscience in a certain sense. But the notion of autonomy that would be appropriate for classical Catholic teaching on conscience is very different from the ideology of autonomy that is widespread in our popular culture.

Prevailing Ideas of Conscience in the Popular Culture

The popular sense "conscience" has among many contemporary Americans differs little from the notion of "moral opinion." Put another way, public discourse about morality rarely indicates that issues of conscience have as their source identifiable principles from which the stated moral opinion proceeds and on which it depends for its authenticity.

Robert Bellah's *Habits of the Heart* describes our culture's individualism as marked by "therapeutic relationships" and claims that our society's psychological sophistication has been bought at the price of moral impoverishment:

> The ideal therapeutic relationship seems to be one in which everything is completely conscious and all parties know how they feel and what they want. Any intrusion of "oughts" or "shoulds" into the relationship is rejected as an intrusion of external and coercive authoritarianism. The only morality that is acceptable is the purely contractual agreement of the parties: whatever they agree to is right.[1]

This reductionistic account of public morality can be traced to the social contract philosophy that shaped our American constitutional documents. The heart of John Locke's philosophy of society is that "[t]he individual is prior to society, which comes into existence only through the voluntary contract of individuals trying to maximize their own self-interest."[2] An economic fundamentalism which expresses this principle to devastating effect in the world economy is the "trickle-down theory" of economics. Whether in personal morality or in the economy, this Lockean philosophy leads to a self-interested individualism which has no place for a genuine theory of the common good.[3]

At the same time, it is important to acknowledge that social contract theory and constitutional philosophy came out of a unique historical situation two hundred and twenty years ago when the American founders had as their project to form a single nation out of immigrants coming from distinct national and religious backgrounds. The social project of forging a single republic out of varied ethnic, traditional, and cultural components has given an understandable bias toward tolerance of diversity and toward free appropriation of values. Catholics would not be the largest religious body in the U.S. today except for this extraordinary achievement of a pluralistic nation of competing moral communities which allowed us, strange as we seemed upon our arrival here, to become rooted as neighbors among the great diversity of others who made North America their adopted homeland.

If we Catholics have assimilated in large part to the prevailing ethos of this pluralistic nation, it has been most of all in our sense of moral community that we have been influenced by our fellow citizens. We have come to inhabit with them the Enlightenment myth that tells us that by reason and self-interest alone we will fulfill ourselves as human beings.

An example of this influence might be the endorsement by the Religious Education establishment in the U.S. of the theory of moral development proposed by Harvard's Dr. Lawrence Kohlberg in the 1960s and 70s. Kohlberg endeavored to produce an account of universal stages of moral development based on the maturation of reasoning. Kohlberg reserved his definition of "conscience" to stage 6 in his life-span description of moral development stages, identifying "conscience" with a rational "autonomy" that had been shaped by cultural influences but had moved beyond their constraints.[4] This theory expresses some very characteristic qualities of our popular ethos. Conscience or ethical autonomy is seen as a rational pursuit based upon individual reflection and rooted in a moral sense that is a sort of "faculty" or endowment of the human person. Conscience is literally beyond the law and is expressive of a personal or philosophical idealism justified not necessarily in communal dialogue, but in reflective sincerity.

In his last years, Kohlberg integrated into his theory the idea that "role playing" or taking the perspective of others was the normal path to achieving adult moral stages. But this appeal to empathic concern never caused Kohlberg to vary his description of his stages. His idea of conscience remained essentially individualistic, rationalistic, and divorced from persuasive principles of action. As many critics of Kohlberg repeatedly charged, he never demonstrated that higher stage reasoning (as he described it) would usually lead to the parallel behaviors or actions.[5]

The principal reason Kohlberg's influence among religious educators has been so unfortunate is that it has reinforced the prevailing notion that morality is principally about ideas. So seen, conscience becomes but a rational fragment of the moral person, rather than the totality of the moral person in a moment of decisive self-commitment. In responding to the rationalist idealism that its authors judge to be the at the heart of our American culture, *Habits of the Heart* evokes the moral power of what it calls "communities of memory." Such a community, which draws upon past tradition for its present identity:

> is involved in retelling its story, its constitutive narrative, and in so doing, it offers examples of men and women who have embodied and exemplified the meaning of the community. . . . The stories that make up a tradition contain conceptions of character, of what a good person is like, and of the virtues that define such character.[6]

Robert Bellah and his co-authors indict contemporary American moral imagination for an individualism detached from affective and communal roots. Kohlberg's moral development theory illustrates a central problem which pervades popular moral imagination, namely, a failure to distinguish between speculative and practical reason. By appealing to "communities of memory," Bellah touches one aspect of this problem: moral education proceeds not by reasons alone, but by discipline and by example. Moral education needs to offer guiding images of the good life and persuasive examples of moral goodness.

This is an area where a significant voice in contemporary philosophy [Bellah's] coheres with an aspect of classical Thomistic moral theory. In order to illustrate how Catholic moral theology may rise above the limitations of popular moral thought, I will attempt to develop a key idea of St. Thomas Aquinas in understanding conscience and its role in the moral life.

Practical Reason and Moral Mastery

One of the principal points in Aquinas's teaching on conscience is to insist that conscience is not itself a faculty—a special moral sense in the person[7]—but an act of judgment which draws upon several sources. In this section of my paper, I will strive to develop a sense of the moral anthropology of St. Thomas which may serve in this area of conscience as a healthy alternative to some tendencies in more contemporary moral theories.

Josef Pieper observes the contrast between St. Thomas, who deals specifically with conscience in only one article of his Summa Theologiae, and more contemporary moralists who make of conscience a treatise on rational autonomy. Aquinas, of course, devotes ten questions (56 articles in all) to prudence, in which he sees the working out of the discernment process which we have come to name exclusively by the title of conscience.[8] St. Thomas dealt with what we call conscience today in his treatment of the operations of the virtue of prudence.

What is especially useful about St. Thomas's account is the description which he provides of the functioning of practical reason. He offers a picture of human intelligence in constant dialectical undulation between reasoning and choosing. Practical reason is not a separate compartment of intelligence, but the gradual transformation of intelligence through dialogue with the appetites into a force that savors, weighs, judges and commands human action. Faced with reality, we respond with a two-fold relation—the relation of *insight* before reality perceived as the true and the relation of *moral energy* before reality perceived as the good. Moral insight is intelligence; moral energy is desire.

The principal difficulty in moral education is that it is not just a learning of methods of reasoning, but also a shaping of sensibilities. Alasdair MacIntyre correctly stresses the importance of the rectification of the appetites or sensibilities of the moral subject to allow practical reason to function meaningfully:

> We have to begin by acquiring enough of the virtues to order our passions aright, so that we are neither distracted nor misled by the multiplicity of the goods which they seem to propose to us and so that we acquire the initial experience of rule-following and action-guiding from which we can begin to learn both how to understand our precepts and maxims better and how to extend the application of those precepts and maxims to an increasing range of particular situations.[9]

There are few aspects of St. Thomas's theology more elaborate or complex than his theory of prudential choice and of conscience. So without hoping to give here an adequate exposition of his theory, I will nonetheless strive to make some central points and draw some parallels to our contemporary situation.

First, every significant moral choice presupposes some situation of struggle or reckoning. It is extremely rare to be faced with a succession of alternatives where only one is clearly good and all the others evil. Conscience involves a sorting through of different kinds and levels of attachment. Thomas's moral theory is helpful more because of the overarching perspective which it provides than because it might offer more specificity to the difficult weighing of concrete alternatives.

For Aquinas, the dialectic between moral insight and moral energy leading finally to a choice which is both reasonable and effective of action, is the heart of conscience. Confronted with a moral dilemma, the person perceives the issues both of truth and goodness and possesses the moral apparatus to proceed to weigh both aspects. This is, by the way, already significantly different from the context of much contemporary moral theory where the notion of "good" is secondary to the notion of "right or permissable" and the notion of the desirable is considered at most a distraction (to a uniquely rational endeavor). Failure to account for moral energy or for desire is one of the principal weaknesses of most contemporary ethical systems. Yet moral action is not explainable without factoring in the power of desire.

In weighing the goodness of an object and of action toward that object, a person has reference not first to an extrinsic law, but to an intrinsic need for fulfillment. Thomas makes one of the first steps in moral deliberation the invoking of *synderesis* (what Pieper calls "primordial conscience").[10] This is the elemental perception of what good is appropriate to a human person. One recent Catholic account expresses it thus: "It is good to live, to eat, to know the truth, and to love, etc."[11] This is knowledge of an intuitive order which provides the fundamental orientation to moral discrimination.

Two things are needed for someone to proceed further toward weighing the realism of a choice: first, a continuing resonance between reason and appetite such that the approval of primitive conscience is echoed by a movement of striving toward grasping the good, and second, a sequence of practical considerations which represent the witness of what Thomas would call wisdom and science. This practical consideration of the fittingness of a proposed good to the concrete circumstances of a person's life is the exercise of what Aquinas named prudence. Rather than attempt a reconstruction of this complicated theory of moral action, I will limit myself to showing some of the implications of this point of view.

The Richer Dynamics of Moral Discernment

Unlike a purely rational account of moral development such as that of Kohlberg (or of Rawls and Hare on whom he greatly depends for his moral conceptions),[12] Aquinas's account drew upon deep threads of feeling and imagination and wove them into the dialectical interchanges that are part of moral discernment. I mentioned above primordial conscience (synderesis), which St. Thomas called the "first habit" of the practical intellect. Put in today's language, we could say that primordial conscience is the instinctive leaning of human intelligence toward the fundamental goods of life.

This instinctive sense of what is good is primordial in that each morally sentient person possesses it as an endowment integral to their humanity. Yet here I go beyond Aquinas to suggest that primordial conscience is nurtured and enriched by family, community, and ecclesial experiences. Our rituals of closeness, caring, compassion, and concern both embody primordial conscience and develop it. Even though each person is born with a primordial conscience (if Aquinas is right), the resonance of that instinctive level of moral discrimination can be encouraged or discouraged, made relevant or irrelevant, by our social conversation.

In addition, wisdom informs our sense of the moral good, forging a link between the essential orientations to the good that belong to primordial conscience and a more concrete sense of moral options. Wisdom here represents the culture's embodiment of the good life. Wisdom is the shaping or landscaping of the imagination to establish a repertory of images of authentic humanness and of our ultimate divine destiny. Here conscience is instructed by divine law and by the human law of church and society. Aquinas's account of conscience and the discernment of good moral action clarifies in a way that is often lacking in other theories of conscience the role of moral imagination.

In each culture, there are repeated articulations of fundamental moral goals. Some cultures enflesh these in maxims, moral sayings, and stories. In our own culture, I wonder if we don't negatively program our potential for moral wisdom by the extraordinary influence which television exercises in disseminating its typical store of narratives and images of the good life. At the least, the point should be made that TV and the media have a powerful potential to contribute—positively or negatively—to the formation of moral imagination and thereby to moral discernment.

A third source of moral sensibility is what Aquinas called "science," but which in our context we could call practical experience. In sorting out the implications and weight of concrete facts in the circumstances of a moral action, the person depends upon a wealth of information and an ability to draw consequences relevant to the case.[13] Conscience is "informed" at this level by moral instruction. Experience of the world and its workings provides the quality of lucidity that enables prudent persons to be confident about their judgments and persuasive in argumentation. Moral "science" is above all based upon experience in successfully drawing practical conclusions that lead to positive action as a fruit of attraction, weighing of goods, and the forceful pursuit of chosen means.

In all three of these sources of the judgment of conscience (primordial conscience, wisdom, and science), we see the way in which practical reason is bathed in affective and communal dimensions of life and how conscience is formed by drawing upon more than purely rational motions. This helps us to understand how both the good and the desirable are aspects integral to moral discernment, for the knowledge of the good in the context of family, community, and church is enmeshed with concrete experiences of belonging, being satisfied, celebrating, and striving for mutually engaging goals. These dynamics of primordial conscience, wisdom, and science parallel significantly the qualities of what Bellah refers to as "community of memory" (referred to above).

Autonomy in Aquinas's Moral Theory

Earlier I noted that the sense of autonomy that one finds in Aquinas's theory of moral action is quite different from that common in contemporary usage. For Aquinas, "autonomy" of conscience would mean the unique experience that the moral subject alone can have in moving from an attachment to the good to an action implementing that good. Autonomy here alludes to the flavor of the particular moral experience and the imaginative landscape within which the dialectic of reason and appetite occurs and reoccurs.

The presence of exceptional circumstances also contributes to the quality if autonomy, in that many circumstances are known in depth only to the moral agent. Aquinas teaches that although one may err unwittingly in the considerations and judgments of prudence by invincible ignorance, one's actions may still be morally good. It would be rare, however, that one would so err in a serious matter without being in dialogue through counsel or conversation with others who could offer a corrective view. Nonetheless the power of conscience is binding precisely because it is the judgment that in good heart one chooses the best one can in the light of available understanding.

While autonomy does mean here that one person's moral action is irreplaceable, it does not mean that it proceeds from some sort of hidden inner courtroom—a moral sense apart—whose proceedings are beyond analysis or uncommunicable. In some contemporary writings, however, this is just what I take from the use of the idea of "autonomy"—that moral action proceeds from a privileged inner sanctum of moral feeling that requires neither dialogue with a community nor rational justification.[14]

In Dialogue with God

The two most celebrated texts of Vatican II touching conscience express the importance of the autonomy of the moral agent and add to that the valuable emphasis that in conscience one is in radical dialogue with God's own Spirit. Paragraph 16 of *Gaudium et Spes* teaches:

> Conscience is the most secret core and sanctuary of [persons]. There [they] are alone with God, whose voice echoes in [their] depths. In a wonderful manner conscience reveals that law which is fulfilled by love of God and neighbor. In fidelity to conscience, Christians are joined with the rest of [people] in the search for truth, and for the genuine solution to the numerous problems which arise in the life of individuals and from social relationships.[15]

This text evokes the privileged quality of conscience: "For [we] have in our heart a law written by God." The phrase here, "to be alone with God," evokes the seriousness and attentiveness which is presupposed by this statement.

The *Declaration on Religious Freedom* states:

> This sacred Synod likewise professes its belief that it is upon the human conscience that these obligations [to

know and respect the truth] fall and exert their binding force. The truth cannot impose itself except by virtue of its own truth, as it makes its entrance into the mind at once quietly and with power.[16]

Both of these texts suggest that the influence of divine illumination provided by the light of conscience is more than a mere philosophic insight and is expressive of God's love for the person. One of the major topics which might be chosen to elucidate St. Thomas's teaching on moral action is the identification of the ultimate goal of moral action with communion with God. In the light of that mystery, individual acts of conscience would find their unity in their shared orientation to pleasing God and approaching God as the perfection of our human yearning. This orientation comes from God's proclamation of love and is experienced concretely in expressions of that love perceived as forgiveness, compassion, and caring providence.

One aspect of the autonomy of conscience, then, is the categorical experience of being called and loved by God and the spontaneity of personal response which God's call provokes. One might say that the inner authority of conscience is rooted in a convincing experience of God's concrete presence to and concern for my own life. It is this religious experience of divine love that transforms moral ideas into moments on the faith journey toward communion with our loving God.

Themes for a Catechesis of Conscience

In the light of these reflections, I suggest that the following three themes need to be integral to an adequate catechesis of Christian conscience:

(1) Conscience is self-awareness and self-disposition lived in the light of God's call and God's tenderness. This implies a vivid understanding that communion with God is the destiny of human life. Apart from that principle of finality and apart from an experience of God's tenderness met in forgiveness and compassion, conscience cannot have an authentic orientation. More important than a specific analysis of the structure of moral action is the

awareness that our moral actions are a response to God's empowerment of us in creation and they are an embodiment of our striving to grow in intimacy with God.

In terms of the church's proclamation, we must stress the principles of destiny and of sacramentality. We will not find satisfying happiness apart from the communion with God. St. Thomas's tract on our ultimate end in the first five questions of the *Prima Secundae* would seem to be tremendously relevant to this moment of time (the ethos of the 80s).[17] Also, as Pope John Paul II has done in *Christifideles Laici,* we need to communicate the truth that the lives of Christians are vehicles for God's power and mercy to be expressed. God is not only our ultimate destiny, but also our present destiny if we will accept the mystery that God wills to continue the ministry of Christ sacramentally in the good works of Christian people today.[18]

In terms of the individual's moral awareness, some recognition and experience of divine presence and caring is fundamental for an adult conscience. It is notable that there is a growing literature dealing with images of God and spirituality that bears witness to the widespread phenomenon of religious experience among contemporary people. Both of the texts of Vatican II cited above presuppose significant religious experience on the part of the moral subject.[19]

(2) Conscience is guided both by the intuitive moral sense of primordial conscience and also by the learned aptitudes for responding to the good established by the discipline of virtue. To appeal to the moral sense or to the reasonableness of people before difficult choices that run counter to the inclination of the popular culture will not suffice. Christians must have a readiness to respond to the articulation of the moral good which comes from those strengths of character we call virtues. In this sense, virtue is a discipline as well as an enabling of moral response. Part of the problem with virtue today can be grasped in the following phrase of Thomas Szasz: "Permissiveness is the principle of treating children as if they were adults; and the tactic of making sure that they never reach that stage."[20]

There has been little discourse about virtue in recent decades in the literature of moral education. Oddly, within the past fifteen years, a few American Protestant moralists have rediscovered virtue theory and have begun to grasp that the disposition of the moral subject to recognize and connaturally affirm true human goods is a fundamental aspect of moral education.[21]

In addition, the witness of the community to authentic images of Christian living nurtures the instinctive leaning of primordial conscience toward the good and reinforces the wisdom of the community. It is noteworthy that in recent decades we have made visitation to and cooperation with works of mercy (like soup kitchens) part of the practical moral education of both the young and the adult in Christian communities. This is a good example of nurturing conscience's instinctive inclination to compassion.

(3) The discernment of conscience in difficult cases is normally a work of dialogue—of spouses with one another and with friends, of children with parents and friends, of authorities with counsellors and community. Prudence is normally lived in a social context. This living dialogue of conscientious Christians is itself an image of Christian integrity. It is noteworthy that for one major theorist of psychological development, Jean Piaget, the meaning of "autonomy" is "the capacity for cooperation."[22] The normal path for any community in discerning its responsibility is sharing of vision in a context of faith.

In cases of individuals with conflicted moral stories, pastoral counselling, spiritual direction, and confession are all means to identify and rectify the work of prudence in the major decisions of one's life. It will be important to propose communal as well as individual models of conscience formation. The moral autonomy that will strengthen Christian lives will be the autonomy of interdependence—the capacity to cooperate as peers in the pursuit of the mutual good of a community. This coheres best with the vision of church which *Lumen Gentium* (recently reviewed by Pope John Paul II in *Christifideles Laici*) proposes: each member is an evangelizing element in a changing world, in loving dialogue with the whole Body.[23]

Concluding Reflections on Method

I hope that the points which I have made here are persuasive in suggesting that Catholic Moral Theology may need to re-emphasize some classical elements in its exposition of moral responsibility. Typically today, moral theology proceeds from an orientation based upon God's call to community, the exemplary revelation of Christ, and the structures of divine and human law. I suggest that an explicit integration of the anthropology of virtue, addressing the dialectic between reason and appetite, is needed for two principal reasons. First, the moral energy that can make discernment effective in action is tied to the role of appetite (as transformed by its dialectical engagement with practical reason). Second, the anthropology of moral action implicit in St. Thomas's theory of conscience engages a more comprehensive understanding of the factors which shape moral maturity. This is especially significant where it touches the necessity for the "rectification" or education of the appetites through virtue.

In addition, although I have freely interpreted certain aspects of St. Thomas's teaching concerning "wisdom" and "moral science," I believe that I have shown that a fundamental step in moral education is "the migration of moral imagination" out of the exile of secularized, profit-economy hedonism and into the promised land of some new effort at Christian culture. (I think that this is precisely the strongest contribution of adult catechumenal programs, when they work. They try to generate within the parish the experiences of community and generativity that produce a meaningful mini-cosmos of shared Christian values.)

Concluding Summary

I have chosen to concentrate upon the idea of practical reason and the way it formed the foundation for Aquinas's theory of conscience, which he understood in terms of prudential judgment. It should be clear that precisely because practical reason is the product of a dialectical exchange between intelligence and desire that it entails all sorts of weighing, estimations of fittingness, reappraisals of the measure of self-investment and of the use of means. There is no getting around the need to engage in a practical balancing of means and outcomes. Roman Catholic moral theology is badly polarized on the issue of how to account for the exercise of prudential judgment in painfully disputed and exceptional cases. The epithets "proportionalism" or "consequentialism" are laid upon explanations that strive to struggle with the concrete details of cases where an admixture of good and evil is unavoidable. We must avoid trivializing the contributions of Catholic moralists who have expressed themselves in the categories of a more casuistic literature, invoking the language of values, norms, alternatives, consequences, and consistency.

In this paper, I have attempted to propose a benign re-reading of St. Thomas's classical teaching on what are often called the "twelve acts of the mind." One could easily trivialize this doctrine in the light of contemporary psychology, pointing out that the language of St. Thomas's thirteenth century psychology appears quite naive when confronted with contemporary experimental findings. I have tried to evoke reliable contemporary meanings for St. Thomas's teaching, since (as is evident) I think that there are genuine values for our own moral predicament in what he offers.

Likewise, I would urge a benign rather than a hostile reading of moralists who can be called "mixed consequentialists" or "revisionists." In terms of the summary review of the work of prudence which I have touched here, it is evident that for Aquinas's own moral theory some calculus of values, consequences, alternatives, and choices is inevitable.

Turning St. Thomas's prudential ethics into a deontological or rule ethic is, to my mind, a betrayal of his genius. Let us insist more firmly on the education of appetite through virtue, on the clarification of an act's specification through its object, and on the overarching orientation of each moral act to the finality of a divine destiny. But let us cooperate. While we estrange ourselves from one another by partisan accounts of moral method, the profit-economy engine is producing more and more images of life that are demeaning, demoralizing, and seductive. Let our first task in conscientious cooperation be benign dialogue about what is at the heart of our Christian vocation.

There are many more themes that ought to be touched to address the moral predicament of Catholic conscience formation. My dominant theme, however, has been that we stand to profit from re-appropriating some classical notions about the formation of Christian conscience. I hope that I have shown both that conscience is more complex than perhaps we often imagine and that an adequate theology of conscience offers more resources than we might have thought for addressing the migration of moral imagination toward a Christian vision of the world. I count on my colleagues to correct and expand my efforts to explain.

NOTES

1. Robert N. Bellah et al., *Habits of the Heart: Individualism and Commitment in American Life* (Berkeley: University of California Press, 1985), p. 139.

2. *Ibid.,* p. 143.

3. *Economic Justice for All: Pastoral Letter on Catholic Social Teaching and the U.S. Economy* (Washington, D.C.: National Conference of Catholic Bishops, 1986). See esp. para. 70f, p. 36–49. "Social justice implies that persons have an obligation to be active and productive participants in the life of society and that society has a duty to enable them to participate in this way" (#71).

4. Lawrence Kohlberg, *Essays on Moral Development, Vol. I: The Philosophy of Moral Development* (San Francisco: Harper & Row, 1981), p. 6–28.

5. Gary L. Sapp, ed., *Handbook of Moral Development* (Birmingham: Religious Education Press, 1986). See sp. Tod Sloan and Robert Hogan, "Moral Development in Adulthood: Lifestyle Processes," p. 167–181. Also Hugh Rosen, *The Development of Sociomoral Knowledge* (New York: Columbia University Press, 1980), ch. 5, "Action, Hierarchy, and Logic," p. 95–130.

6. Bellah, *op. cit.,* p. 153.

7. Thomas Gilby, O.P., ed., *Summa Theologiae of St. Thomas Aquinas, Vol. 18: Principles of Morality* (New York: McGraw-Hill, 1966), p. 181.

8. Josef Pieper, *Reality and the Good* (Chicago: Regnery, 1967), p. 81: "Moreover, in the reversal of this situation by the newer 'Thomistic' moral systems, which hardly speak of prudence but much more of subjective conscience, we may rightly see a departure from the actual ontological foundation of the ethics of St. Thomas."

9. Alasdair MacIntyre, *Three Rival Versions of Moral Inquiry: Encyclopaedia, Genealogy, and Tradition* (Notre Dame: University of Notre Dame Press, 1990), p. 130.

10. Pieper, *op. cit.,* p. 63f. Cardinal Ratzinger has re-named this dimension of moral experience "anamnesis." Cf. p. 18 ff.

11. Servais Pinckaers, O.P., *Les sources de la morale chrétienne; sa methode, son contenu, son histoire* (Fribourg: Editions Universitaires Fribourg Suisse, 1985), p. 385.

12. Kohlberg, *op. cit.,* esp. ch. 4: "From *Is to Ought*," p. 101–189.

13. See Gilby, *op. cit.,* p. 173.

14. See Stanley Hauerwas et al, *Truthfulness and Tragedy* (Notre Dame: University of Notre Dame Press, 1977). Ch. 2: "Obligation and Virtue Once More," p. 40–56. Hauerwas considers the Kantian tradition in ethics and William Frankena as an exponent of that tradition to represent an "autonomy" of moral rationalism.

15. W. M. Abbott, S. J. and J. Gallagher, ed. and trans., *The Documents of Vatican II,* "The Church Today" (New York: Guild Press, 1966), p. 213–4.

16. *Ibid.,* "Religious Freedom," para. 1, p. 677.

17. Thomas Gilby, O.P., ed., *Summa Theologiae of St. Thomas Aquinas, Vol. 16: Purpose and Happiness* (New York: McGraw-Hill, 1969). See pp. 144–155.

18. John Paul II, *Post-Synodal Apostolic Exhortation: The Lay Members of Christ's Faithful People* (Boston: St. Paul Books, 1989).

19. On the importance of God-imagery see: Antoine Vergote and Alvaro Tamayo, *The Parental Figures and the Representation of God* (The Hague: Mouton, 1980); Ana-Maria Rizzuto, *The Birth of the Living God: A Psychoanalytic Study* (Chicago: University of Chicago Press, 1979); William F. Lynch, S.J., *Images of Hope: Imagination as the Healer of the Hopeless* (New York: Mentor-Omega, 1965); P. J. Philibert, "Symbolic and Diabolic Images of God," *Studies in Formative Spirituality,* Vol. VI, 1 (Feb., 1985), p. 87–101.

20. Thomas Szasz, *The Second Sin* (Garden City, N.Y.: Anchor Press, 1973), p. 21.

21. Some key works of this sort are: Stanley Hauerwas, *Character and the Christian Life* (San Antonio: Trinity University Press, 1975); James M. Gustafson, *Can Ethics Be Christian?* (Chicago: University of Chicago Press, 1975); Gilbert C. Meilaender, *The Theory and Practice of Virtue* (Notre Dame: University of Notre Dame Press, 1984).

22. Jean Piaget, *The Moral Judgment of the Child* (New York: The Free Press, 1965), ch. 4, p. 327f.

23. John Paul II, *op. cit.,* esp. ch. III, p. 79f.

Chapter 7

FIRST RESPONSE

The Reverend Richard Gula, S.S., Ph.D.

Father Philibert's search for an adequate theory of conscience respects the totality of the person in every moment of choice. His proposal underscores that conscience is not just the ability to make rational decisions about what to do, and that forming conscience is not just equipping oneself to make the right decision. Conscience is above all the pervasive condition of the heart, of the kind of person I am at the core of my being. It involves the whole person in being both expressive and creative of the self. As such, we ought not to limit our understanding of conscience to just an activity of the intellect, though it certainly engages critical reason; nor is it just an activity of the will, though it certainly involves desire; nor is it just a strong feeling, though affections make a difference; and, while conscience is always the judgment *for* oneself, it is never formed in a vacuum *by* oneself. Conscience is a community achievement, formed not in isolation but in dialogue with many sources of wisdom.

Two aspects of Fr. Philibert's proposal deserve more attention. These are the imagination, which helps us examine the lens through which we see the world, and the art of moral discernment, which is at the heart of exercising the virtue of prudence.

To appreciate what the formation of conscience requires, we might consider the goal toward which we are striving in forming conscience. This goal is expressed better by a story than by a rule, so I want to use a story.

> When I was seven I had to have my tonsils removed. The operation was scheduled for early in the morning, and I was forbidden to have any food or drink after dinner the evening before. The operation was delayed, and I recall lying for several hours on a surgical bed in a corridor outside the operating room. My mouth was so dry that I couldn't swallow. My lips were so parched they hurt.
>
> There I was, a child all alone, sobbing and begging for a glass of water. Every now and then a nurse passed by, saw me crying, explained why I couldn't have a drink, and went back to work. Then one nurse I had not seen before stopped and asked if she could help. Again I pleaded for water. Like the others, she explained that she couldn't give me anything to drink, but then she did something totally unexpected: She told me that her lips were moist with lipstick and that maybe a kiss would make my lips moist, too. She bent down, kissed me, wished me well, and went back to her work. . . .
>
> I don't remember if her kiss made my thirst go away, but I do know it made my loneliness go away. It was a kiss that spoke volumes about the ties of love that bind us—better than a thousand Sunday sermons.[1]

Where did this Good Samaritan nurse get the courage to stay and not run away from another complaining kid? Where did she get the practical wisdom to know that moist lips kissing parched lips was the right thing to do? No medical-moral principles prescribe

96

it. How did she know? What goes into forming such a conscience to produce such a character? I am going to suggest imagination and discernment.

Imagination

Fr. Philibert's approach to conscience rightly draws on an anthropology of virtue, for becoming a person of virtue is the goal of forming conscience. In an anthropology of virtue, the imagination plays a special role.

The moral life is rooted in the imagination, in the way we see things. The imagination, after all, is not to be equated with our capacity for make believe, but it is our capacity to construct our world. In the imagination our affective and cognitive capacities play together to give us a picture of the world. When we examine the images in our imagination, we are examining the lenses through which we see the world.

The way we see is not so much chosen as it is inherited. It is almost totally dependent on our relationships and the worlds in which we live with their beliefs and values, causes and loyalties that speak about what is "good" and how we ought to live. The formation of conscience takes place by interacting with overlapping worlds: family, church, school, profession, politics, sports, entertainment, and others. If conscience literally means "knowing with," then our moral vision and our moral sense of who we ought to be and what we ought to do are conditioned by others whom we take into our consciousness, whose vision we entertain, whose voices we hear, whose lives we imitate. No wonder parents worry about where their children go to school, about the friends they make, the television shows they watch, or the books they read. They worry because they have an intuitive, prediscursive sense that our inner spirit is shaped by the company we keep and the stories we live by. It reflects the values, vision, and virtues of those who are most influential on us. This is what makes it possible to say that the people who fascinate us and the stories which captivate us have a greater influence on our moral lives than abstract principles do.

Each of the overlapping worlds in which we live communicate values and vision more by stories, images, and rituals than by rules. Fr. Philibert rightly draws from Robert Bellah's sociological analysis to underscore the influence the American story of individualism has had on us already. By living within this story we have acquired a respect for autonomy as a value that we compromise only at our peril. This respect for autonomy is embedded in the Horatio Alger story and in the American dream. On the positive side, the right "to life, liberty, and the pursuit of happiness" (the script of our story) has attracted the world's tired and poor. It also fuels the fires of ambition and creativity. On the negative side, it has led to the cruel treatment of Native Americans, to the exploitation of the environment, and to blaming the victims of poverty, injustice, and disease.

The more we participate in the stories and language of a community, the more we begin to take on its way of seeing and responding. After all, we acquire habits of the heart in the same way we learn a language—by being immersed in it so that we can observe and practice the behavior of others. Formation in virtue requires guiding images, or persuasive models of moral goodness like the Good Samaritan nurse. So when we want to know the most influential sources forming conscience, we need to ask about the most important sources of influence on the imagination.

The stories and images of the Christian community are in considerable tension with those of other communities. The images of the Christian community are not always the most influential for shaping the way we see the world. William F. Fore's book, *Television and Religion: The Shaping of Faith, Values, and Culture,* maintains that television is usurping the role of the Church in shaping the imagination and our system of values. He says,

> Television, rather than the churches, is becoming the place where people find a worldview which reflects what to them is of ultimate value, and which justifies their behavior and way of life.[2]

Fore goes on to show the powerful influence television has had on our attitudes and behaviors in the areas of violence and sexuality. Soap operas, situation comedies, and police dramas transmit many images of what is "good" and how life ought to be lived which stand in direct conflict with the images of the Gospel and rob religious stories and images of their power to move people.

Moral behavior, then, is not so much a function of moral principles we hold true as it is a function of the imagination holding the images which give us a "picture" of the world. The images in our imaginations influence what we see and so affect how we respond. From the point of view of the imagination, forming conscience is a matter of influencing the imagination, with stories and images. Christian morality believes that the stories and images which come to us in the Christian story provide a truthful way to seeing the world and they portray the good in the moral life. An anthropology of virtue which respects the role of the imagination puts forth a twofold challenge to moral education and to forming a Christian conscience; (1) tell the Christian story in a captivating way so that we can meet Jesus, and (2) provide persuasive examples of moral goodness shaped by these stories so that we can model habits of the heart of a Christ-like identity.

But ethics cannot be left solely to the imagination. Issues have to be sorted out. Hard decisions have to be made. But until we take into account the images and the imagination which shape our moral vision, we are taking ethics out of context and short-circuiting the formation and function of conscience. An adequate theory of conscience must link the imagination to discernment, to the ways we know who we ought to be and what we ought to do.

Moral Discernment

Our tradition holds that God is the ultimate source and end of morality and that what God enables and requires is an unconditional moral obligation. Morality can only be objective if it is ontologically based on God—the unconditional ground of moral values, norms, and their justification. An adequate theory of conscience, then, must include something about the ways we know what God is enabling and requiring us to be and to do. This is the challenge of moral discernment. Documents of the Church, such as *Lumen Gentium* (n. 25) and *Dignitatis Humanae* (n. 14), make clear that a Catholic must pay attention to the teaching of the Church in the formation of her or his conscience. What we still need to develop, however, are the links between this way of informing conscience and the role of Scripture, the practice of virtue, a lively feeling for value, prayer, sensitivity to the Spirit, and broad consultation. Showing the link between these resources for knowing what God enables and requires puts us in the realm of moral discernment.

To link these elements is to explore the ways faith and reason work together to inform conscience. The Magisterium bases its moral guidance on claims to know the objective moral order. How do we know this objective order? *Gaudium et Spes* says that it will consider the urgent needs of the day "in the light of the gospel and human experience" (n. 46). This document, along with many others, favors "reason informed by faith" as the way we come to know what is right. What does that entail?

The epistemological role of faith in coming to moral truth is not to be a thesaurus of answers to moral questions. Rather, faith is the light by which we see what is going on. The Chinese proverb that says ninety percent of what we see lies behind our eyes is apt for explaining the relation of faith to morality. The Christian mysteries, symbols, and stories influence the believer's imagination to shape the way we see and interpret human experience in relationship to God. For example, the paschal mystery of Jesus and the symbols of the cross and resurrection insist that death is not as final as it may seem. In light of these mysteries, the Christian need not fight death at all costs but can face death with the hope that something more will rise out of it. Relating faith and morality this way links conscience to the imagination and to discernment.

The Bible, too, informs morality. Critical approaches to the Bible oppose using it as an occasional ornament to "proof text" positions reached on philosophical grounds. Rather, as the pastoral letter *Economic Justice for All* illustrates, the Bible provides a "deeper vision" (n. 29) of God and human dignity to enlarge the environment within which the moral life is lived and to authorize or exclude certain values or norms for moral living. In brief, faith informs morality by giving us a particular view of what it means to be human, by influencing the attitudes we ought to take toward the world, by authorizing values and norms, and by helping us interpret the morally relevant factors of a situation.

Reason works in a critical-dialogical fashion with faith. Our tradition of natural law claims that what God requires is mediated through the structures and experiences of being human. The truly human becomes the proximate or mediate standard of objective morality. Thus, reason's grasp of what befits human well-being at discursive and prediscursive levels is a valid source of moral truth.

A great deal of attention has already been given to the discursive level of providing publicly defensible reasons for our claims to moral rightness and wrongness, and how these reasons instruct conscience. As Fr. Philibert has indicated, religious education's endorsement of Kohlberg's theory of moral development based on the maturation of reasoning has reinforced the myth that tells us that morality is about ideas and that conscience is a rational fragment of the person. Against Kohlberg, Fr. Philibert correctly notes that conscience is not a one-sided rationalism. It must integrate the affective aspects of the person as well. Right moral living is not reducible to knowing principles and having analytic skills to apply them. Right moral living also requires virtue, honest self-appraisal, imaginative insight, well-digested experiences, and a lively feeling for values.

Along with discursive reasoning, the art of discernment engages the prediscursive side of recognizing moral value as well. In that way, moral knowing is much more like the discerning heart of the mystic than it is like the calculating mind of a computer analyst. Paying attention to affective dispositions is an essential prerequisite for making reliable decisions. Our sense of outrage or feelings of peace and harmony are valuable sources of knowing what befits human well-being. As moral theology expands its range of interest beyond act-analysis to include character and community, it will need to appeal to a richer model of moral knowing than discursive reason provides. The rise of narrative theology is helping us to expand the range of moral deliberation to include the importance of affectivity and images in making decisions. The future of moral theology will have to explore the relation of affective conversion to practical wisdom in the process of coming to moral truth. Only when the mind and heart work together can we say that we are following a properly informed conscience.

In the end, the claims we make about knowing what is right and wrong will always need some epistemological modesty. This is, we must be careful to avoid claiming to know more than our methods and data allow. The more we realize how context-dependent our knowledge and subsequent moral judgments are, the more modest we need to be about claims to absolute certainty. Bernard Lonergan has well pointed out that coming to truth involves the constantly unfolding process of the recurrent operations of experience, understanding, judging, and deciding. The processive character of knowing reminds us that we are always on the way to a fuller account of all that makes up the moral reality of an action. The moral certitude which we can achieve along the way is a modest claim because we cannot be sure in advance that the uniqueness of individuals, the variations in cultures, the changes of history, or even the involvement of God would ever introduce significant differences to give a new meaning to an action.

In conclusion, Fr. Philibert's proposal for a theory of conscience suggests that the development of conscience is the matter of getting straight three sets of stories: the story of our lives (our own experience), the stories of our culture (the images society provides us), and the stories of faith (the traditions in which we ground our identities). The process of forming conscience engages the whole person in the critical dialogical interaction of these three sets of stories in order to deal with the whole of our experience.

NOTES

1. Joseph Allegretti, "A Person of Character," *Health Progress* 71 (April 1990): 88.

2. Fore, *Television and Religion* (Minneapolis: Augsburg Publishing House, 1987), p. 24.

Chapter 8

SECOND RESPONSE

John Haas, Ph.D.

Catholic moral theology is in a frightful muddle today. That institution which used to be a paragon of lucidity and clarity, the Catholic Church, has, at least in the area of morality, degenerated into an assortment of partisan camps hurling epithets at one another: physicalists, voluntarists, deontologists, teleologists, consequentialists, proportionalists, situationists. The labels themselves, which ought to facilitate debate, have only led to further confusion. Richard McCormick himself speaks of "the malleability of terms such as teleologist, utilitarian, consequentialist, and deontologist."[1]

Indeed, there must be something fundamentally wrong with categories which would place Kant, Fichte, the Catholic tradition, Germain Grisez and W. D. Ross in the same group even though, as McCormick says, a chasm separates them.[2] They are all termed deontologists because they all hold that there are certain acts which may never under any circumstances be done despite the consequences. Yet the conviction that certain acts are never morally permissible surely does not qualify them all as deontologists without further significant qualifications. Plato himself saw that there was a significant difference in approaches to the conclusion that certain acts are always wrong. In the Socratic dialogue Euthyphro the question is posed: "Is something wrong because the gods have forbidden it or have the gods forbidden it because it is wrong?"[3] The way in which one would answer that question is critically important for moral theory and simply would not justify categorizing both approaches the same way.

The Catholic Church used to be the one institution to which anyone could look to find certitude and help in resolving difficult moral conundrums. Even today I remember my excitement as a 25 year old Protestant seminarian when I discovered the Doctrine of Double Effect which was developed principally by Catholic moralists to assist conscientious Christians avoid sinning when faced with moral dilemmas which seemed to involve them in evil even as they resolved to do good. It is admittedly a subtle moral principle but not a particularly difficult one to grasp.

There are certain presuppositions which must be in place for the principle of double effect to work, however. One is that a person *can* avoid sinning with God's grace. Bruno Schueller points out that the Principle of Double Effect is virtually an exclusively Catholic doctrine.[4] Actually this should be no surprise. I do not think such classical Protestant doctrines as total depravity and *simul justus et peccator* are irrelevant to the fact that the Protestant tradition never developed such a doctrine as double effect. If it is believed that one can never avoid sinning then it is hardly to be expected that one will expend great energy devising moral principles to help one avoid the inevitable.

Another presupposition of the principle of double effect is that there are certain acts which may never morally be done under any circumstances. As we all know the Catholic tradition has insisted that there are some acts which are intrinsically evil. A corollary of that position is that there are absolute moral norms which may not be violated because they specifically keep us from committing intrinsically evil acts. Most of contemporary Catholic polemics in the area of moral theory address the question of intrinsically evil acts and universal moral norms. One of the principal casualities in these polemics has been the doctrine of double effect. Richard McCormick edited and contributed to a volume on the principle of double effect entitled *Doing Evil to Achieve Good*. He concluded the book by saying that his interlocutors had surely "provided (an assist) toward achieving, if not clarity, then at least more intelligent confusion about the ambiguities of moral choice and of moral thought about such choice."[5]

But "intelligent confusion" is not what we seek! In fact, it is a contradiction in terms. In 1982 McCormick said of the continuing debate over whether there are indeed intrinsically immoral acts: "This discussion is almost stalemated by now. It is growing repetitious, arid, and fruitless, especially so when carefully crafted positions are summarily dismissed with terms such as 'consequentialism' and 'proportionalism.' "[6] But if proportionalism were an effective moral theory why do intelligent people have such difficulty grasping it?

The bottom line for proportionalists seems to be the claim that there are no exceptionless material norms. There are *virtually* exceptionless material norms but with all the explanations of that expression found in Father Gula's book *Reason Informed by Faith* it is clear that, in the last analysis, "virtually" means that there are no exceptionless material norms.[7] But where are the certitude and clarity in the moral life if there are no universal material norms, no absolute values which may never be violated. One cannot even say that innocent human life is an absolute value in the proportionalist approach. Bruno Schueller claims that the killing of noncombatants to repel an aggressor would be unnecessary in "perhaps 99 out of 100 cases."[8] Of course, that leaves it justifiable in perhaps 1 out of 100 cases if it is *necessary* to repel the aggressor. If such is the case, then we cannot say that it is always wrong ever directly to kill noncombatants. McCormick adopts a similar position when he says that the proportionalist approach would allow killing "when the killing is the *only way imaginable* to prevent greater loss of life."[9]

In describing proportionalism Father Gula also speaks of "virtually exceptionless material norms" succumbing to "necessity"— which is why they are only "virtually exceptionless." He writes:

Or take the case of the married couple who have all the children for whom they can care in a reasonable way. They cannot enlarge their family without compromising the well-being of their present children. At the same time, the couple feels that fairly regular sexual expression *is necessary* for the growth and development of their marriage. They do not feel that they can respond adequately to both values and follow the proscription of contraception in *Humanae Vitae.* What do they do?[10]

The clear implication is that the couple can contracept because of necessity, just as Father Schueller suggested we could kill noncombatants out of necessity. Contraception and the taking of innocent human life have always been proscribed by Catholic tradition regardless of the circumstances. Father Schueller and Gula suggest they may be done out of necessity. There is, however, no necessity to doing evil ever. The necessity claimed for the married couple is "fairly regular sexual expression . . . for the growth and development of their marriage." But the use of natural family planning would require abstinence for 8–9 days a month. Would use of the 20 or more infertile days a month not constitute "fairly regular sexual expression"? Just how many days are required for "fairly regular sexual expression"?

Father Schueller does not indicate what would necessitate the taking of innocent human life, but his fellow proportionalist Father McCormick says it becomes necessary when it "is the *only way imaginable* to prevent greater loss of life." But the only way imaginable is according to whose imagination? God forbid that any of us should be innocent bystanders when the one trying to prevent greater loss of life does not have much imagination!

This is no way to provide clarity for the people of God as they seek to do the will of Him who only wills their happiness. Not only the people of God, but the entire world used to look to the Catholic Church to give clear guidance to the tackling of moral problems. There were certain clear, universal, material norms which sketched out the parameters within which the righteous person pursued the good. "Thou shalt not steal." "Thou shalt not murder." "Thou shalt not commit adultery."

"Thou shalt not bear false witness." But according to Father Timothy O'Connell in his *Principles for a Catholic Morality,* the Ten Commandments are "a cultic text with some minimal ethical components."[11]

Our desire for and search for clarity do not constitute an attempt to escape the struggle and agony of making our own moral choices for ourselves in concrete, tough circumstances. However, it is precisely because of the ambiguity in many moral choices that it was so good that Father Philibert concentrated his attention on St. Thomas' teaching on the virtue of prudence. It is precisely this established, good habit of making the right choice in concrete situations which gives us facility in making lucid decisions in cloudy circumstances. Prudence is, as Josef Pieper tells us, the *Situationsgewissen,* the conscience of the concrete situation.

Father Gula writes in his book *Reason Informed by Faith:*

> The gourmet version of the moral life does not dispense with the recipes of moral norms, but the moral gourmet is not so bound by the recipe that he or she would not adjust according to taste. Discernment (and here I think I would use prudence) is what helps the gourmet make the proper adjustments. So if the moral life is going to be a personal response to one's hearing the call of God in this instance, moral discernment of spirits is indispensable.[12]

Prudence would keep Father Gula's delightful metaphor of the moral gourmet from degenerating into an Epicurean.

Father Philibert is certainly correct in locating in St. Thomas' 56 articles on the virtue of prudence what we are accustomed to calling today conscience. Unfortunately there was a period in the Church's history when morality was preoccupied with law and its application to concrete situations. The critical moral question became whether one were bound by or free from the law which was seen as the work of conscience. The reflex principles were devised to deal with the degree of certitude one would have to have of freedom from the law before one could act. Moral schools developed around epithets as freely hurled as those of today: tutiorists, probabiliorists, probabilists, aequi-probabilists, laxists.

However, in the approach of St. Thomas the principal moral concern was personal growth and fulfillment in God. As he pointed out in his *Summa contra Gentiles,* "God is offended by us only when we act against our own good." St. Thomas' treatise on beatitude at the beginning of the *prima secundae* of his *Summa Theologica* identified happiness, not duty and obedience to law, as the motive for the human life, a happiness which could find its fullness only in God.

Law is viewed in the thought of St. Thomas not as an oppressive taskmaster but rather as a "kindly tutor" leading us to the true freedom of the children of God. Human beings have been blessed not only with the kindly tutor of the Decalogue but also with their own dynamic, open-ended natures created in the image and likeness of God. As St. Paul said, "Ever since the creation of the world (God's) invisible nature, namely, his eternal power and deity, has been clearly perceived in the things that have been made."[13] Within our very beings are "dynames," dispositions ordered toward goods, and when we act on behalf of them in a reasonable manner we realize our fulfillment. As Father Philibert points out, "In weighing the goodness of an object and of action toward that object, a person has principal reference not first to an extrinsic law, but to an intrinsic need for fulfillment." The virtue, the settled disposition, which enables us to choose the appropriate means to our fulfillment is the virtue of prudence.

The reason this virtue can play such a key role in clarifying difficult moral situations for us is that it is both an intellectual and moral virtue. And I believe it is by virtue of this characteristic that prudence enables the moral agent to avoid ever violating a moral absolute while at the same time responding to the demands of the concrete situation with all the vicissitudes and exigencies of a never repeatable, historical moment. Prudence is an intellectual virtue *sub ratione veri,* under the aspect of the true, and a moral virtue *sub ratione boni,* under the aspect of the good.

Prudence is prevented from degenerating into situationism as it orders action to a given situation because it is also an intellectual virtue and as such ordered to that which is. In fact, the preeminence of prudence over all the other virtues derives from the metaphysical insight that Being precedes Truth and Truth precedes the Good.

As St. Thomas tells us, ends serve the same role for the practical intellect that principles do for the speculative. In other words, what makes the practical intellect "work," as it were, are the ends or goals on behalf of which we act. Intelligible, reasonable behavior is understood as ordered toward an end perceived as a good. The intellect sees the truth of things and perceives them as goods on behalf of which acts are formulated. The will spontaneously moves toward an end when it is perceived as good, that is, lovable.

Since prudence is an intellectual virtue first and foremost it must receive its measure, its form, from reality itself before as a moral virtue it grants measure to a given act. It must know the goods which lie before the moral agent as possibilities before it commands their realization. In fact, St. Thomas calls prudence "directing cognition."[14] He also refers to it as the "virtus intellectualis circa moralia," the intellectual virtue concerned with morality.

Although prudence is not concerned with moral norms as such, it is concerned with the true and the good. Because of its orientation toward being it orders the moral agent toward the good. For example, innocent human life is perceived as a good, indeed one of the basic human goods on behalf of which human beings formulate actions. Human life is a good toward which we are spontaneously disposed and which we seek to nurture. In fact, to act against human life as though it were not a good, as though it were an evil, would undermine its role as an end on behalf of which we might act. Indeed, it has the character of an end which would make certain of our actions not only intelligible but even possible. Consequently innocent human life may never be directly violated for this would undermine the very intelligibility of our actions.

Anyone should be able to recognize and acknowledge the incomparable value of each innocent life. Anyone should be able to understand that it is incommensurable with any other value. It cannot be placed in the scales and found wanting. It cannot be measured against any assemblage of other goods, no matter how impressive or appealing, and found to be liable to direct violation.

If innocent human life can be subjected to assault and destruction, then no other proposal for moral action makes any sense, no other proposal for moral action can be compelling, for it too could be overturned by another arbitrary assemblage of goods.

But it is precisely the virtue of prudence which saves us from arbitrariness and subjectivism. It is the settled good habit of making the right moral decisions in concrete situations. It can do this because its eye is fixed squarely on the true which is loved as the good and sought in the concrete situation. As Servais Pinkaers writes, "Reason reveals the good to the will and the will loves the true as its good . . . Reason is like the eye of the will which shows it the lovable object . . . How could the will love the good for itself if it did not first know it as it is in its truth?"[15]

Again, it is prudence which can play a pivotal role in ordering the intellect, the will and the passions of the moral agent toward the good. It is so important that Thomas calls it the "mother of all the virtues." But it serves this role by ordering us toward reality, God's reality, which, as we all know and believe, is good and justifiably the object of our pursuits. And within God's creation there is no higher good than the human person created in the very image and likeness of God Himself. Because every human being has been directly and explicitly called into being by God Himself and therefore constitutes an absolute value, no human being may ever be directly violated. He may never be unjustly deprived of his goods, he may never be murdered, he may never be lied about. There are universal moral norms because there is an absolute value, the crown of God's creation.

Jesus Christ revealed to us not only God but also the human person. He showed us who God is and He has shown us who we are. As we are taught in *Gaudium et spes,* "In reality it is *only* in the mystery of the Word made flesh that the mystery of man truly becomes clear. . . . Human nature, by the very fact that it was assumed, not absorbed, in him, has been raised in us also to a dignity beyond compare. For, by his incarnation, he, the son of God, has in a certain way united himself with each person."[16]

When a Christian denies that there is an exceptionless norm against the direct taking of innocent human life, then that Christian must of necessity contemplate a willingness to take the life of the Child held in Mary's arms.

Trying to be faithful to McCormick by relying on his own words, I ask, when may one take an innocent human life? McCormick insists that "When . . . (killing of innocent life) is reluctantly caused because *necessary* . . . it does not entail a bad moral will, or 'turning against a basic good.' "[17] But then he himself asks, ". . . when and on what grounds must a killing action . . . be said to be *necessary?*" and answers "when the killing is the *only way imaginable* to prevent greater loss of life."[18] But how does this rationale differ essentially from the chilling words of Caiaphas which attempted to justify the crime of all ages: "You do not understand that it is expedient for you that one man should die for the people, and that the whole nation should not perish."[19]

Innocent human life is an absolute value because it is the image and likeness of God before which we ought to stand in awe and reverence. Innocent human life is an absolute value because the Word made flesh is innocent and just and worthy of all love— in every circumstance without exception.

The attempt of many contemporary Catholic moralists to acknowledge more readily the contextual character of all moral choices and to free Catholic moral thought from a crippling legalism is admirable. But it cannot be done at the expense of moral absolutes and universal moral norms which manifest and protect our humanity. Perhaps a recovery of the significance of the teaching on prudence so brilliantly hit upon by Father Philibert will assist in overcoming the polarization which seems to exist today in Catholic moral thought. Prudence has no other concern than the determination of the morally good action in a concrete, historical situation by holding tenaciously and uncompromisingly to a love of the true and the good.

NOTES

1. Richard A. McCormick, "A Commentary on the Commentaries," in *Doing Evil to Achieve Good,* ed. Richard A. McCormick and Paul Ramsey (Chicago: Loyola University Press, 1978), p. 199.

2. Ibid.

3. This is a paraphrase. Cf. Plato, *The Last Days of Socrates: Euthyphro, The Apology, Crito, Phaedo,* Tr. Hugh Tredennick (New York: Viking Penguin, 1969), p. 31. (*Euthyphro* 9A–10B)

4. Bruno Schueller, "Neuere Beitraege zum Thema 'Begruendung sittlicher Normen'," *Theologische Berichte* 4 (Einsiedeln: Benziger, 1974), p. 126, Cf. McCormick, "A Commentary," p. 197.

5. McCormick, "A Commentary," p. 265.

6. Richard A. McCormick, *Notes on Moral Theology 1981 through 1984* (Lanham, Maryland: University Press of America, 1984), p. 118.

7. Richard M. Gula, *Reason Informed by Faith* (New York: Paulist Press, 1989), pp. 294–295.

8. Bruno Schueller, "The Double Effect in Catholic Thought: a Reevaluation," in *Doing Evil to Achieve Good,* p. 181.

9. McCormick, "A Commentary," p. 262.

10. Gula, *Reason,* p. 290.

11. Timothy E. O'Connell, *Principles for a Catholic Morality* (New York: The Seabury Press, 1978), p. 39.

12. Gula, *Reason,* p. 315.

13. Romans 1:20.

14. *De Virtutibus Card.,* 1.

15. Servais Pinckaers, "La nature de la Moralite: Morale Casuistique et Morale Thomiste," *Les Actes Humaines. Tome II* (Paris: Desclee & Cie, 1966), p. 248.

16. *Gaudium et Spes,* 22.

17. McCormick, "A Commentary," p. 262.

18. Ibid.

19. John 11:50.

Chapter 9

PASTORAL CONCERNS
METHODS IN MORAL THEOLOGY

FATHER PHILIBERT: I would like to observe that the fundamental question we have all been dealing with is the question of effective moral education and effective conscience formation. A variety of different speakers have said that our moral education and conscience formation has lacked effectiveness because we have failed to engage the rectification of appetites. Also we have failed sufficiently to engage the moral imagination.

One of the strengths of Father Gula's observations was to note that we are really more shaped by our images than we are shaped by our principles.

We also heard from John Haas a response which picked-up the question of prudence and pointed toward the whole question of the debate on method.

I believe that the polarization among Roman Catholic moralists on the question of method in the United States at this time is a scandal. I really believe that there must be some way to establish a consultation which would bring together representatives of the moral theological community and representatives of the bishops, not as a shoot-out, not as a kind of debate to end all debates, but really as a quest for sympathetic mutual understanding, so that we can get beyond the impasse of the misunderstandings that exist.

Part of the problem of the debate in methodology is that those who are more preoccupied with good ends are not sympathetically trying to dialogue with those who are preoccupied with the right choices.

ARCHBISHOP: In regard to method, was it a mistake to separate moral theology from ascetical theology in the sense that the ideal of the Christian life can be falsely considered apart from a norm of the Christian life?

FATHER GULA: That's an excellent observation about what has happened in the development of moral theology since the Council and of how there has been a movement toward integrating moral theology with the great mysteries of faith. We have come out of a long tradition of isolating the moral life from our religious convictions. As a result, we have almost made moral theology not a theology at all, but a moral philosophy pursued by believers. We are beginning now to see that the great mysteries of faith—Trinity, Jesus, Church, and Sacraments, for example—are integral to understanding the moral life.

ARCHBISHOP: How can this integration of the moral imagination help us to be far more effective in trying to share this gift which is our heritage?

FATHER PHILIBERT: First of all, let us think about what Father Gill said this morning in terms of the impediments to our capacity for proper moral agency. The wrongly formed super-ego guilt of fear can only dissipate when someone enters as a peer into a community of moral conversation where the community itself is constantly forgiving, constantly reaffirming, and constantly empowering.

You all know that there are some parishes which have resisted the sign of peace as an "intrusion" upon a liturgy which formerly was very impersonal, very quiet, and very domesticated. Although that gesture may not be necessarily the best way to express the sense that we mutually forgive one another as we

114

are forgiven by God, it is nonetheless a sign of very great importance.

FATHER GULA: There is a film that has been very provocative with regard to moral development and moral response called "The River's Edge." In this film, one of the teenage boys kills his girlfriend and leaves her lying at the river's edge. He goes back to his friends at school and brags about this deed. Several of his friends then go to the river to look at the body. After taking a look, they go back to school and carry on with business as usual. What is striking in the film, and what is very dramatic about it, is that no one ever says anything to any authority. No parents are informed. No school officials are told. Not even the police know. The teenagers just looked and went home.

The power of the film lies in its demonstration of moral business. It shows how our moral sensitivity can grow dull from being overexposed to the many images of violence that fill our lives. Exposure to so many images of violence can numb our moral sense of empathy. The moral conversion at stake here is fundamentally a matter of the imagination. Moral conversion happens as a response of being loved. It requires that kind of affective bonding which a person has with someone he or she admires.

I remember an account John Tracy Ellis gave when he was commenting on the vocation scene in our country. He was asked how, in his view of the history of the American Church, might he account for this vocation crisis. His response was to ask: where have all the heroes gone? It was a sense of the loss of someone to admire, someone whom a younger person wanted to imitate, or to model, and to have that kind of life for one's self.

BISHOP: Do you consider that there is any real dialogue going on right now among the schools of moral theology or that what is happening in the journals is really talking past one another?

FATHER PHILIBERT: I would just point to a couple of things where I think there is some convergence going on.

And as John Haas correctly said, the reintroduction of virtue theory has been the reintroduction of a concern for prudence. The more we work with prudence the more we see how integrative it is.

I also believe that some theologians are, in fact, working to try to harmonize these positions. I believe that we are polarized by a very strongly deontological (or rule-oriented) ethic on the one side, and a more prudential, consultative, community-based kind of ethic on the other. These should be in harmony.

FATHER GULA: I would like to address this issue by stepping back to examine the foundation of method in moral theology. The roots of conflict and controversy in Catholic morality today lie there. Not until we can appreciate what is at stake in these foundations can we have any fruitful dialogue.

I want to approach these foundations through the image of an earthquake, coming from California where we have had a recent experience of one. When seismic shifts occur beneath the surface, those things which we thought were quite stable begin to topple and sometimes collapse.

As I have tried to follow the discussion during the years of theological renewal, I find Bernard Lonergan has put his finger on a very foundational shift. We talk about the shift of worldviews. The paradigmatic shift that is going on is between the classicist worldview, which has shaped so much of our theology, and the worldview of historical consciousness.

In the shift to historical consciousness, I think we must be alert to what the sociology of knowledge is telling us about how all of our knowledge is context-dependent, and how we really look at everything from a particular point of view that is conditioned by history, culture, and linguistics. The shift in worldviews in theology is of seismic proportions.

Another seismic shift is anthropological. I think the understanding of the human person that underlies our theological reflection is key. The major shift here is the shift from nature to person.

A third shift is epistemological. How do we know? I think Lonergan has made a great contribution when he talks about all of knowledge as a process of the recurrent operation of experiencing, understanding, judging, and deciding. The recurring process of these operations brings us toward truth.

PROFESSOR HAAS: I would agree that there has to be some forum that provides for debate among the various current schools of moral methodology in the Catholic Church. I agree with Father Philibert that scandal is not too strong a word.

One of the reasons we haven't been able to get further with the debate is because we too easily fall back into categorizing various moral theologians rather than really zeroing in and addressing their respective positions.

There was at least an initial attempt on the part of the Pope John Center to provide a forum for this kind of debate made this year. I would hope that an even fuller opportunity would be provided some day, perhaps not in front of the college of bishops here, but some forum in which we can pursue these questions as brothers and sisters in Christ.

I agree with Fr. Gula that there is a significant paradigmatic shift taking place within the theological community.

But what truly fascinates me are those moral positions that remain constant while significant paradigmatic shifts are occurring. For example, we find the directive "thou shalt not commit adultery," in the Decologue of a nomadic, semitic people. Yet we also see that Aristotle in classical Greece writes, "There are some actions and emotions whose very names connote baseness and shamelessness, and among these actions are adultery, theft and murder."

Here is a philosopher writing in Athens and a religious, political leader on a mountain top in the desert in Sinai, and both are saying "Thou shalt not commit adultery." So despite the paradigmatic shifts, which inevitably occur within cultures, what fascinates me are the constant elements that we find within moral reflection among civilized peoples.

BISHOP: I think this series of Bishops' Workshops has heard the various theological positions and methodologies in moral theology discussed. In 1984 the workshop included John Connery and Lisa Cahill. They really let the issues emerge.

The question is what can you actually do now? We have tried an experiment in the diocese in which I am serving. The diocesan bishop and myself decided we could not wait for the Catholic Theological Society of America to start to talk with the fellowship of this group and that group. We would be here for years waiting. There are an awful lot of strong emotional feelings.

We invited the theological community that exists in our diocese, the three colleges and the university and we said, would you please serve as a theological consultation? We didn't say anything about who's good, who's bad. But, we said, here are the non-confidential documents of the Conference.

The first document we started out with was the one on doctrinal responsibilities. We were asked to go to our own diocese to consult and come back and vote on the language and the concepts of that document to see where we stood.

We started out with that. It's an experiment. It wasn't the disaster that everybody predicted it was going to be. We didn't go to public relations officers. We just said, would you as a theological community come down and talk with us about this?

We have met now almost six or seven times. It's been a very fruitful, helpful situation. Those who really don't want to meet with us because we are the enemy, don't meet with us. But the vast majority want to meet. They do want to interact. We are not claiming we are the best theologians. What we are saying is, we want to hear their best thoughts.

There is something positive that takes place as a result of such interaction. I am saying, to date it looks promising. There is a similar possibility in each individual diocese, if you have a Catholic college, university, to convoke these folks and say, would you advise me?

ARCHBISHOP: I think Professor Grisez actually presumed that the results of that dialogue would be that everybody would tranquilly go off and accept whatever the bishops, after having heard this dialogue however long it would have to go on, would in their sagacity and wisdom decide at some plenary or ecumenical council.

Well, that's another matter.

I am not saying that what was proposed as a structured dialogue is the best way to do that, but it was one attempt to move in that direction.

The Pope John Center should sponsor such a major dialogue, but this is not the mother of all academic fora. It is only an annual Bishops' Workshop put on by the Pope John Center for the values that the bishops more or less tell us they think are helpful in their on-going discussions and ministry.

I can speak for the Board of this Center in responding to you bishops by fashioning a program that would be helpful to you. But, we are the Pope John XXIII *Medical*-Moral Research and Education Center. While we have been rather theoretical around the theme of conscience, we will be having later in the program some discussion of the medical aspects of this, true to our inspiration as a center and as an institute. But we are clearly open to the suggestions of those things that you think would be helpful.

BISHOP: I read the scandal referred to in this discussion in terms of a failure on the part of some to give the rightful place to authoritative teaching of the Church, which, in the anamnesis of the Catholic person struggling to make a right conscience judgement, has to have a priority of place. For me, the scandal is that the richness that I perceive in contemporary magisterial teaching on the part of the Holy Father, on the part of the instructions of the Congregation for the Doctrine of the Faith, is really not taken and developed, but too often ignored, and not taken into account. Somehow I think that that dialogue that needs to take place ought to be taking place within the theological community, not to exclude us.

FATHER PHILIBERT: I think your observation is very much to the point, that it is not so much a question of theologians debating with bishops.

We in the academic world are amphibious beings. On the one hand, we exist in a world of faith and a faith community. But we also exist in a tough, critical, hermeneutical world of broad academic conversation, on the other hand. It is St. Anselm I think, who coined the phrase that theology is faith seeking understanding.

I think we have a unique situation in the United States for Roman Catholic theologians. Our Roman Catholic theologians, in their own corporate life of faith, dialogue with the faith community—with the community that celebrates the wisdom of the magisterium; but theologians also seek understanding in dialogue with partners who may not be Roman Catholic and who may not be in Catholic universities. Such persons have a great deal to offer in terms of understanding the anthropological and human dimensions of moral problems.

Perhaps the problem is a lack of what Aquinas used to do, namely, a kind of benign or sympathetic reading of people with whom he had some theoretical problems. I think there may be a lack of benign reading of each other's texts or perhaps even an ignorance of others' points of view.

I agree that whatever kind of dialogue might emerge, it would not be so much theologians debating with bishops. Perhaps it would not be best if this happened first of all in front of a college of bishops. Perhaps the needed dialogue should happen in a context in which tentative efforts at mutual understanding could take place in less threatening environment.

Structured Dialogue:

Moral Teaching and the Mission of the Church to Form Consciences according to the Mind of Christ

Chapter 10

THE BISHOP, CONSCIENCE AND MORAL TEACHING

The Most Reverend Donald W. Wuerl, S.T.D.

Your Eminences, Brother Bishops, Friends of the Pope John XXIII Medical-Moral Education Center:

It is a privilege to be a part of this workshop and be asked to make these reflections.

The theme of this presentation is the relationship of the bishop (magisterium), conscience and moral teaching. In short, how does the teaching office in the Church relate to, affect and inform Christian conscience.

Basically, we address two questions:

1. How is content-laden moral imperative applied in changing circumstances and in diverse ages and cultures? The question is one of function.
2. What is the communal—ecclesial—dimension to an intimate, radically personal act? The question is one of context.

Another way of addressing this issue is to say that bishops have the spiritual authority to bind in conscience. What does this mean when we also believe that the individual has an obligation, a serious moral obligation, to follow his or her conscience?

The question of context is of particular importance because we also believe that the truth—not one among many truths—but *the truth* is found in Christ who identifies Himself as the Way, the Truth and the Life. We also believe that truth—incarnate in Christ—continues in the Church, the visible community of the faithful gathered around the apostles and alive in the spirit sent to teach us all things and bring all things that Jesus said to us to remembrance (John 14.26).

How do we relate the teaching function of the bishop in the Church (the magisterium) to the conscience of the believer, which is the guide to correct moral action? On the surface, the magisterium seems to be an external institutional guide while conscience appears to be the personal internal one.

In order to highlight the role of the bishop, the magisterium, in the formation of conscience, I will touch on the following major points:

1. The nature and definition of conscience, and the Catholic understanding of the freedom and inviolability of conscience.
2. The relationship of practical judgment (conscientious judgment) to the knowledge on which judgment of conscience is based.
3. The role of the bishop (magisterium) in forming correct conscience.
4. The elements involved in the proper exercise of conscience:
   a. objective moral norms;

b. adequate knowledge of the validity of these norms;

c. the application of these norms in a practical judgment to a specific situation and act.

5. Finally, we shall speak of the relationship of bishops and theologians in the effort to understand more fully the proper application of the gospel mandate in specific circumstances. This involves a reflection on the collaborative relations of bishops and theologians taking into account that the "living magisterium of the Church and theology, while having different gifts and functions, ultimately have the same goal: preserving the people of God in the truth which sets them free and thereby makes them a light to the nations" (*Instructions on the Ecclesial Vocation of the Theologian,* n. 21).[1]

Definition of Conscience

In pre-Christian writers, the Greek word for conscience is *syneidesis,* translated into the Latin *conscientia.* Used by such writers as Democritus, Plato, Denys of Halicanossis, Diodorus of Sicily, Philo and Josephus and such Latin writers as Cicero and Seneca, it takes on primarily the meaning of a judicial conscience, i.e. when an action is performed conscience passes moral judgment on it. If the judgment is favorable, one experiences peace of soul. If the judgment is not favorable, one experiences guilt and remorse.[2]

While not abandoning this meaning, a richer, more expanded meaning is given to conscience in the Judeo-Christian tradition. For the most part, the Hebrew scriptures describe experiences of conscience without using the word itself. (The word first occurs and only in isolated instances in the Wisdom books.) The expression we find in the Hebrew scriptures is "heart" or "reins" or other such images. Conscience is thus always related to the human person as oriented to God in the hearing of God's word, the acceptance of the divine will, together with a consciousness of one's own position and responsibility before God, and an awareness of the divine judgment.[3]

Although the term for conscience is not found explicitly in the gospels, the teaching of Jesus moves the emphasis from external action to the heart, to interior dispositions and the need for purity of intention.

Since previous speakers have in considerable detail outlined the traditional definition on conscience, I would like to move beyond the historical portion of this paper into some reflections of the concept of conscience from the Christian tradition. Saint Paul takes the Greek word *syneidesis,* popular in the philosophical tradition, and gives it added meaning. Without developing a systematic teaching on conscience, Paul indicates the essential functions of conscience in Christian life.[4]

Conscience includes the knowledge of God's judgments which oblige us to specific action. It is an organ of the religious life to which the apostolic revelation of truth is made (2 Cor. 4.2) and which preserves the mysteries of faith in their purity (1 Tim. 3.9).[5] This is an innate disposition—an orientation—the atavistic recognition of moral imperative. With Saint Paul there are two new aspects associated with the word "conscience", i.e. that of having authority to apply the new law of love and that of being subject to error.[6]

For the writers of the Christian scriptures, "conscience meant a consciousness of the true moral content of human life as seen by faith, the basic outlook on life governing all one's actions. But it involved also a prudent assessment of each human situation in light of Christian responsibility and love."[7]

This basic approach was handed down by early Christian writers to succeeding generations until it was constructed into a critically reflective science of moral theology by Saint Thomas Aquinas. The thoughts of Saint Thomas, scholastic theology and later moral theology are influenced by a distinction made between *conscientia* (syneidesis) and *synteresis* or *synderesis.*[8] In the scholastic tradition synderesis came to mean "that profound quality which makes man have conscience and qualifies him to perceive the moral order and moral values as his obligation."[9] For Aquinas it is the most profound innate disposition (*primus habitus*) of the practical intelligence.[10] *Synderesis* endows the intellect with the highest moral principles insofar as they are immediately perceived as binding oneself and every human being. Examples of such principles would be "the good is to be done" or "love your neighbor as yourself."[11] Emanating out of *synderesis* comes the prudential judgment of conscience as to what is actually the good or right expression of love, neighbor, justice, etc. in a given situation.[12] Hence, Saint Thomas uses "synderesis" for awareness of principles, "practical reasoning" for the process of moving from principles to conclusions, and "conscientia" for the concluding judgment. Therefore, conscience according to Saint Thomas is an intellectual act of judgment which is primarily practical and forward-looking, corresponding to and guiding each choice one is about to make. It is one's last and best judgment concerning what one should choose and with this judgment in mind one chooses either in agreement with conscience or against it.[13]

Inviolability of Conscience

In the Catholic tradition we affirm the inherent freedom of the human person to make choices for good or bad.[14] The instrument for this choice in the area of morality is conscience which one is bound to follow even when mistaken. Experience, scripture, and Church teaching agree that judgments of conscience can be in error. The law of God written in one's heart can be misapplied in one's judgment. Mistakes are possible in formulating principles, reasoning from them, and considering the facts to be morally evaluated.[15] Still, conscience holds primacy and must be followed; if one acts against one's conscience, one is certainly in the wrong. Hence, Saint Thomas can say that if a superior gives an order which cannot be obeyed without violating one's conscience, one must not obey. To obey the superior in this case would be to disobey what one believes to be the mind and will of God.[16]

However, if the error is one's own fault, one is responsible for the wrong one does in following an erroneous conscience. Such "conscientious" action does not entirely free one from guilt. Scripture speaks of this as guilty blindness and associates it with hardness of heart. (Cf. Is. 6:9–10; Prov. 28.14; Jn. 3.19–21; 3.39–41; 12.35–43). Catholic teaching also recognizes a conscience voluntarily fixed in error through rationalization and self-deception.

Vatican Council II speaks about a conscience "practically sightless as a result of sinning."[17] Since we recognize the distinction between subjective innocence and subjective culpability in regard to objectively wrong acts, we must recognize that conscience can indeed err and that we have an obligation for the formation of conscience.

While the basic law of love written in our hearts urges us to good actions, the multiple voices of the world in which we live challenge, ignore or contradict our God-given disposition and can and do drown out or overwhelm the inner voice of conscience.

The Relation of Practical Judgment to Antecedent Knowledge

The knowledge in which judgment of conscience is rooted and out of which it flows is more than mere intellectual knowledge. It is knowledge in the biblical sense of the word "heart" as the whole person, mind, and will as oriented toward God, the *Summum Bonum*. For the believer it is a profound personal knowledge of salvation and wholeness.[18] In the Catholic tradition, this orientation toward the good as known, although weakened and wounded by the fall, is, nevertheless, always present and operative.

According to Thomas, "the natural inclination of the will is always bound up with knowledge of the practical reason. Thus, by the very nature with which it is created, there is in the will a profound disposition that urges it, of itself, to strive for the good conceived by reason . . . It presses toward the good as known by reason (bonum rationis)."[19]

Drawing on the insights of Augustine and Aquinas, Newman understands "conscience" as being the divine law "as apprehended in the minds of individual men".[20] From his description of divine law, it can be said that for Newman "conscience" is the individual's apprehension of the "rule of ethical truth, the standard of right and wrong, a sovereign, irreversible, absolute authority in the presence of men and angels."[21] For Newman, conscience serves a twofold function, acting as both a judgment of the reason (moral sense) and a sense of duty (magisterial dictate).[22] In distinguishing right from wrong and imperatively constraining or sanctioning one's actions, it serves as a "personal guide."[23]

The Role of the Magisterium in Forming Correct Conscience

We now come to the question of the content of the knowledge out of which the practical judgment of conscience flows. This brings us to the issue of the role of the norm, the Church's teachings, the magisterium, in the formation of a correct conscience. While asserting the moral sense of conscience, Newman emphasizes conscience as a sense of duty, an authoritative voice bidding the human person by command, praise, promise and threat to do certain things and avoid others.[24] For Newman, as we have seen in scripture and in Aquinas, conscience has both affective and cognitive dimensions, that is, it involves the whole person, the will holding reason and emotions in an essential balance.[25] Conscience, according to this view, is more than a mere psychological or sociological phenomenon, it is intricately bound to the Creator and His law, and any notion of conscience which does not recognize and accept this was meaningless to Newman. He makes it quite clear that the right of conscience is never the "right thinking, speaking, writing, or acting according to [one's] judgment or [one's] humour, without any thought of God at all."[26]

Pope John Paul II reaffirms the freedom of conscience and the obligation that conscience be properly formed and related to God's law: "To claim that one has a right to act according to conscience, but without at the same time acknowledging the duty to conform one's conscience to the truth and to the law which God Himself has written on our hearts, in the end, means nothing more than imposing one's limited personal opinion."[27]

Conscience does not come forth fully formed as Athena springing fully clad from the head of Zeus: it needs to be informed by moral teaching. De facto human moral action is conditioned by the social, familial and personal experiences that mold and give structure to the values a person accepts as his or her own. Given the fallen condition of the human person, this moral teaching by competent authority is even more necessary. By moral teaching we mean that body of information that conscience uses together with the other data available in making a practical judgment in a specific instance about the rightness or wrongness of an action.

Newman recognized this need for the support and cultivation of conscience:

[Conscience] cannot perform adequately without external assistance; it needs to be regulated and sustained. Left to itself, though it tells truly at first, it soon becomes wavering, ambiguous, and false; it needs good teachers and good examples to keep it up to the mark and the line of duty; and the misery is that these external helps, teachers, and examples are in many instances wanting.[28]

Conscience, at its best, seeks guidance through prayerful reflection on the gospel, use of reason and the human sciences, the "sensus fidei," the insights of theologians and the teaching of the Church. However, because the ultimate source of moral teaching is the revelation of Jesus Christ and because the Church is charged with the mission of understanding, interpreting, and applying that revelation in the formation of conscience, the teaching of the Church assumes a preeminent position.

As recognized by Newman, revelation, as guarded and passed on through the Church, is the most authentic complement to conscience. It was his belief that the sacredness and freedom of conscience, together with its fallenness, showed that "the Church, the Pope, the hierarchy are in the divine purpose the supply of an urgent demand."[29] In our Catholic tradition, especially as articulated by Newman, moral teaching and conscience, or moral authority and conscience, are not opposed: they complement and require one another. One is the living action, the other the "understanding" out of which the action flows.

The importance of Church teaching to the proper functioning of conscience was recognized as well at Vatican Council II:

In the formation of their consciences, the Christian faithful ought carefully to attend to the sacred and certain doctrine of the Church. The Catholic Church is, by the will of Christ, the Teacher of the Truth. It is her duty to give utterance to and authoritatively to teach that truth which is Christ Himself and also to declare and confirm by her authority those principles of the moral order which have their origin in human nature itself.[30]

The follower of Christ lives and acts as part of the Body of Christ, a member of the ecclesial community, in communion with the living tradition of the whole body, united with its head, Christ the Divine Teacher.

While asserting the traditional Catholic teaching that "everyone of us . . . is bound to obey his conscience,"[31] the Council fathers recognized the fact that "conscience frequently errs from invincible ignorance without losing its dignity."[32] This ignorance or error, however, is not excusable when it results from negligence in the pursuit of truth and goodness. If one's conscience errs because of one's complacency, prejudice, rashness, or self-centeredness, one will be in the wrong whether one rejects or follows its dictates. Therefore, a true Christian conscience cannot be individualistic; it must be conformed to the teaching of Christ. While a Christian has the right and duty to follow his or her conscience, there is always present the responsibility to form that conscience in accord with the truth and in the light of faith."[33]

The Church as it works out its perfection in history must, if it is to be responsive to Christ and His message, teach, explain and apply its experience of Christ. The authentic teaching office in the Church does this with the authority of Christ. The Church's *magisterium* is a central part of the communal character of the faith and something that is of the very constitution of the Church to provide it direction, stability, self-awareness, unity and secure teaching and guidance that is faithful to Christ's gospel.[34]

The magisterium functions in a variety of ways. Bishops teach and oversee the teaching of others. They lead the community in worship and specifically in the celebration of the Eucharist. There is a sense in which every exercise of the liturgy and, in a most particular way the Eucharist, is a form of teaching because it brings us closer to the life of the Spirit who is the ultimate teacher in the Church. The primary exercise of the teaching office is found in the pastoral context of preaching and includes a host of catechetical efforts: homilies, pastoral letters, reflections, articles and other means to proclaim the Church's teaching.

The goal of such teaching is to convince others of the truth of the Church's message or confirm those already so persuaded. This is the point of contact in its most effective moment between the role of the magisterium and the conscience of a believer. This bishop, by proclaiming in a way that leads another to accept the teaching of the Church, helps the believer form his or her conscience.

In the act of the supervision of what is taught in the name of the Church, the bishop oversees the teaching of the faith by those who recognize him as the local chief shepherd and join with him in the nurture of the flock. This can take a wide variety of forms and finds expression as the bishop challenges those who teach the faith to do so in a way that provides a complete and accurate presentation of what the Church believes and leads others to accept it.

On this level, when the bishop proclaims the faith and oversees the proper exercise of teaching by others, the magisterium functions, for the most part, not only to touch individual hearts but to establish that doctrinal/moral context for the individual's act of moral judgment. In one sense the bishop's task is to elaborate for the community of believers that attitude of belief and openness in trust that characterizes adhesion to the proclamation of the faith represented by the profession "credo Ecclesiam."

At the same time, the bishop may be required to address more specific and tentative judgments and provide particular cognitive content that allows the faithful to make certain judgment concerning moral matters not so closely and evidently related to the first principles. This specified theological teaching takes the form of articulated judgment that can be described as "final" in the sense of "defined," if it is, or "final" in the sense of coming from the highest expression of the teaching office.

Christ's promise to remain with His Church until the end of time takes on a special significance when we address the matter of the continual, authentic teaching of the truth. Individual judgments about the content of Christ's teaching need to be verified. The judgment on the authenticity of any particular teaching rests with the bishops, who are charged to foster the unity of the Church. There can be no unity with multiple, contradictory teachings.[35] The bishop, as teacher, is assisted by the grace of his episcopal ordination to teach the truth of the gospel and the doctrine of the Church. Bishops are also charged to maintain the unity of the Church.

This divine assistance, we are reminded in the recent *Instruction on the Ecclesial Vocation of the Theologian,* is given to the successors of the apostles teaching in communion with the successor of Peter, and in a particular way, to the Roman Pontiff as Pastor of the whole Church, when exercising their ordinary magisterium, even should this not result in an infallible definition or in a "definitive" pronouncement but in the proposal of some teaching which leads to a better understanding of revelation in matters of faith and morals and to moral directives derived from such teaching.[36]

The guidance of the Spirit is the foundation and inspiration for the exercise of the Church's teaching office. Obviously this is not a question of some sort of "infused" knowledge. We are dealing with a case of the best practical judgment on an issue that is complex and multifaceted. The judgment of the teaching office—guided by the promise of the Spirit—carries a weight and presumption of truth that no other teacher can rightfully claim.

The innate *habitus,* the primordial "memory," is formed and oriented by the direction it receives from a wide range of voices. In a world in which there are dissonant voices competing for moral allegiance—voices that work to form a new "collective memory" and sense of obligation, it falls to the teaching voice of the Church to articulate Christ's will and message, not as one more among many but as part of the process that clarifies from inside the movement of the Spirit who is the soul of the Christian community.

Catholics turn to the magisterium of the Church for divinely inspired guidance in living the Christian faith. The reliability of the Church as interpreter of the gospel allows one to accept its teaching even when it is not irreformable. Given the guidance promised by Christ to the Church, it is eminently reasonable for believers to place their trust in the authoritative guidance that the magisterium gives for Catholic life. This practical conviction is at the root of Newman's assertion: "Ecclesiastical authority, not argument, is the supreme rule and appropriate guide for Catholics in matters of religion."[37]

The Proper Exercise of Conscience

For the Catholic, formation of conscience according to the teaching of the Church is necessary if the acts of conscience are to be ordered to the truth as revealed and taught in the Church. The proper exercise of conscience, then, involves four elements:

1. objective moral norms;
2. adequate knowledge of the validity and truth of these norms;
3. knowledge of the pertinent facts in a particular situation;
4. the application of these norms in a practical judgment to a specific situation, instance, or act.

One of the basic principles concerning Catholic moral teaching is the existence of an objective moral order in which some actions are right and other actions are wrong. The moral order is not fleeting or capricious, although throughout history we continually gain greater insights into the exact nature of the moral order. In such an understanding, if an action is, in fact, objectively immoral, no circumstances or intention can make it objectively moral.[38]

Moral norms can in themselves be known. Out of the Church's experience of applying the gospel values to daily situations, a body of moral teaching has developed which the bishops proclaim with authority as part of the teaching of Christ. The believer has an obligation to be aware of the teaching of the Church and, to the best of his or her ability, to appropriate that teaching as an expression of the will of Christ.

In specific practical situations when the Christian attempts to act conscientiously, he or she does so by the sincere application of the moral norms as articulated by the Church in a manner that is consonant with the Church's application of those same norms.

134

Hence, for a Catholic to act in a subjectively moral manner, he or she must not only seek to know and to make their own the teaching of the Church, but also apply that teaching in a sincere manner.

Relationship of Bishops and Theologians

It is within the context of both the Church's teaching office and the need to understand more fully the consequences of the application of that teaching in practical situations that we place our discussion of the relationship of bishops and theologians. As the *Instruction on the Ecclesial Vocation of the Theologian* points out, the vocation of the theologian is awakened "by the Spirit in the Church."[39] The theologian's role is to pursue in a particular way an ever-deepening understanding of the word of God "found in the inspired scriptures and handed on by the living tradition of the Church. He does this in communion with the magisterium which has been charged with the responsibility of preserving the deposit of faith."[40]

The *Instruction* proceeds to note that the theologian's work responds to a "dynamism found in the faith itself."[41] Theology's proper task is to understand the meaning of revelation. To do this, the theologian must apply a methodology and philosophical system or concepts in a reflection upon revealed doctrine. It is the theologian's task in this perspective "to draw from the surrounding culture those elements which will allow him better to illumine one or other aspect of the mysteries of faith. This is certainly an arduous task that has its risks, but it is legitimate in itself and should be encouraged."[42] It is in this sense that we say that theologians have the responsibility of helping the faithful (bishops included), through their expertise precisely as theologians, to understand more fully the implications of the faith for moral living.

There can be a variety of responses in practical situations to the application of the Church's teaching in any given instance. Theologians using different methodologies may come to tentative conclusions or opinions at variance with one another on the application of the Church's received tradition when dealing with the complex and many-faceted issues of contemporary society. In their effort, however tentative, theologians make a real and substantial contribution to the life of the Church by addressing the moral teaching of the Church in its relationship to specific new issues of our times.

Nonetheless, since all the faithful, including bishops and theologians, receive the revelation and the teaching of Christ through the Church, and since within the Church bishops are the ones who have been charged and empowered by the Holy Spirit to make the practical judgment about the conformity of any one teaching to the truth of revelation, it falls to the bishops to have the final word in judging and verifying the relationship to revelation and to the teaching of the Church of any opinion proposed by theologians.

As the *Instruction* points out:

> The magisterium, therefore, has the task of discerning, by means of judgments normative for the consciences of believers, those acts which in themselves conform to the demands of faith and foster their expression in life and those which, on the contrary, because intrinsically evil, are incompatible with such demands.[43]

Judgment does not mean that there is no discussion or even divergent views during the development of thought on a given subject, but at some point in dialogue, discussion and even disagreement give way to decision. We cross a line from discussion about various theological conclusions to the approbation and application of the conclusions. Here we find the real center of some of the present-day confusion and conflict—the distinction between the role and functions of bishops and theologians. Theologians make their claim on the faithful through the cogency of their arguments and their understanding of the issues under debate. Bishops make their claim on the faithful because of the office they hold in the Church and because of the promised guidance of the Holy Spirit in the exercise of that office. Both theologians and bishops (magisterium) make judgments. When in the practical order there is a clash of judgments, that of the magisterium enjoys the benefit of unique divine protection. This is true even if the judgment itself is proclaimed as tentative and non-irreformable.

When there is a disagreement about the application of the Church's teaching in a moral dilemma, the practical, pastoral judgment for the good of the Church under the guidance of the Holy Spirit falls to the bishops. Hence, they place a claim on the conscience of the faithful (theologians included)—a claim that cannot be made by anyone else in the Church. It is a claim which is qualitatively different from any claim of any theological hypothesis or any theological opinion.

The distinct role of the bishops and the theologians helps us to understand why it is the teaching of the Church that must inform conscience and is necessary for the right and proper function of conscience. In the formation of conscience, the teaching of the magisterium offers content that enjoys a unique guarantee of truth. It offers the surest and safest way to know God's will for us in our concrete situations. It is the surest way for us to find our way to the verdant pastures promised us by the Good Shepherd.

The Church's moral teaching binds conscience, not because it is the fullest possible expression of the moral value being addressed and not because it may very well be an irreformable statement of truth, but because in the expression of the best judgment, given the present circumstances, it is the teaching office that enjoys the promised abundance of the Holy Spirit.

Given the promise of divine guidance to its teaching action even when not proposing non-irreformable teaching, the magisterium can make a claim on conscience which cannot be rejected because one "asserts that the validity of the teaching is not evident, nor upon the opinion that the opposite position would be the more probable. Nor would the judgment of the subjective conscience of the theologian," as the Instruction points out, "justify it because conscience does not constitute an autonomous and exclusive authority for deciding the truth of a doctrine."[44]

Conclusion

In summary, conscience is the practical judgment about the rightness or wrongness of one's acts. Such a practical judgment is to be followed because it is the ultimate personal norm for moral behavior. Conscience acts out of the knowledge available to the person making the practical judgment. For the Christian, Christ's teaching and that of His Church must form the context out of which the practical, moral judgment of a believer is made. In that context the believer, in faith enlightened by the Spirit in and through the Church, can with trust and confidence walk in a way that allows us to claim it to be the Way of Christ.

NOTES

1. Cf. Congregation for the Doctrine of the Faith, *Instruction on the Ecclesial Vocation of the Theologian* (May 24, 1990), n. 21, reprinted in 20 *Origins* (July 5, 1990), p. 122.

2. Cf. Eric D'Arcy, *Conscience and Its Right to Freedom* (New York: Sheed and Ward, 1961), pp. 5–8.

3. Cf. Rudolf Hofmann, "Conscience," *Sacramentum Mundi,* 1 (London: Burns and Oates, 1968), p. 412.

4. Cf. Sean Fagan, S. M., "Conscience," *New Dictionary of Theology,* eds. Joseph Komonchack, Mary Collins, and Dermot A. Lane (Wilmington, Delaware: Michael Glazier, Inc., 1987), pp. 226–227.

5. Hofmann, "Conscience", p. 412. '

6. Cf. D'Arcy, p. 9.

7. Fagan, p. 227.

8. This word seems to have entered into theological use as the result of an error. A copyist of St. Jerome's Commentary on Ezekiel accidentally wrote "synteresis" for "syneidesis." Cf. F. L. Cross and E. A. Livingstone, eds., *The Oxford Dictionary of the Christian Church* (London: Oxford University Press, 1974), p. 335.

9. Ibid., p. 230.

10. St. Thomas Aquinas, *Summa Theologica* 1, q. 79, a. 13 (hereinafter the Summa will be referred to as "S. Th.").

11. Cf. Haring, p. 230.

12. Ibid.

13. Cf. S. Th. 1, q.79, aa. 12–13; 1–2, q. 94, aa. 2, 6, cited in Germain Grizez, *The Way of the Lord Jesus: Volume 1—Christian Moral Principles,* (Chicago, IL: Franciscan Herald Press, 1983), p. 76.

14. Cf. S.Th., 1, q. 83, a. 1; 1–2, q. 1, a. 1; q. 6, a. 1; q. 18, a. 1.

15. Cf. S.Th., 1–2, q. 19, aa. 5–6; q. 94, aa. 4, 6; q. 48, a. 1.

16. Cf. S. Th., 1–2, q. 19, a. 5, aa. 2; 2–2, q. 104, a. 5.

17. *Gaudium et Spes* 16.

18. Cf. Haring, p. 231.

19. Cf. R. Hofmann, *Die Gewissenslehre des Walter von Bruegge und die Entwicklung der Gewissenslehre in der Hochscholastik* (Muenster, 1941), pp. 107–108, as translated in Haring, *Free and Faithful in Christ,* p. 231.

20. John Henry Newman, *Letter to His Grace the Duke of Norfolk* (1875), reprinted in *Newman and Gladstone: The Vatican Decrees* (Notre Dame, IN: University of Notre Dame Press, 1962), p. 127.

21. Newman, *Letter to the Duke of Norfolk,* p. 127.

22. Cf. John Henry Newman, *An Essay in Aid of A Grammar of Assent* (Notre Dame, IN: University of Notre Dame Press, 1979), p. 98.

23. Ibid., p. 304.

24. Cf. John Henry Newman, *Sermons Preached on Various Occasions* (London: Longmans, 1919), pp. 64–65.

25. Cf. F. J. Kaiser, F.S.C., *The Concept of Conscience According to John Henry Newman* (Washington, DC: Catholic University Press, 1958), p. 113.

26. Cf. Newman, *Letter to the Duke of Norfolk,* p. 130.

27. John Paul II, *Respect for Conscience: Foundation for Peace—1991 World Day of Peace Message,* reprinted in 20 *Origins* (Dec. 27, 1991), p. 472.

28. John Henry Newman, *Discourses Addressed to Mixed Congregations* (London: Longmans, 1929), p. 83.

29. Newman, *Letter to the Duke of Norfolk,* p. 133.

30. *Dignitatis Humanae* 14.

31. *Dignitatis Humanae* 11.

32. *Gaudium et Spes* 16.

33. *The Teaching of Christ,* eds. Ronald Lawler, O.F.M. Cap., Donald W. Wuerl, Thomas Comerford Lawler (Huntington, IN: Our Sunday Visitor, 1976), p. 284; cf. Bishops of Canada, *Episcopal Statement: Formation of Conscience,* December 1, 1973; National Conference of Catholic Bishops, "The Church in Our Day," November, 1967 and "Human Life in Our Day," November, 1968, reprinted in Hugh Nolan, ed., *Pastoral Letters of the United States Catholic Bishops,* 3 (Washington, DC: U.S.C.C. Publications, 1983), 98–154, 164–194.

34. *Lumen Gentium* 19–21; cf. Donald W. Wuerl, "Natural Law, the Community, Authority," *The Priest* (May, 1969), pp. 272–282.

35. *Lumen Gentium* 24–25; cf. Donald W. Wuerl, "Academic Freedom and the University," 18 *Origins* (September 8, 1988), pp. 207–211.

36. Cf. *Instruction on the Ecclesial Vocation of the Theologian,* n. 17.

37. John Henry Newman, *The Idea of a University* (Garden City, New York: Image Books, 1959), p. 54.

38. For a treatment of this subject, see Eric D'Arcy, "Natural Law," *Encyclopedia of Bioethics* 3 (New York: Macmillan and Free Press, 1979), pp. 1131–37 (with an extensive bibliography) and Philip Keane SS, "The Objective Moral Order: Reflections on Recent Research," 43 *Theological Studies* (1982), pp. 260–278.

39. *Instruction on the Ecclesial Vocation of the Theologian,* n. 6.

40. Ibid.

41. Ibid., n. 7.

42. Ibid., n. 10.

43. Ibid., n. 16; cf. Pope Paul VI, Encyclical, *Humanae Vitae,* n. 4 & n. 11; and First Vatican Council, Dogmatic Constitution, *Dei Filius,* ch. 2, (DS 3005).

44. cf. *Instruction on the Ecclesial Vocation of the Theologian,* n. 28.

Chapter 11

FIRST RESPONSE

The Reverend Avery Dulles, S.J., S.T.D.

We hear so much about freedom of conscience that it comes almost as a shock to be told that a person's conscience may be bound. This, however, is what Bishop Wuerl has asserted. He argues his case persuasively on the basis of Catholic tradition, with appropriate citations from Paul, Thomas Aquinas, Newman, and Vatican II. If I correctly understand his paper, Bishop Wuerl is saying that the individual always has a subjective obligation to follow the biddings of conscience, but that conscience itself prompts one to seek out objective norms of right and wrong. For the Catholic the moral teaching of the ecclesiastical magisterium is always an important factor; in fact, it is, generally speaking, the safest norm to follow.

Bishop Wuerl does not limit his thesis to the simple faithful. He insists that the judgments of the hierarchical magisterium are binding in conscience on all members of the Church, including theologians. As Catholics they are obliged to accept the official teaching of their Church with sincere religious assent as well as with external conformity. Since the conscience of the theologian, like that of other Catholics, must be shaped by the teaching of the Church, theologians cannot normally appeal to conscience as giving them a right to dissent.

Bishop Wuerl performs a real service by showing the positive links between conscience and the moral magisterium. Too often the impression is given that the two are alternatives, even antithetical. The magisterium is described as though it took the place of conscience, and conscience as though it liberated one from the need to listen to the magisterium or submit to it.

Relying in part on Bishop Wuerl's remarks, I would like to suggest that there is a dialectical relationship of mutual support and tension between conscience and the magisterium. They support one another because conscience impels a person to obey God's injunctions as intimated by the organs of revelation, including the Church as God's authorized representative. The magisterium fulfills the aspirations of conscience by enabling it to find the moral good at which it aims. Far from taking the place of conscience, the magisterium enables the individual to act conscientiously, with full personal responsibility before God, the transcendent judge to whom we are absolutely accountable.

There is no perfect identity between conscience and the magisterium of the Church. Conscience is an interior, not an outer, voice. Conscience, moreover, exists in all human beings, even those who belong to no Church. Paul in the second chapter of Romans speaks of Gentiles, who do not have the law, observing by nature what the law commands, inasmuch as the law is written on their hearts, accusing or defending them by its testimony (Rom 2:14–15). For members of the Church, the magisterium is one, but only one, informant of conscience. Bishop Wuerl mentions several other fonts of moral knowledge, including prayerful reflection on the gospel, the use of reason and the human sciences, the *sensus fidei,* and the insights of theologians. To this list one could add, as Newman does, the example of people esteemed for virtue. Conscience, therefore, is not abjectly dependent on the magisterium.

Moral pedagogy, in my opinion, should strive to make people ever more sensitive to the inner biddings of conscience. It should lead people to pray and to invoke the guidance of the Spirit. Jesus, as I understand him in the Gospels, evoked the inner resources of his hearers. When questions were addressed to him he rarely laid down specific rules. He taught now by hyperbole, now by parables, and now by questions. When questioned, he would propose counter questions such as: Is it lawful on the Sabbath to do good or to do harm (Lk 6:9)? Which of the three was the neighbor to the man who had fallen among thieves (Lk 10:36)? He knew the right answers but he wanted to activate the hearers' own power to answer these questions for themselves. He was educating his disciples for freedom.

During the centuries between the Reformation and the Second Vatican Council Catholic moral theology tended increasingly to exalt the authority of law, which was sometimes depicted in voluntaristic terms as depending on the mere will of the legislator. The Church and its magisterium were too often understood in primarily juridical categories. Moral rectitude was depicted as a mater of compliance with divine decrees as relayed by ecclesiastical authorities. Toward the middle of the 20th century there was a commendable return to a moral theology centered on virtue or moral excellence. Morality was once more seen, as it had been in earlier centuries, as a free and rational pursuit of the good. Less emphasis was placed on adherence to an extrinsic moral code; closer attention was given to the inner dynamics of nature and of grace. Law itself was seen as a pedagogue (cf. Gal 3:4), enabling a person to respond to true inner imperatives. For Thomas Aquinas the ideal was to be so moved by the Holy Spirit that one would spontaneously fulfill what the law commanded (*Summa theol.* 1–2.93.6c and ad 1). The precepts of the new law, he maintained, were intended primarily to instruct the faithful so that they would be inclined freely to obey the impulses of grace (ibid., 1–2.106.1).

During and after the Second Vatican Council there was a strong reaction against legalism and authority. Many Catholics have been veering toward a kind of antinomianism, making an absolute out of the individual's freedom of conscience. People tend to forget that the individual can never be totally autonomous, and that docility (teachability) is an integral part of prudence. The Catholic, of course, has special motives for heeding the voice of authority. In view of the commission of the magisterium to teach with the divine assistance all that Christ has commanded, the teaching of the Church must be for the Catholic, not indeed the sole and all-controlling norm, but the preeminent objective element to be consulted. The Catholic who follows an erroneous conscience without due regard for the teaching of the magisterium may be at fault for having failed to inform his or her conscience. (For the teaching of Thomas Aquinas on this point see *Summa theol.* 1–2.10.6)

This does not mean, however, that submission to magisterial teaching is an adequate norm of morality. In many cases the magisterium has not laid down any binding rule, and has left it to the faithful to apply the norm of prudence. Even where the Church has spoken, it does not follow that the word of the Church should be the sole or principal motive for good behavior. In most cases people ought to be able to see for themselves what is right or wrong. In the area of natural-law morality, the Church has not thus far seen fit to make definitive pronouncements, involving the infallibility of the teaching office. In certain instances, rather rare I believe, church authorities have made an authoritative but nondefinitive pronouncement, clearly rejecting the opposed position and putting an end to legitimate public debate within the Church. This is what Bishop Wuerl means, I presume, when he speaks of the magisterium having the "last word."

Bishop Wuerl has given good reasons for holding that in such cases no Catholic, however expert in theology, is entitled to disregard or contest the official teaching. Even so, a serious thinker may be personally convinced that some noninfallible teaching of the magisterium is not fully consonant with other sources of moral judgment, such as reason, biblical teaching, the opinions of reputable theologians, and the general sense of the faithful. The difficulties can indeed appear so great that a given individual is unable to give sincere assent. It is increasingly recognized that in situations of this kind further dialogue between theologians and the magisterium may be useful. The National Conference of Catholic Bishops, in its meeting of June 1989, approved a set of principles for formal doctrinal dialogue to resolve apparent disputes.

The Instruction of the CDF on "The Ecclesial Vocation of the Theologian," published in May 1990, likewise recognizes the value of dialogue. While discountenancing strident opposition and laying down loyal submission to the magisterium as the rule, the CDF acknowledges that the theologian may raise questions regarding the timeliness, the form, and even the contents of particular magisterial interventions (no. 24). Such critical questioning is most likely to be appropriate when the magisterium is making prudential decisions in which solid principles are intertwined with contingent applications linked to transitory conditions. By calling attention to these variables, the theologian can help the Church to achieve true doctrinal progress. According to some historians, the teaching of the Church has developed over the centuries with regard to matters such as torture, usury, witchcraft, religious freedom, and Church-State relations. The passage of time is normally required for a final discernment to be made between the permanently valid principles and time-conditioned applications that may be somewhat tentative and conjectural.

It is difficult to decide to what extent the current positions of the magisterium on contentious matters are subject to further revision in the light of new historical developments. Although a general obedience to the decisions legitimate authority must be the rule for the theologian, as for other Catholics, some scope must be given for further questioning by competent experts who are convinced that a given decision is too much influenced by limited presuppositions or passing circumstances.

Cardinal Newman, in his *Letter to the Duke of Norfolk,* said that if the pope were to speak against conscience in the true sense of the word, he would be cutting the ground from under his own feet (in the edition cited by Bishop Wuerl, p. 132). The same may be said of the magisterium in general. What properly moves people to adhere to the moral teaching of the Church is nothing other than the voice of conscience. A nervous effort to substitute law for conscience would be a self-defeating policy. It might even incite opposition by creating the impression that the Church is more interested in conformity than in free and responsible behavior. The most pressing need of our day is not to lay down more and stricter rules but to educate the consciences of the faithful so that they may be able to make reliable judgments based on personal insight and virtuous inclination. A particular value of Bishop Wuerl's paper is that it helps to integrate the inner authority of conscience with the external authority of the Church's magisterium.

Chapter 12

SECOND RESPONSE

The Reverend Monsignor James J. Mulligan

When I first had the opportunity to read Bishop Wuerl's fine presentation on conscience, I was not sure what, if anything, I would be able to say in response. It is clear and complete, and any effort on my part to explain the meaning of conscience would end up, I feared, as little more than repetition of what had already been better said. And so I decided, rather, to come at it from another point of view and to touch on the question of *how* we are to communicate this whole reality of conscience to those who are not theologians. How is the fact of formation of conscience to be communicated to people so that what is clear and logical and true, may be able to capture not only the mind, but the heart and imagination as well?

Bishop Wuerl spoke of Cardinal Newman's concept of conscience. One author has referred to this in the form of five propositions: "(1) Conscience consists in a habitual orientation of the whole person toward God; (2) conscience develops in the person a profound awareness of the presence of God; (3) conscience implies that a person desires to serve God with a perfect heart; (4) this orientation to God and perfect service will be manifested by consistency in conduct; (5) finally, conscience imposes the duty of habitual obedience."

Every one of these propositions points to conscience as being far more than a matter of reasoned and intellectual decisions governing the choice of right actions. Instead, *at every stage it involves the relationship of persons,* for at every stage it involves a point of contact between the individual and the living God. Since it is a relationship that is at stake, it also becomes a question of love and that is far more than an intellectual proposition. It involves, as well, a lived experience.

In this presentation, I am going to use two particular sources: Saint Paul and George MacDonald. Of course, I feel no need to explain who Saint Paul is, but it might be well if I were to say just a few words about George MacDonald. He was born in 1824 in Scotland, the son of tenant farmer. He completed his education in 1851 and became a Congregationalist minister—and was married in that same year. His ministry continued for the grand total of almost three years, and in 1853 he was forced to resign. His preaching had become unpopular because of his strange ideas—such as that all men, even Catholics, might be saved. For the rest of his life he earned his living writing novels and children's stories. Being a writer he was, of course, almost always poor. He also produced three volumes of sermons which he never really preached.[1] The material that I will use is from those sermons. He died in 1905.

In the First Epistle to the Corinthians Saint Paul presents a vision of our relationship to Christ which has much to do with an understanding of conscience and its relationship both to theology and to the living Church itself. His vision begins in the very first sentence of the letter. He says:

> Paul, by the will of God called as an apostle of Jesus
> Christ, and our brother Sosthenes, to the church of God

at Corinth, to those who are consecrated by union with Christ Jesus, and called as God's people, like all those anywhere who call on the name of Jesus Christ, their Lord as well as ours; God our Father and the Lord Jesus Christ bless you and give you peace.[2]

One theme of his epistle will be union and it is set out clearly in these few words. Furthermore, it is not just a union into which we happen to enter by common agreement; it is, rather, a union to which we *are called*. Paul himself is called as apostle. The Corinthians are called as God's people. All those who call on Jesus are likewise called. And, indeed, he addresses himself to the Church, and even the word church in Greek means the "assembly," those who are "called together." At every step the initiative is God's.

He tells the Corinthians, "You have grown rich in everything through union with [Jesus]—in power of expression and in capacity for knowledge. So your experience has confirmed the testimony that I bore to Christ."[3] What he speaks of as "power of expression" and "capacity for knowledge" are, I think, far more than a talent for clear verbal expression and a good grasp of theology. They are, rather, the lived reality of expressing the presence of Christ in all that we are and all that we do, and the growth of a knowledge that comes far more from relationship than it does from academic pursuit. The testimony that he bore to Christ was the testimony of a living savior who would enter into and transform their lives. He has no hesitation in appealing to their own lived experience to verify this.

When we approach the question of conscience with people, we should not fail to appeal to their experience as well—and to our own. Even though at times we would possibly prefer not to admit it, we are always better off when we obey the dictates of conscience and make every effort to live in union with Christ. The Corinthians, coming as they did from a pagan city noted for its immorality, must have found their own transformation startling— more so, I suspect, than do we, who were almost all born and raised in a society that at least claimed to be Christian.

To what experience can we appeal? Certainly to the experience that we all have at one time or another, the experience of the painfulness of sin and the peace that comes from conversion. We are all too easily led into the error of thinking that sin is the mere breaking of law and so conscience is just as easily taken as a rationalizing process that helps to find a "legal" way out. This situation arises from what I would call a misinformed image of what sin really is. Father Gula spoke yesterday about imagination, and I agree fully that the way we image things is essential.

We tend to look at moral law as though it were somehow on a par with human laws. We have probably all, at one time or another, bent the traffic laws just a bit. We speed. We park illegally. We make exceptions for ourselves—and then honk our horns when others make their own exceptions. We see law as frequently arbitrary—and so it is. The speed limit in many places is 55—a reasonable but certainly arbitrary number. It is a legal limit chosen from a range of possible safe speeds. If you violate it and get caught you pay the penalty. But if you are not caught and you do not have an accident, then it would seem that nothing bad has happened. Many people, in my opinion, have just this image of moral law. "Thou shalt not speed," may be a law, but its violation, nine times out of ten, brings no bitter consequences. They also see sin as little more than violation of a law.

There is a far better image available to us. When you buy a bottle of rat poison it is marked with a label bearing the image of a skull and the words, "Thou shalt not use internally." You can, of course, use it internally if you want to. After all, you bought it and it is now yours. If you are scrupulous you might write to the manufacturer for permission before using it internally. But whether you sneak a taste or do it right out in the open with full permission, you will be just as dead. The rule here was not at all arbitrary. It expressed an essential relationship between your body and the contents of that bottle. There is a much better image of sin and moral law. Sin kills. Formation of conscience is the formation of the ability to discern between what kills and what gives life. It is not a mere legal matter.

We are called to a union with Christ which will, among other things, enable us to begin to make this sort of discernment. Amazingly, however, it is the relationship itself which will teach us most and *not* our own capacity to understand things with human wisdom alone. "For since in God's providence the world with all its wisdom did not come to know God, God chose, through the folly of the gospel message, to save those who had faith in him."[4]

The source of this sort of wisdom is far deeper than the mere acquisition of knowledge. For Paul the first sign of this is to be found in his own experience of preaching Christ and the amazing consequences that emerged from that preaching. On his first trip to Corinth, he had just come from Athens. It was there that he preached at the Acropolis and waxed philosophical, speaking of the God "in whom we live and move and have our being."[5] He spoke glowingly of the divine nature and of the resurrection. Some of the listeners scoffed and others said, "Good show! You'll have to come back and tell us more some time."[6] But there is no record of mass conversions or of the sudden emergence of a thriving Christian community in Athens.

Paul left, probably downcast, and went to Corinth—possibly falling ill on the way. But when he preached in Corinth—that seaport famous throughout the empire as a den of iniquity—he was heard and people's lives were changed. In his First Letter to Corinth he recalled that incident and wrote:

> So when I came to you, brothers, I did not come and tell you the secret purpose of God in superior, philosophical language, for I resolved, while I was with you, to forget everything but Jesus Christ and his crucifixion. For my part I came among you in weakness and with a great deal of fear and trembling, and my teaching and message were not put in plausible, philosophical language, but they were attended with convincing spiritual power, so that your faith might rest, not on human philosophy, but on the power of God.[7]

There is more in Paul's preaching than just Paul's words. There is, in some way, the power of God himself to convert and transform. It is not Paul who changes their lives, but God.

We have been drawn into such a union with Christ that we are given a whole new vision of reality, a whole new way of thinking and acting—a way that surpasses the limits of our own limited logic. We are not called to act against logic, but beyond it. "Just so, no one understands the thoughts of God but the spirit of

God. But the Spirit we have received is not that of the world, but the Spirit that comes from God, which we have to make us realize the blessings God has given us."[8] In Paul's eyes we are so transformed by union with Christ that a whole world of new values is opened up to us. "The spiritual man is alive to all true values, but his own true value no unspiritual man can see. For who has ever known the Lord's thoughts, so that he can instruct him? But we share the thoughts of Christ."[9]

In union with Christ we are drawn into the life and power and knowledge of God. Without ever using the word, for it had not yet been coined, Paul was speaking of the Trinity. We have become one with the living Word, the expression of God's own being. We have become one with His love—that love which is the one Living Love that exists between Father and Son. Our knowing and loving is made one with God's own knowledge and love. From this bond of unity comes the reality of true Christian conscience. This reality is not just a question of *my individual* relationship to God. It is a relationship which exists in such a way as to draw me into relationship with a whole community of believers—the Church.

It is that Church which becomes a living and visible expression of this reality of the saving presence of God in the world. Within that Church there is a visible unity with visible leadership. Indeed, there could be no real community without such visibility, for we live in a world in which the deepest reality of spirit, in order to be known, has to manifest itself in the weaker reality of the visible world. If that Church is to be a sign and source of salvation, then those who lead it must be able to do so with the assurance that they do not ultimately lead the Church into error. This, of course, is where we begin to enter into the first hint of the meaning of infallibility, but I will not pursue that concept at the moment.

We are also human beings who learn things bit by bit and piece by piece, even in the area of that which is spiritual. And so we develop a theology—an effort at clear and logical presentation of that which we believe and experience at a level which always goes beyond the limits of logic itself. We are also human beings who grow only gradually into the fullness of that to which God has called us.

It should come then as no surprise that there will be discussions and disputes about doctrinal matters. This we should expect from the very fact that what we believe cannot, in the final analysis, be limited to what we attempt to put into words and concepts. Nor should we be shocked that there will be discussions and disputes about moral matters. These may well emerge from honest disagreement among honest people. Still we should be completely honest with ourselves and admit that our disagreements can also come from our unwillingness to confront our own sinfulness. Dissent may arise from what we feel sometimes as an onus placed upon us by the weight of the truth.

It makes sense that in the Church there should be those who attempt to *explain* both doctrine and morality. These are the theologians. But there must also be those who, with full authority to do so, *proclaim* the truth. These are the bishops. The two may seem to clash at times; but in the end, if the unity we claim is real, they must come together. And, as Saint Paul said, our faith must finally rest not on superior, philosophical language, but on the power of God.

I spoke earlier of George MacDonald, and let me now turn to an insight which emerges from one of his sermons. The real question of conscience is not simply one of what we must *do*. It is, rather, a question of what we must *be*. MacDonald writes:

The Lord cared neither for isolated truth, nor for orphaned deed. It was truth in the inward parts, it was the good heart, the mother of good deeds, He cherished. It was the live, active knowing, breathing good He came to further. He cared for no speculation in morals or religion. It was good men he cared about, not notions of good things, or even good actions, save as the outcome of life, save as the bodies in which the primary live actions of love and will in the soul took shape and came forth. Could He by one word set at rest all the questionings of philosophy as to the supreme good and absolute truth, I venture to say that word he would not have uttered. But He would die to make men good and true. His whole heart would respond to the cry of sad publican or despairing pharisee, "How am I to be good?" . . .

We have to do with Him to whom no one can look without the need of good waking up in his heart; to think about Him is to begin to be good. To do a good thing is to do a good thing; to know God is to be good. It is not to make us do all things right He cares, but to make us hunger and thirst after a righteousness possessing which we shall never need to think of what is or is not good, but shall refuse the evil and choose the good by a motion of the will which is at once necessity and choice.[10]

There remains yet one final point to be made. As important as it is that conscience be properly formed and as important as it is that we be transformed to the fullness of God's goodness, we must never fail to treat each other with mercy. We must proclaim and we must explain and we must call ourselves and all others to the completion of that which God has offered us. We must give away all else and hold on to this alone. It may take a mighty struggle for this to happen, but, in the end, there is no other real choice.

Jesus said to the rich young man: "If you want to be perfect, go! Sell your property and give the money to the poor, and you will have riches in heaven. Then come back and be a follower of mine."[11] MacDonald wrote of this call to perfection and of the fact that the young man went away sad. Perfection is not easily arrived at, even though it is the goal to which we are called. In regard to the commandments he said:

Is there no keeping but a perfect keeping? [You may well be tempted to say:] "None that God cares for."

There I think you utterly wrong. That no keeping but a perfect one will satisfy God, I hold with all my heart and strength; but that there is none else He cares for is one of the lies of the enemy. What father is not pleased with the first tottering attempt of his little one to walk? What father would be satisfied with anything but the manly step of the full grown son?[12]

As bishops you are to teach. You are to proclaim the truth of the saving power of God. To do that you will, I hope, make use of

154

all that you know from your study of theology. But even more so, I hope that you will reflect on your own lived experience in prayer and the depth of your own continued conversion. This will fill your preaching with all the power of God. Your living union with Christ and with each other will do more to form consciences than theology or psychology can ever hope to do. Your living experience will help to give meaning to the experience of others and will bring those first tottering efforts to the full grown stride of real sons and daughters of God.

NOTES

1. *Unspoken Sermons*, published in 1870, 1885 and 1891. Some of these have been published in condensed form as *Creation in Christ*, edited by Rolland Hein, Harold Shaw Publishers, Wheaton, Illinois, 1976.

2. I Cor 1–3. The Greek text reads: Παῦλος κλητὸς ᾿απόστολος Χριστοῦ ᾿Ιησοῦ διὰ Θελήματος Θεοῦ καὶ Σωσθένης ὁ ἀδελφὸς τῇ ἐκκλησίᾳ τοῦ Θεοῦ τῇ οὔσῃ ἐν Κορίνθῳ ἡγιασμένοις ἐν Χριστῷ Ιησοῦ, κλητοῖς ἁγίοις, σὺν πᾶσιν τοῖς ἐπικαλουμένοις τὸ ὄνομα τοῦ κυρίου ἡμῶν ᾿Ιησοῦ Χριστοῦ ἐν παντὶ τόπῳ, αὐτῶν καὶ ἡμῶν· χάρις ὑμῖν καὶ εἰρήνη ἀπὸ Θεοῦ πατρὸς ἡμῶν καὶ κυρίου ᾿Ιησοῦ Χριστοῦ.

3. I Cor 1,4–6.

4. I Cor 1,21.

5. Acts 17,28.

6. Cf. Acts 17,32.

7. I Cor 2, 1–5.

8. I Cor 2, 11–12.

9. I Cor 2, 15–16.

10. MacDonald, *Creation in Christ*, pp. 110–111.

11. Mt. 20,21.

12. MacDonald, *op. cit.*, p. 113.

Chapter 13

PASTORAL CONCERNS
CHURCH AUTHORITY
AND CONSCIENCE FORMATION

BISHOP: I wonder if it is possible for some people not to have any conscience at all?

FATHER DULLES: I think everybody is born with a conscience, so I would suspect that if they really have no feeling of conscience it is not inculpable on their part that they have somehow extinguished the voice of conscience. On the other hand it is initially, I think, rather faint and vague. It has to be educated to become acute and sensitive, and people may not have had the opportunity for an education of their conscience. So, as a matter of fact in practical decisions they are not motivated to any perceptible degree by conscience.

BISHOP: The Second Vatican Council speaks of conscience being "numbed" in the face of sin—repeated sin—even being silenced. I am not certain that it really speaks of the existence or nonexistence of conscience.

BISHOP: I have two short questions for Bishop Wuerl. First question: what is the relationship of the magisterium of the Church and its power to bind the conscience of Catholics who do not accept *Humanae Vitae?* The second question is somewhat similar. What is the relationship of the Magisterium of the Church and its power to bind the conscience of Protestants?

BISHOP WUERL: We distinguish between teaching and the appropriation of the teaching. When we attempt to aid the formation of conscience we are trying to provide people the material they need and in a way that it will be persuasive. But ultimately it is individual conscience itself, that binds.

And out of the faith that motivates a person and therefore substantially directs that person's conscience, there should be a predisposition to accept as part of the interior formation of that conscience the teaching of the Church.

MONSIGNOR MULLIGAN: I am thoroughly convinced that what we call sin is wrong, not because there is a rule against it. That's not what makes it wrong. Rather, there are rules against it because the thing in itself is destructive, hurtful and deadly.

I remember someone who came to me one time and he told me he really felt bad. He thought he had a guilt complex, and I asked him why. He explained the whole thing to me. I said, "I have wonderful news for you, you don't have a guilt complex. You are guilty. If you would just stop doing this then you would feel 100% better." And he did. He stopped doing it and he felt 100% better.

BISHOP: Father Dulles, you point out the various sources we go to to help us form our conscience in addition to the magisterium. And I certainly think the sources you pointed out are the appropriate ones. And the magisterium is among them. But, I would like you to comment on the fact that it seems to me that the magisterium serves a second function, too, which is to be interpreter and judge of the others in the final decision or analysis. So, it's not one among several, it's preeminent and definitive. So, I would like you to reflect on that for me, please.

FATHER DULLES: I think that's a valid point. The Magisterium does reflect on and interpret the others. I don't know that the others are reducible to the interpretation that the magisterium gives to them. For example, the sense of the faithful or the consensus of theologians can exist without being officially identified as such by the magisterium. So, I think they still remain distinct sources, and when the magisterium does give the interpretation of these other sources, it has to be seen as a credible interpretation. The discrepancies, or apparent discrepancies, have to be overcome before one has a settled judgement of conscience; otherwise one is hesitating between alternative norms that seem to contradict one another.

BISHOP: I don't know if I understood you, so I would like to ask a further question. I think that you point out well the process that the Magisterium needs to do in terms of consulting before coming to a definitive judgement and if that's what you are saying I can agree with you. But, I think that's a different kind of answer than the question I was asking. Isn't it our understanding as Church that when it comes to a conflict between interpretation of the Scriptures or of the other sources through which our consciences are formed, the faithful must submit to the Magisterium? And the Magisterium carries the burden of teaching in those moments.

FATHER DULLES: Of course, there are all sorts of degrees of definitiveness in the way the magisterium speaks and sometimes it does not speak in a completely definitive way. There might be a passing statement, in an encyclical, or a bishop's pastoral or something like that. A person reading it would say, well, this does not jibe with my reading of scripture or with my sense of where people are at today. And some further dialogue is necessary. Of course, if the Magisterium speaks definitively I do think that is an overriding consideration for the faithful Catholic, though even there may be some interior difficulty in assenting to it if one feels it is opposed to other sources of faith.

BISHOP: The first line of Bishop Wuerl's summary says "Bishops have the spiritual power to bind in conscience." And my question concerns the power of bishops within an episcopal conference to bind in conscience with specific reference to the case of the bishop who does not accept the vote or the decision or the teaching of the episcopal conference.

Now, I know that the Holy See is studying this question. The standard answer which I have read in regard to this is that a conference has considerable moral power because of its access to a number of the bishops. But, what does that mean for the faithful of a diocese whose bishop has not accepted the teaching of a conference?

FATHER DULLES: Bishops' Conferences may be reiterating what is already the general doctrine of the Church, teaching through Popes and councils. But if they are making prudential pastoral application without obligatory force, I don't think there is any obligation for the individual bishop to agree. The question is, does the joining together of a group of bishops add a new quality to the teaching or does it merely provide a vehicle for the ordinary magisterium of the individual bishops? That would be one serious theological question that's still under a great deal of discussion.

BISHOP: I want to return to the subject of conscience. You rightly referred to sin as being one of the causes of that gradual silencing of the voice of conscience. But, it does seem to me that we have to advert to the fact that there are other causes also of this silencing of the voice of conscience. For example, a great problem for our priests, a question they frequently raise, is that so many young people today are living together without being married, and seem to think nothing of it. Their conscience does not seem to trouble them. Given the overwhelming quality of this problem, does anyone see any different ways of responding to it, or remedying it?

Not all of the acts that we find fault with are the result of formal sin. Many judgments coming out of our current societal matrix would be subjectively innocent judgments. At least in the sense that persons working out of everything they know, come to conclusions we would find fault with.

What expectation can we have that our understanding of marriage would be accepted by someone who grows up today watching the television, living in a family that is single parented, and having divorce as the normal expectation of all their class-mates? Out of that matrix is going to come another judgement.

What used to be normal, generally accepted moral principles are no longer so accepted. And how we form conscience against that matrix seems to me to be the question of how we once again re-evangelize.

FATHER DULLES: Just to accentuate the problem rather than give a solution, I have here a digest of a recent Gallup survey on college students. The survey divided them into three categories, Protestant, Evangelical and Catholic, and checked their attitudes on religious and moral questions. Now, it said the Catholic students were 29% of those studied. On every single issue they come out as disagreeing with the traditional morality more than either the Protestants or the Evangelicals.

So, for instance, on pre-marital sex, 75% of the Catholic students sanctioned it. Sixty percent of the Protestant peers and 39% of the Evangelicals agreed with them. And so on with trial marriages, importance of religion, abortion, divorce, adultery, etc.; on every one of these issues the Catholics come out more permissive than either the Protestants or the Evangelicals.

I suppose they are all exposed to the same media. And yet we have more vigorous church teaching in the Catholic Church against all these things than they have in either the Evangelical or Protestant groups. So, the problem must be somewhere else. And I suspect it's that we are not educating conscience. We are not evangelizing our people, but we are handing down laws, which are rejected.

MONSIGNOR MULLIGAN: We need to watch out for something that exists in our culture—and it's very strong in the United States—a sense of toleration of pluralism. I am not proposing we should turn to intolerance, but what I mean is this. "Pluralism" people sometimes interpret as meaning that you can't say that anybody is wrong about anything. I think pluralism means that we can live in a society where I can say to someone, "I don't agree at all with what you are doing and I think it's absolutely wrong and here is why," and expect to be heard fairly when I say that.

BISHOP: My main point is, is the moral teaching of the Church binding on the conscience of an individual Catholic or in a Catholic institution, and if so, how binding?

I would ask how binding is the Church teaching on birth control, on sterilization, on abortion, on in-vitro fertilization. A bishop from Europe told me two weeks ago that in his country some Catholic hospitals, not a majority, but some Catholic hospitals perform abortions on the grounds that the doctor has made a decision in conscience that it's all right.

I think that there is a problem here. Does binding really mean binding only in some cases? I am not talking about the local bishop not having the same authority as the pope, but in many cases the teaching is clear cut and proposed by the highest authority. What's the bishop's obligation to see that the instruction given in the confessional is in accordance with clear cut binding teaching, for example, on birth control? What's the obligation of a bishop with regard to teaching proposed as Catholic in Catholic institutions that contradicts clear cut teaching on practical matters?

I guess I am back to the question, how binding is the teaching and what action are we prepared to do to reaffirm to the public that it's binding? Part of the reason we have so much dissent in practice in our people on contraception is the fact that we have not by our own actions conveyed the impression that this teaching is important.

BISHOP WUERL: Bishop, I would like to underline that in my response I am addressing the question of how do we lead others to accept the Church's teaching that we have announced as binding, so that conscience itself becomes the focus of that binding.

One question has to do with the function of how do we get the teaching internalized in a person who has a difficult time either knowing or appropriating the teaching. The other concerns the content of that interiorization. That has to be the Church's clearly articulated teaching.

It is the function of the bishop to see that those who accept him as the chief shepherd of the local church and except also that they have an obligation to follow the teaching of the Church articulated by the local bishop. And the bishop an obligation to oversee all the teaching that is done in the name of the Church.

FATHER DULLES: Let me speak to just one of the many points that was raised regarding Catholic institutions, I think a great deal of study has to be made as to the nature of the particular institution. Various institutions have, as you know, different relationships to the bishops and to the Holy See. Consequently, the power of the Church authority has to act within an institution might be considerably limited.

I think those distinctions are made in the latest apostolic constitution which does speak of the relationship of the bishop to a Catholic institution that is not controlled by the Church. The bishop simply can't reach in and suspend faculty members or cancel courses within an institution by direct action, but the bishop should be in relationship to the trustees and officers of such an institution to try to get something done about what is contrary to Catholic doctrine if such is being taught within the institution. There are contracts or legal aspects, tenure aspects and so forth that all have to be considered here.

BISHOP: To look at how official teaching is actually communicated to our people I need to examine my conscience, and if you will pardon me, examine yours a little bit, in three areas.

The homily is the primary way in which most of our people come into contact with the on-going articulated sense of Catholic teaching. Religious education programs in our schools and parishes and the Rite of Christian Initiation of Adults into the Church are. . . . .

As I look at these recently, I find that in the area of moral teaching it is a rare homily that successfully communicates an articulate sense of traditional moral teaching. For liturgical reasons that classical Sunday sermon for many of us, and certainly for many of our priests, is no longer able to serve that purpose.

Secondly, in many of our Catholic schools there is a high number of non-Catholic, and many times non-Christian, persons. The religion teachers are diffident about communicating Catholic values as Catholic because they feel that it is really not appropriate to do that for people who are not Catholic. And, of course, our Catholic children are not hearing, in many cases, what is a classical Catholic teaching.

In the third case, in my meetings with those in charge of the R.C.I.A. programs, I have found that in one program I participated in, I gave the entire instruction on Christian morality. I was assigned to do this in a forty-five minute class and that would be all that was taught about Catholic morality for these people who were approaching their Easter baptism in three weeks!

BISHOP WUERL: We are really speaking about the new evangelization that has to take place, the effort to make come alive again that which most of our hearers assume. I think when you are given a scripture text for the liturgy and the sure fire way to make it a disaster in the homily is to begin by saying, "In today's reading we have," because minds are already clicking off. They have heard that reading a thousand times; they presume they know what you are going to say. A new evangelization is needed to catch the attention of a new generation.

Sometimes the other voices beat us to the punch before we even have an opportunity to get our side out there. For example, a document comes out, something that would be of importance to our church, for example, the instruction on the ecclesial vocation of the theologian.

This document is presented at a press conference. Either the U.P., the A.P. or Reuters is the first to get the story out to the local newspaper. The first interpretation of this document to our people and to our priests is usually a story by a stranger whose job was to get the story out there, and to pick the one point they thought important. After that it's very hard mediating the rest of the document.

MONSIGNOR MULLIGAN: I don't think we should ever hesitate to communicate what the Church teaches and to communicate it with all the conviction and force at our disposal, no matter to whom we are talking. There is nothing offensive about that, nothing wrong with it. And, in fact, it seems to me if I really believe what the Church teaches, I must say it. I am eternally grateful for what the Church has given me. I think that in and through the Church I have received the gift of faith and gifts that are beyond compare and it is a joy to share them with other people.

In regard to our preaching, so often we preach and we tell the truth, but do so too blandly. We need to bring our imagination to bear on what we are saying to touch people, not only in their minds, but in their hearts and to try to draw for them a sense of the urgency that we feel about what we preach, the joy that we have in it, the conviction that we have about it. I think sometimes documents that come from Rome, documents that come from episcopal conferences, are dealing with the most wonderful topics, but in a style that is so hard to read, and hence so difficult for people to deal with. They need to be interpreted and I realize that part of our job is to interpret these documents. But, I would like to see the documents done in a style that people could pick up and read and want to read, and enjoy reading.

It would be a magnificent thing to have the documents in the conference well ahead of time and not released to anybody until conferences have had a chance to think about them and say something about them, and then release them with a real positive expression of what they mean.

PART TWO

AREAS OF CONSCIENTIOUS ACTIVITY

Chapter 14

PSYCHIC MANIPULATION, INDOCTRINATION AND THE CAPTIVE CONSCIENCE

The Reverend James LeBar

The foundation of the Judeo-Christian moral system from a practical point of view is the conscience. Properly formed and understood, the conscience is the tool by which people have, for centuries, determined what is right and wrong. There may be different words used to identify this process in different cultures, but the elements of choice, reflection, decision, and application will be found in each.

Our awareness of the power and ability of the human mind is constantly expanding. We have reports that human faculties can be transferred to another place in the brain when the original site is damaged beyond repair. We all are aware of the developmentally disabled people, called **savants,** who may not be able to utter a word, or even put their own clothes on, but who can, total up and speak the total of a series of numbers faster than a computer. A savant is also able to sit down at a keyboard a play a piece of music, having heard it but a single time.

We cannot be unaware of the influence television has on our modern society, and its way of thinking . . . and **judging.** Television can and does form values in minds, willingly or not. What child, for example, does not know how to sing the *McDonald's* or *Burger King* jingle? Does that same child know how to sing a hymn, or say a prayer? Unfortunately, the response here is often in the negative. Why? From what I can see it is simply because no one has ever taught the child.

Today, many people will label our society as materialistic, or secular or humanist or any combination thereof. It certainly cannot be termed religious, or value oriented, at least in the normal manner. There are values but they are not wholesome ones, and they do not lead to holiness, but to despair, in so many cases.

And it is not only values to children that cause the problem. The **New York Post** is not generally a source of positive reinforcement for the Church. But on Wednesday, January 9th, columnist Ray Kerrison wrote about a court decision which came down two days previous:

> "Monday night might have been one of the darkest days in the history of this city. It was the day that a court of law rules that desecrating a house of worship is so trivial that it is less offensive than spitting on the sidewalk, hawking hot dogs without a permit, or smoking in the subway.
>
> "In Manhattan Criminal Court Judge Jo Anne Ferdinand all but gave a pass to six homosexual and abortion radicals who committed the most vile acts during Mass celebrated by John Cardinal O'Connor in St. Patrick's Cathedral on December 10, 1989.
>
> "She ordered them to do some community service, refusing to sentence them to any jail time (they could

have gotten up to a year) or imposing so much as a 10 cent fine.

"Not only that, Judge Ferdinand actually invoked the names of Mahatma Gandhi and Dr. Martin Luther King Jr. in her sentencing—a comparison so utterly bizarre that it besmirches the memory of two genuine historical figures."

Mr. Kerrison concludes his column with these significant and telling words:

"So why the homosexual blitz on the cardinal? Simple. **Their expressed goal is to make homosexuality acceptable to the community.** (emphasis mine) Their publications claim the only way to do that is to dismantle prevailing moral standards. They are doing that with devastating success through political action, intimidation and pushing repugnant sex-ed courses in the public schools. These courses emphasize detailed instruction on sex acts and promote condoms and anal intercourse.

Activists see the Catholic Church and the cardinal as the chief obstacles in their path. So they rage at him— while much of the city looks the other way.

As convicted church defacers, the so-called Safe Sex Six may be contemptible, but the judge who let them off is a menace to all of society. She has placed every house of worship in this city in jeopardy."

And I might add here, that every person who seeks to worship is in jeopardy, too.

* * * * *

There is no instance of a more dedicated effort to destroy prevailing beliefs and moral values than the cult phenomenon. For the past twenty years and more, cults have been attracting thousands of people, and not only our youth, but hard working adults, and senior citizens as well. They prey on the highly idealistic individual who really wants to do something in life, but who, up to now, has not been able to reach that goal. It is estimated that 40% of cult members come from Catholic families, 30% from Jewish families, and only 12% from Protestant families, the remainder being of no religious persuasion. There are, according to the latest statistics more than 5,000 different cultic groups operating today. Some are quite small; others have a huge membership. All seek one thing: **the control of the individual.** Once a cult has achieved this all things are possible. And to put it quite simply, they are able to succeed because our (young) people do not have a solid religious formation with strong values in behavior and morals. Cults sense this deficiency and seek to fill it with their own ideas. They capture the conscience of the individual through manipulation and deceit.

Cults can be divided into several main groups. Some cults overlap this grouping, and can be both *religious* and *biblical,* or perhaps both *shepherding/discipleship* and *biblical.*

First are the *psuedo*-**religious** cults such as the Hare Krishnas, or the Unification Church; they claim to be religious, but in fact are not at all. Some of these may also claim to be **biblical,** such as the Way International or the Church of Bible Understanding, but it is their own version of the bible that they produce and follow.

Secondly, we find the **shepherding/discipleship** cults such as the Boston Church of Christ or the Greater Bible World Outreach, formerly known as the Bible Speaks. These groups practice an adherence to the bible teachings so narrow and strict that the leader has total control over the individual.

In the third spot we find the **therapy cults,** also known as **human potential movements.** Life Spring, the Forum (called EST at one time), and Transcendental Meditation all fit this category.

Fourthly, we find **NEW AGE** groups. These groups deify themselves, create their own reality and seek communication with the nether world through channelling and seances.

The fifth group brings together the **eastern meditation** groups, each one led by a guru. Sri Chinmoy and the Maharishi Mahesh Yogi fit into this category. They can be distinguished from legitimate gurus by the degree of control and isolation they practice.

Lastly, there are the **satanic** cults, which seek to glorify evil and worship the devil. Within this grouping we find the experimenters, the satanic churches, and the mind controlling groups which capture the minds and bodies of people of all ages.

If we look for a dictionary definition of the term, *cult,* we would find a simple statement such as *"a system of religious worship or ritual."* Since this can apply to any religious group, we must look elsewhere for a definition. Therefore people involved in this work for many years have come up with six characteristics to identify a cult:

a) there is a charismatic leader who directs all attention to him(her)self instead of to God;
b) there is an excessively high degree of deceit used in recruiting;
c) During the indoctrination into the group, there is excessive mind control, manipulation and elimination of certain previously acquired knowledge;
d) there is a tunnel-vision approach which allows for no questioning or discussion;
e) excessive fear is placed in the individual should he or she desire to depart the group;
f) the group collects great amounts of money, and few people know where it goes.

Mind control is a devastating concept. It robs the person of freedom, choice, individuality and thought. It is not a new concept, however, and it does not belong to the cults alone. Ancient societies practiced it, and in recent times, you will no doubt recall the difficulties Cardinal Mindzentzy was forced to undergo before he was put on trial at the end of the Second World War. Robert J. Lifton, Professor of Psychiatry at the John Jay College of Criminal Justice at the City University of New York, wrote about brainwashing in China in his book, *Thought Reform and the*

Psychology of Totalism originally published in 1961, and reissued in 1989. He isolated eight criteria to identify the degree of thought reform or mind control. It will be useful to use his ideas as a framework.

Summed up in a few words we might say that **thought reform** or **mind control** can be accomplished through the management of human communication, so that all information is manipulated through deception, a search for purity, and a use of loaded language that thoroughly confuses right reason.

Mind control strangulates the conscience. It renders the normal processes of evaluation, choice and decision making inoperative. In effect it makes the conscience of an individual a captive. An individual under mind control cannot follow the dictates of the conscience, for this faculty in unavailable. The channels are blocked.

Conscience needs communication to exist. Messages, so to speak, must travel between the brain and the will. Human beings need to communicate with the environment around them. They need to relate in order to grow. In the use of **milieu control** the cult victim is deprived of this kind of communication. Physical control is used such as taking the person to an undisclosed location, away from all that is familiar. Mental control is used also such as a warning that "if you tell (*what is happening to you*), something will happen to you or your loved ones." The individual is often kept so busy with little things that there is no time to communicate with one's self. Thus the delicate balance needed between external information and internal reflection, (as Lifton says) is upset and the person cannot test the reality of things around him. One's own feelings are not only said to be unimportant, but are to be totally ignored—as being in error.

Our society is based on truth and in the mutual exchange of ideas, we presume the person with whom we are talking holds to the same value of truth and honesty as we do. We don't generally doubt the sincerity of another. But when a person has been subjected to mind control, the usual rules do not apply. For there has been a **mystical manipulation** of the person so that things are not always what they seem. Lifton sees an effort "to provoke specific patterns of behavior and emotion in such a way that these will appear to have arisen spontaneously . . . and [depend upon] an appeal to a higher purpose."

Conscience is thereby deceived into thinking it is perceiving reality, when in fact it is seeing illusion. Mind controllers will use staged rituals (for example, making it appear that a baby has been sacrificed in a satanic ritual so that fear will generate obedience.) Some cults will use drugs, but the power of mind control is so strong that drugs are not a common tool at all. Hypnosis and altered states of consciousness are used too, so that in effect the ability of the conscience to determine right and wrong is rendered useless.

One of the things we have learned over the years is that for mind control to have a lasting effect, it must be constantly reinforced. Psychological techniques are used so that a person becomes extremely sensitive to all kinds of cues. The person's own sense of reality and the exercise of the faculty of the conscience actually flows with the tide of information flowing into his mind from the cult environment, instead of reacting against thoughts, words or actions that are at variance with right reason.

For example, a startling and disturbing situation was discovered in the McMartin Day Care Center scandal. It was reported that a number of the young people that were abused as little children actually became the abusers as they got older. It was considered a privilege to take part. They never learned that such actions were wrong.

Adults, too, can fall victim to the same thing. The person brought into a satanic cult, for example, willingly participates in rituals which perpetrate on others the same atrocities that were practiced on them in a prior ceremony. What is so powerful that the operation of a person's conscience can be suspended? It is this **mystical manipulation,** of Lifton.

Closely allied with mystical manipulation is the third of Lifton's steps, that of **demand for purity.** It is here that most people find it so difficult to believe that a normal, healthy, robust young person could be so changed that he would see good when it is actually evil. Aristotle once wrote that "No one acts for an evil end". This is a principle that is the foundation of our teaching on conscience and free will. As you well know, no one can choose something evil. A choice is made under the appearance of being a good.

The conscience is held captive. The decision making abilities of the individual is not based on **truth,** but rather on the **pure ideology of the group.** Anything relating to the individual is to be eliminated in favor of the group. Guilt and shame are used here to achieve the desired change in the person to reflect the new way of thinking. Guilt over not being perfect, or of having done something personal is used in a badgering manner. Frequently a person is ridiculed before the entire group, and shamed into believing they have acted wrongly, when in fact, they were only acting naturally, but it was not according to the group's ideology. Fellow cultists, particularly the leaders, shame the person into compliance, obedience or submission.

In cultic life, there has to be a statement, usually public, renouncing one's former way of life, acknowledging that the *new* way of life is the only true one. Lifton calls this fourth criterion the **cult of confession.** Recall the Cardinal Mindzenty affair and you can appreciate this step in the process. Having been influenced severely by the manipulation, the person is now asked to confess to crimes never committed, and if this is not done, then public humiliation follows. Immersed in this step are successful efforts to get the mind to surrender all independence and to have the conscience understand that there are no longer any private thoughts or ideas. All belong to the group.

Once this has been achieved, a positive effort begins which will place the person squarely in the control of the cult (or other group) with no real desire to do otherwise.

Lifton's fifth step is called **Sacred Science.** Here we find the ultimate moral vision for the ordering of human existence. *God has it all wrong.* "We (say the cult leaders) know better and will gradually let you in on our secrets. But remember that only a few will ever be privileged to know the complete truth."

This criterion might compare to the formation of conscience as we know it. Here the basic principles for action are induced. This is the indoctrination phase. How well does it work?

One need only talk to a parent whose child has been inducted into one such group. Let me quote from a letter from such a parent, written recently:

"Before (my son's) association with the group, he was a vibrant, intelligent, articulate, outgoing person with a charismatic personality that attracted people not only to him but also to the Lord through him. . . .

"Well, . . . all this has changed. (His) personality has changed, and not for the better. He not only has become *beyond* extremely spiritual, but his personality (as his parents and all his friends know it to be) has changed to a degree that is very frightening. We started to see this change last fall.

It is as if all that this young man had learned in his formation at home was held in suspension while another schema was laid on top.

You have all been bothered at one time or another by some of your people claiming that we teach no conscience formation any more. Well, I can assure you that in cults and some other groups there is a definite formation going on of erroneous and mal-formed consciences, and it corresponds to this fifth step of Lifton: **Sacred Science.**

Have you seen any of the 900 number TV ads on lately? You can solve almost every problem with one of these numbers. You can find a date, or a mate; you can talk to an astrologer. You can even make your confession to someone who will listen. The small print indicates that each call is more than $2.00 a minute, and market analysts tell us that this service is extremely successful and growing by leaps and bounds.

What does this tell us if not that people want to be guided, and they want to know what is good and what is not. We have here, in a sense, an example of Lifton's sixth characteristic, **loading the language.** Lifton states in explaining this characteristic, that the most far reaching and complex human problems are compressed into brief, highly reductive definitive-sounding phrases, easily memorized and easily expressed. **In a sense, easy answers, always right, always proper.**

Within the cult group, the person is taught to be highly judgmental of the outside world, and to see everything as right and proper only in the group. What the individual may think, feel or experience is not important. Words you and I might understand in one fashion, have an entirely different meaning for the cultist. For example, to us the word *father* might mean the male parent, the priest, the First Person of the Blessed Trinity. But for the member of more than one cult, it means *the leader.* For the satanist, all our Catholic terms and ceremonies are inverted, and mean the direct opposite. So such a person might easily agree to something we say, while all the time understanding the words we use in their own language.

Conscience also needs to understand reality in order to operate correctly. We have always taught that a person is not culpable if he or she acts on a faulty conscience. The loaded language of the cultist throws the use of conscience into utter confusion.

Lifton's seventh criterion is the *preeminence of* **doctrine over person.** The individual's human experience is totally subordinated to the doctrine of the group. Here, I can almost hear the objections of many present here now: ***Isn't this what we have in our Catholic Church?*** My response to that query is a *qualified* yes, with a **but** attached. Yes, it is true in the abstract, **but** no doctrines are imposed by force. Nor do we hide our doctrines from one studying the Faith. Here, too is an instance where one has to understand the meaning of the words when applied to the cult problem. For **doctrine** does not mean religious belief; it means the rules and directions of the group. *Preeminence* has a totalistic and all inclusive meaning, often placing obedience above right reason. In a mind control group, a distance is placed between the individual and the real world, between fantasy and reality. There is also a vast chasm between an individual's personal experience and the highly abstract, and often impossible interpretations of such experiences. Under mind control history is changed, rewritten or ignored. Sin and crime are denied.

The **preeminence of doctrine over person** prevails in the indoctrination process of the group. One's character and conduct must be re-formed according to the group. The person's own identity is reshaped to fit the group, and not vice-versa. Personal talents and abilities have no place in this concept, only the will of the group. Any attempt to act independently of this process is met with swift retribution.

Yet, people do occasionally leave cults without external assistance. Why? How? The answer is found in **the conscience,** which can burst through all this control and submission to bring the person to a realization that there is an objective norm for right and wrong. There is in every individual, whether under mind control or not, a permanent, inborn disposition of the mind to think of general and broad truths of moral conduct that become the principles from which a man may reason in his own moral activities. St. Jerome, in the fifth century, referred to it as *a spark of conscience.* St. Thomas Aquinas saw it as a habitual quality of the intellect, enabling it to know the basic principles of practical reasoning.

St. Thomas Aquinas never confused this action of the intellect with **conscience** proper, which is defined as the action of the practical intellect to decide, immediately, whether a particular action is right or wrong. **Conscience** is the conclusion which reason reaches only after duly applying moral laws to specific action. In a cult, or with a person under mind control, this ability is overwritten so that the conclusion reached is always what the cult wants.

Strong as the influence of the cult may be, this "spark" sometimes breaks through with an amazing tenacity. In **Michelle Remembers,** a true story of a year long contest between innocence and evil, Michelle Smith tells of how she hung on to her "goodness" in the midst of terrifying abuses forced on her by a group of satanists. No matter what these people did, Michelle would not give in. Though she was too young to read at the time of her experiences, she saw how a Bible was so important to another sufferer, and she took a page of this bible and kept it. In later life, after a miscarriage and a horrible dream, at age 27 she went for professional help, and what she and her psychiatrist learned was both revolting and almost unbelievable. But it was awesome and inspiring too, as they both learned of the power of God, Who ultimately came to her rescue.

I have met both Michelle and Dr. Pazder, and if you really want to know how awful the satanic cults are, I urge you to read *Michelle Remembers* (Congdon & Lattes, New York, 1980. 310pp; also Pocket Books, New York, 1981).

The final criterion on our list today can be called the **dispensing of existence.** When a group becomes so important in its own eyes that it feels it can control anything and everything, it eventually develops a doctrine of **we** and **them.** From that point it is only a short jump to a statement that *no one else has any right to exist but us.* In political terms, this can mean that non-party members are *non-persons* who must either conform (join the party) or be annihilated. Things are not quite so drastic in the cults. What we find in the cults is that anyone not in the group is considered to be non-existent. Unification Church members, for example, have taught consistently that anyone outside the group is Satan, and thus *anything goes* in dealing with them, truthful or not. This is **heavenly deception,** which is identical to the Hare Krishna's **transcendental trickery.**

Here we might mention a variation on this point: the denial of existence at will of anyone not in harmony with our group or with me, an individual. You will find this idea in some cults, but it is primarily in the **NEW AGE Movement** that we see this fulfilled. A primary tenet of **NEW AGE** is that a person can create his/her own reality. To put it another way, only what I (a New Ager) consider to be in existence, is in fact real.

How does this affect conscience? Immensely. For in a society, such as we have at the present time, we find people seeking to rewrite history to obliterate unpleasant or unflattering happenings. We find people making decisions not from the Judeo-Christian principles, but from a combination of comfort, convenience and pleasure. Moral values, and thus conscience, has no place in this thinking.

Have you been cut off at the intersection by another vehicle lately? Have you seen a driver **not** stop on red before making the right turn? In a sense such people are denying your existence in their behavior. Perhaps **denial of existence** is also one of the reasons why we have so many prisoners and homeless people. Prisoners commit their crimes because they never used their conscience. Perhaps they did not even avert to the effect their action would have on another person. That person for them, just did not exist. Have some of the homeless people lost an awareness of their own existence so that they no longer care what happens?

Has their conscience ever given them a message of what **right** thing to do?

There are indeed captive consciences today, and not all exist in the minds of the cult people. Radio, television and other media are tools of manipulation as they seek to have us buy their product. The content of dramas, and even the sit coms put forth a message each time they air, and these days the messages are not good. They are not moral, most of the time, and they are not even a respecter of the value of human life.

A perplexing problem for both the mental health professionals and religious leaders is the uncanny attraction cults and satanism has for youth and adults alike. No segment of society is safe from the influence of these groups. Without a solidly formed conscience anyone can fall victim to a cult which will form the individual, remake the conscience and remold the person into a dependent, fear-filled group member. The normal is reversed into the abnormal. Language and the meaning of words are modified for their own purposes so that what is standard and traditional in the moral sense seems to be abnormal.

I hope that our look at cults today has given you a new perspective on the formation of conscience. I have tried to show the importance of conscience formation as a tool in countering the cults effectively.

This is a dangerous situation—one we must rectify!

Thank you very much for your attention.

Chapter 15

CONSCIENCE, CULPABILITY
AND CO-DEPENDENCE

Mary Ellen Garvey-O'Brien

You may be wondering, as I have, how I managed to get on the speakers roster with so many well-known theologians. Could it be that a priest once heard me speak at a Catholic hospital where I worked in the Department of Drug and Alcohol Services— and liked what I had to say? Could it be that I attended Catholic schools from age 7 to 27 with only a one year break while studying abroad? Could it be that the headmaster of the Catholic high school I attended is now a local bishop? Could it be that my husband is an active Knight of Columbus? I believe it's probably partly all of these things *and* God's will that I present this paper.

I learned to generalize about the world from what I observed in my family of origin. I will elaborate on this theme later. For now, suffice it to say that I was rather naive growing up. My parents were devout Irish-American Catholics who prayed to St. Jude, St. Anthony, said the rosary and novenas; I believed everyone's family experience was the same, that everyone was just like me. I learned later that those who are different still experience the same feelings I do. This is the same principle by which AA and Alanon function—sharing common feelings. I will also elaborate on this topic later.

Because both of my parents were recovering alcoholics, growing up meant helping others and going to AA meetings. That's how it was throughout my developmental years. Little did I know that both would die prematurely of alcoholism—my mother when I was 17 and my father when I was 26. Without a doubt, I am a codependent and have sought treatment for it.

Today I will attempt to clarify the relationship between conscience, culpability and codependence. It is a fascinating combination, only the surface of which I will touch upon today. I will share my experience of nearly 12 years as a clinician working with substance abusers in varied settings and in an employee assistance program. I want to stress above all else that addiction and codependence are treatable diseases that are not anyone's fault or choice. Many people are genetically predisposed to addiction and others emotionally predisposed to codependency.

Conscience, Culpability and Codependence

At the outset, I wish to define the terms used in the title of my talk. "Conscience" is knowledge or sense of right or wrong with a compulsion to do right. "Culpability" is associated with being responsible for wrong or error, blameworthy or deserving censure. It often is thought to be related to guilt. The Latin "culpa" translates to fault or guilt.

But for many Catholics, including me, conscience has been equated with guilt, regardless of culpability. It is often discussed by clients in the context of going against authorities (i.e., parents, the Church, ethnic traditions).

Let's clarify at this time, however, that conscience formation is not the primary focus of this talk but rather that codependence in relation to conscience and culpability is. So, what is codependence?

"Codependence" is an obsession with another person or his behavior which interferes with the ability to care properly for self. Deprived of a firm foundation in their ability to tell right from wrong, codependents are set adrift in a sea of uncertainty as they deal with relationships. Just as the alcoholic becomes obsessed with the next drink, the family member or codependent becomes obsessed with the alcoholic's behavior.

I will use the words "chemically dependent, alcoholic, addicted, dependent and substance abuser" all interchangeably in reference to the addicted individual or one the codependent is obsessed with. Also, although the pronoun "he" is used throughout, dependency and codependency know no barriers, including that of gender.

One's self-identity is lacking or distorted if the family of origin is dysfunctional. That is, with any dysfunction, and specifically addiction in a parent, a child learns to define self in relation to the addict. Think of some adjectives that describe an active addict: sick, angry, preoccupied, self-righteous, blaming, out of control, silent, rigid, cold, phony, grandiose, lonely, violent, superficial, manipulative come to mind. Now think about which of these adjectives could be applied to an addict's spouse or codependent. Many, if not all of them, could also be applied to the codependent. Together, these two adults provide the scripts or role models for their children. The children, therefore, often have no consistent healthy parenting. Instead, they may lack love in the form of a parent's positive engagement with them. Both parents are caught up in the addiction process. Consequently, since one parent uses a substance and is dependent upon it and the other is obsessed with the dependent's behavior, the kids share in the disease process by any one or a combination of the following:

a) parenting the parents
b) manipulating to get what is needed
c) learning to rely only on themselves to get things done
d) becoming fearful of asking for help

e) feeling super-responsible for everything
f) maturing early
g) experiencing a loss of childhood.

It is clear then the addicted family shares the disease. Nobody escapes without being effected.

The unspoken laws that govern and control a chemically-dependent family, as Claudia Black has explained at length, are the following:

a) Don't talk
b) Don't trust
c) Don't feel.

In any family, children generalize that what happens in their family happens everywhere. Therefore, if a child is taught to focus on the needs of others (i.e., an alcoholic parent), that child learns to dismiss his own needs and gain approval by caring for the parents. His identity is unclear except in relation to the needy parent. He is taught to respond, "I am fine. How are *you?*", (with an emphasis on "you") when asked how he is doing. Consequently, self-esteem is low and rarely nurtured within the family since those involved are often enmeshed with the addicted person.

In short, the codependent learns not to discuss what is going on at home because his perceptions are not validated. That is, if a child says to a parent, addicted or codependent, "I heard you fighting last night. What happened?", the parent may respond with, "Nothing. You must have been dreaming!" As a result, the child feels confused, lied to, or at best awkward, because the parent disapproves of his inquiry. He practices, therefore, the "don't talk" law.

The "don't trust" law which evolves in addicted families results from broken promises when the addicted person tells the family: "I'll never drink or use drugs again." Codependents are disappointed if the substance use is resumed; consequently, they don't believe what the addict says. Again, they generalize to the whole world what they learn in their family of origin—not to trust.

In the case of the "don't feel" law, which codependents abide by, there is a chronic predictable unpredictability and a consistent inconsistency at work. These result in anxiety and fear whenever one stops to think about what to expect in the family. For the child or the codependent spouse, then, anticipating what might be found upon returning home is blocked out. Just as the alcoholic may "black out" and forget, since he's in a temporary state of amnesia, codependents learn to block out so as not to feel the pain of fear and anxiety. Each learns to deny or numb their feelings; this is referred to as having frozen feelings.

The codependent's self-esteem certainly is not enhanced if he lives life avoiding feelings, not trusting others and not talking about life at home. The codependent ties his self worth to the addict or the addict's behavior. A particular codependent client described her situation, stating, "I shoplift because my boyfriend demands Reebok sneakers, coffee that costs $7.35/lb. and filet mignon steak twice a week. I'd do anything to pacify him." She gave him power over her and her self-esteem. Unfortunately, since he was chemically dependent, he did not take good care of himself or her. With the progression of his addiction, her self-esteem plummeted lower and lower.

Before discussing relationships further, let us highlight the problem with self-identity. Specifically, when a child grows up around parents who have no understanding of the proper boundaries between individuals, he cannot but perceive identity as something that is shared. The child does not sacrifice independent identity to stay connected with an addicted parent but rather the child never received the opportunity to develop that independent identity. It is my impression, therefore, that conscience becomes equated with the guilt parents impose upon the children. We commonly call this shame.

Shame refers to feelings about one's own needs. Catholic clients have told me they feel selfish and ashamed when considering their own needs. I have attempted in therapy to help them relabel their selfishness and reframe it as taking care of one's self.

Because codependents look for approval from others and care so deeply about how others see them, they place great importance on how they appear. They develop a certain mask and posture to complement their "I'm fine" attitude. They use the facade when dealing with the outside world and with those they are most intimate with. Because the facade works and is pleasing to others, it is maintained and protected at all costs. Before very long the codependent identifies with this facade as it is familiar and accepted by others. It becomes automatic. So, the false self replaces the true self. The true self is lost or hidden from the codependent. The facade is shaped by the needs and wishes of others while the true self becomes the repository for unwanted and unmet personal needs—and, consequently, a source of shame. The codependent's energy goes into keeping up the "I'm fine" front, the need to be forever smiling, the facade of "I'm in control" while internal guilt and suffering feed the shame.

Regarding relationships, codependents are caretakers who often rescue, feel persecuted and then end up victimized. In her book *Codependent No More,* Melody Beattie discusses the phenomenon known as Karpman Drama Triangle. This triangle is depicted in handout #1. My interpretation follows: This triangle is a pattern repeated by codependents in reaction to the dependent. However, codependents, whether they grew up in alcoholic families or not, take on certain roles as part of their facade.

According to Lawrence Kohlberg, development in moral thinking comes from "role-taking" experiences. These experiences are those social encounters in which a person takes the point of view of another. Because codependents are enmeshed with the dependent and have no separate identity, their conscience and moral thinking mirror the alcoholic's. This occurs naturally as part of the codependent's development. As a result, I feel the codependent is not culpable or responsible for his own behavior *until* such a time, if ever, when treatment and recovery occur.

The roles in the family which codependents assume are spelled out in detail on handout #1 labeled "Family Disease Concept." Codependents uniformly feel that they cannot turn their backs or leave the alcoholic, someone they love or once loved, just when the dependent needs them most. This happens at any point in the progression of the addict's disease. Consequently, the codependent usually chooses to stay with the alcoholic and adapt to the illness. There is no healthy way, however, to adapt to addiction. The codependent or co-alcoholic can best be understood when seen realistically as an equal and opposite reaction to the alcoholic's actions and attitudes. As the alcoholic's disease progresses, often aggressively blaming the codependent, the codependent becomes more passive and guilt-ridden. He often feels that his values are violated; many times an overwhelming hopeless, helpless posture results.

The protector role described in the handout is the rescuer whose characteristics revolve around absorbing the alcoholic's defenses. As a result, the codependent's self-image, even the facade, deteriorates. People rescue and protect because they don't feel good about themselves. Although the feelings are temporary and artificial, caretaking provides a brief moment of good feelings, self-worth and power. Just as a drink helps an alcoholic momentarily feel better, a rescue or protective act distracts from the pain of who the codependent is. Codependents don't feel loveable, so they settle for being needed. They don't feel good about themselves, so they feel compelled to do a particular act to prove how good they are (i.e., call employer with excuses for addict).

After rescuing, comes persecution. Codependents become resentful and angry at the person they "helped." They did something they did not want to do, something that was not their responsibility while ignoring their own needs and wants. Anger results, and to make matters worse, the addict does not appreciate what the codependent has sacrificed. Controller, blamer and isolator on the handout fit into this persecution area of the triangle.

Finally, the victim role parallels the enabling section of the handout. The victim corner of the triangle portrays predictable and unavoidable result of rescue. Feelings of helplessness, hurt, sorrow, shame and self-pity abound.

The triangle and shifting roles described are an observable process codependents experience. The process may take hours or years to complete.

The most detrimental aspect of the caretaking or enabling, as we clinically refer to the process most often, is that codependents become and stay victims. Victims attract perpetrators. Victims believe they need someone to take care of them because they feel helpless. Often victims present themselves to somebody or some institution needing to be taken care of mentally, physically, financially or emotionally.

Treatment of codependents is on-going and life-long. Timmen Cermak, M.D., in his recent book entitled *Diagnosing and Treating Co-Dependence* describes four stages of recovery for codependents which are very similar to those of the dependent. He writes, "It is not surprising that the two should parallel each other so closely, given that the 'ism' of alcoholism is shared equally by both the drinking and the non-drinking members. If the diseases are essentially the same, so too should be the recovery process."

For the dependent person in Stage I, the Survival Stage, denial is confronted and the pain one feels or causes is addressed.

In a similar fashion, codependents undergo a Survival Stage which is characterized by denial that a problem exists. The codependent, remember, lives by the law, "Don't feel," and maintains a facade of being "fine." To relinquish the facade would jeopardize his identity.

Both the chemically dependent and the codependent believe their rationalizations. The dependent feels that continued use of a chemical is necessary in order for him to feel normal. In the extreme, the dependent may be convinced that the chemical is necessary for mere survival, emotional and physical. Even at this point dependents believe they can stop using anytime they want.

The codependent, likewise, believes his behavior is voluntary, creating the illusion that he is in control while everything around him is out of control. The technical term given to the contradiction between illusion of control and the compulsive nature of the behavior is "denial of limitation."

When the codependents surrender to their disease, Cermak reports the costs are equally as high as those the dependent experiences when physical withdrawal from a substance occurs. Many codependents in recovery have told me that valued relationships were lost and with them their identity was lost, as, "It was tied so much to that other person."

In Stage II, the Re-Identification Stage, both the dependent and codependent get a glimpse of his true self. The avenues by which the true self may be reached include:

1.) Hitting bottom (i.e., losing a great deal, such as spouse, family, job, friends, financial security).

190

2.) A tragic incident (i.e., a crime, a car accident, injury to self or a loved one).
3.) A fortuitous grouping of crises when many things go wrong and cause pain at the same time, or
4.) Intervention (a clinical process in which a crisis is purposely created in order to access treatment for the dependent or codependent to stop the destructive behavior while the person possesses enough physical and/or emotional resources for recovery to be an option).

Whatever means is imposed, the result is a crack in the denial system through which the person catches a glimpse of his true self, a re-identification.

As mentioned earlier, some dependents use chemicals to feel "normal", and, therefore, with a willingness to abstain and follow treatment recommendations, there exists acceptance at some level of being labeled an alcoholic or drug addict. For the addict, accepting the label or acknowledging having the disease of addiction means relief, allowing a more objective view of one's life, having a new framework for re-interpreting one's past, and a realistic basis for a future in recovery.

As we all know, accepting a label, or for that matter a diagnosis, is not easy. For codependents the diagnosis means renouncing the martyr or persecutor role. It becomes more difficult to continue in the old role once the label or diagnosis is given and the requirement that one take responsibility for his dysfunctional behavior follows.

The rewards are similar, then, for dependents and codependents. Both can assess the past and address the future with hope and make a commitment to change. By addressing their diseases, spirituality (which is the opposite of disease) becomes an option. Ann Wilson Schaef, in her book *Co-dependence—Misunderstood—Mistreated,* states that recovery from codependence is impossible without recognizing and working with spiritual issues as healing issues.

Another aspect of the Re-identification Stage is accepting one's limitations. It is best understood in relation to the First Step of the Twelve Step Program of Alcoholics Anonymous and

Alanon. That is, one must accept that his life has become unmanageable. Cermak believes that, "When one accepts limitations, one can stop attributing this unmanageability to personal inadequacy or insufficient willpower." This also provides a better understanding of the past and hope for the future.

Some people, however, never progress to this stage in recovery as they become stuck and stagnant, not advancing beyond accepting their label or diagnosis. There is a lack of understanding of the "ism"—the way of thinking or feeling that was built around their chemical dependence—and they are very likely to relapse into old behavior.

It is also important for dependents, before moving on to recovery, to acknowledge that willpower alone is not the answer to recovery. Addiction and codependence are three-fold diseases involving physical, emotional and spiritual components. Certainly there is a place for willpower in influencing one's own behavior, but, on the other hand, willpower is totally ineffectual when it comes to influencing another person's emotional world, behavior or one's genetic susceptibility to addiction.

In Stage III, the Core Issues Stage, recognition of powerlessness occurs. For the dependent, it becomes clear that any attempt to control substance use has failed. For the codependent, there is recognition that attempts to stop the dependent's use of substances have failed.

So, recovery continues and lessons about powerlessness are broadened in this stage. Cermak describes a, "winning through losing" idea. He states that chemical dependents and codependents can only move ahead by stepping back. He says, "Successful relationships require that *each* partner be independent and autonomous." For codependents this is very difficult, as they still confuse their own identity with the dependent's. During this stage detachment is necessary, as well as the realization that most human emotions fall outside the range of one's influence. The most one can do is to respond honestly to feelings and hope healthy and appropriate behaviors will follow. Thus, with acceptance, the choice to respond to the best of one's ability results in a certain serenity. This inner peace is drastically different from the struggles which existed because of efforts to control those things which are beyond one's control.

In the fourth and final stage, the Re-Integration Stage, one learns to work at setting priorities to meet his own needs. He has accepted his disease where he has learned the meaning of the phrase, "Let go & let God." Defeat is viewed as surrender, and willpower is viewed as willingness and acceptance. A stage of freedom and health has evolved—having accepted limitations and, relinquishing the power to control that which was not real but perceived, they now reclaim the personal power they possess.

In my opinion, this stage is ripe for recovering religious values one may have had early on in life. Cermak states that during this stage chemical dependents and co-dependents, "weave a belief system which legitimizes self-acceptance. Self worth stops being something that must be earned through one's accomplishments or through relationships with others." By putting the addict's needs in perspective and addressing one's own needs first, the recovering codependent is able to adopt a value system that is far more functional. Rebuilding or creating a conscience is primary. With this, it becomes possible to accept culpability when warranted.

Cermak speaks of self-worth as a by-product of maintaining integrity in most areas of one's life. He recommends achievement of integrity by: 1) awareness, not denial; 2) honesty, no secrecy; and 3) a conscious connection with one's spiritual impulses, not arrogance—all of which a person has the opportunity to now cultivate. For dependents and codependents, individual or group counseling and a Twelve Step Recovery Program offer this opportunity. Specifically, the second step instructs individuals to turn to God as each understands Him, which allows a person to examine his religious beliefs in relation to conscience formation.

Sharon Wegscheider-Cruse, in her book *Choice-Making for Co-dependents, Adult Children and Spirituality Seekers,* paraphrased the Twelve Steps for codependents. (See handout two.) For a complete explanation of the Twelve Step Program, read *Alcoholics Anonymous* (also called *The Big Book*) and/or *Twelve Steps and Twelve Traditions.* The Steps address the spiritual aspects of the addiction or codependence. A common phrase recovering people use is "working the Steps" or "working the program." The purpose of acquiring an understanding of the steps and participation in a program is to empower the person to make appropriate choices for a manageable life with support from others who have had similar feelings and, at times, experiences. "Anonymous" people meet in various locations all over the world for the purpose of discussing their problems and staying away from relapse "one day at a time."

It is in recovery, then, that one takes responsibility for himself—such is the essence of recovery.

In dysfunctional families or relationships, nurturing statements or affirmations often are not provided. Therefore, it is necessary that in recovery one learns to nurture himself instead of looking to another to find his own identity and sense of self.

In summing up, let's take a look at what we discussed today. Codependents, because of their family background or dysfunctional relationships, have formed faulty decision making processes. Often with a cloudy understanding of right and wrong, they take the blame for actions that may not be or frequently are not their own. By placing the needs of the addict above their own, codependents neglect themselves, resulting in a lack of self identification. Only by affirming that his needs are worthwhile can a codependent take charge of or responsibility for his life.

Through therapy or self-help groups, such as Alcoholics Anonymous or Alanon, the individual in recovery can rekindle or create moral and spiritual values that lead to a healthy conscience. With a healthy conscience the recovering codependent is able to make choices that can lead to a more fulfilling life. By being open and accepting, the Church can offer encouragement and assist the codependent in building a deeper spiritual foundation upon which the codependent may rely.

HANDOUT 1
FAMILY DISEASE CONCEPT

An interpretation of Karpman's Drama Triangle, the codependent's reaction to an addict's behavior.

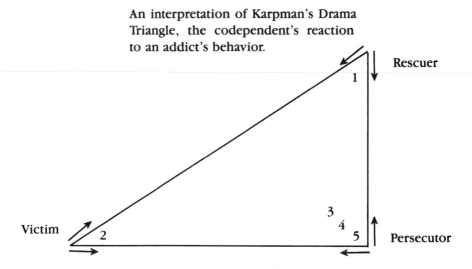

The roles explained below occur in the co-alcoholic when he accepts the alcoholic's version, questions his own recall of situations or suffers through them.

1.) PROTECTOR: Takes on negative feelings about self to take the focus off the alcoholic, minimizes, supports rationalizations, apologizes.

2.) ENABLER: Assumes increasingly more responsibility for the alcoholic's behavior. Attempts to manipulate and control drinking—becomes angry, alienated, inadequate, picks up pieces.

3.) CONTROLLER: Tries to control uncontrollable drinking; the supply, watering down, drinking with him or his supply, sneaking so he has less, states, "If you love me, you'll stop. . . .", etc. Takes responsibility for his behavior.

4.) BLAMER: Feels a failure, hurt, fear, anger. Attacks him, sarcastic, threatens, silent, resentful.

5.) ISOLATOR: Loses self in pity, silence, becomes rigid, fixed, martyr, self-righteous, loner, defensive, antisocial.

THE TWELVE STEPS

1. We acknowledge and accept that we are powerless in controlling the lives of others, and that trying to control others makes our lives unmanageable.

2. We have come to believe that a power greater than ourselves can restore enough order and hope in our lives to move us to a growth framework.

3. We come to a decision to turn our lives over to this power to the best of our ability, and honestly accept that taking responsibility for ourselves is the only way growth is possible.

4. We make an inventory of ourselves, looking for our mental, emotional, spiritual, physical, volitional and social assets and liabilities. We look at what we have, how we use it, and how we can acquire what we need.

5. Using this inventory as a guide, we admit to ourselves, to God as we understand Him, and to other caring persons, the exact nature of what is within that is causing us pain.

6. We give to God as we know Him, all former pain, hurt and mistakes, resentments and bitterness, anger and guilt. We trust that we can let go of the hurt we cause and receive.

7. We can ask for help, support and guidance and be willing to take responsibility for ourselves and to others.

8. We begin a program of living responsibly for ourselves, for our own feelings, mistakes and successes. We become responsible for our part in relationship to others.

9. We make a list of persons to whom we want to make amends and commence to do so, except where doing so would cause further pain for others.

10. We continue to work our program, each day checking out our progress and asking for feedback from others in our attempt to recover and grow. We do this through support groups.

11. We see, through our own power and a Higher Power, awareness of our inner selves. We do this through reading, listening, meditation, sharing, and other ways of centering and getting in touch with our inner selves.

12. Having experienced the power of growing toward wholeness, we find our bodies, minds and spirits awakened to a new sense of physical and emotional relief which leaves us open to a new awareness of spirituality. We seek to explore our meaning in life by honest sharing with others, remembering that BECOMING WHO WE ARE is a lifetime task which must be done one day at a time.

References

Beattie, Melody, "Codependent No More," Hazelton Foundation, 1987.

Cermak, Timmen, "Diagnosing and Treating Codependence," Johnson Institute Books, 1986.

Wegscheider-Cruse, Sharon, "Choice-making for Codependents, Adult Children and Spirituality Seekers", Health Communications, Inc., 1985.

Wilson Schaef, Ann, "Co-Dependence Misunderstood—Mistreated," Harper and Row, 1986.

Chapter 16

PASTORAL CONCERNS
CONSCIENCE, CAPTIVITY
AND CO-DEPENDENCE

BISHOP: Father LeBar, you spoke about cults generally, and very thoughtfully, and probably with great prudence, but you didn't mention any of the groups in the Church, which some people have had some concerns with. Could you give us some guidance as to how we would review them? And for Mary Ellen: so many of our seminarians are the adult children of alcoholics. I don't know really why that is, and wonder if you could comment on it and give us some guidance as to any special way that we should work with these.

FATHER LEBAR: Probably the largest and most serious problem that approaches being a cult in our Catholic Church is, at the present time, the *covenant communities* of the charismatic movement. These groups over the years not only have manifested many of the signs that I described today, but have avoided attention for the most part because they claim to be part of the Church. And most of them are.

Now, again, I must make it clear I am not talking against the charismatic movement. Parish prayer groups are excellent, and the whole idea of the charismatic movement is a wonderful experience. But, somewhere along the line some people in these prayer groups decided to do the "charismatic thing" twenty-four hours a day and they joined into these covenant communities. Where the people elected their leaders things didn't happen too badly. But, where somebody suddenly felt divinely appointed to be the leader and then started to control to an excessive degree, we had problems. Another element that was and is dangerous in these groups is that they are under lay leadership for their spiritual activities. They do not want to be under the control of the local bishop. One of the biggest difficulties in this area is that they are making a concerted effort to establish a "dooms-day" type of theology. This is what becomes theologically very difficult, in addition to all of the mind control problems. Now, some groups are reevaluating their membership. Many people are pulling out, and many are going to the bishop and telling them what's going on.

MS. GARVEY-O'BRIEN: I am not surprised to hear that many seminarians are adult children of alcoholics, gamblers, overeaters, or any other addiction.

I think the reason that you may be seeing an increase in people being adult children of alcoholics is that they are now able to label what they are. In the past they may have had other problems, for example, depression or a need to control, or any of the things that I mentioned, responding to the laws that govern that type of family: don't trust, don't talk, don't feel.

A rule of thumb I use is that one in ten people is alcoholic. If we say one in ten is also a gambler or a sex addict or some other sort of addict and each one affects six to eight other people, we are going to have a majority of people who have been affected by somebody's addiction. Also, it is important to note that the "common cold" for adult children of alcoholics is depression. Depression, like addiction, is treatable. Once people label something, that may be a beginning of getting some help or a beginning of the choice process to do something about it.

200

BISHOP: Father LeBar what are some of the policies that you would suggest as to when people phone in and ask if they can't be exorcised?

And before you answer, I want to address Mrs. O'Brien. I remember attending a conference on co-dependency where the speaker said that from her studies she found that 80% of service people, priests, doctors, notaries, lawyers have alcoholics somewhere in the family. Do you agree?

MS. GARVEY-O'BRIEN: In the family where there is an alcoholic parent or a disfunction in the family, the oldest child often is the hero who goes into the helping profession, which may include careers such as priests, social workers, teachers, nurses, or doctors. In their roles they have certain characteristics which can be used for better or for worse. For the better, they are great employees. I know that from working in employee assistance programs. They are conscientious. They work hard. They never quit. They are successful. They are perfectionist. For the worse, they wear themselves out and eventually may end up depressed, not fulfilling their own expectations or needs, losing sight of who they are, making their priority pleasing authorities or simply focussing on others to avoid themselves.

FATHER LEBAR: I am sure that all of you recall that last March, the first Sunday of Lent, Cardinal O'Connor spoke in the Cathedral and told everybody that we had two exorcisms last year. Ever since then life has been busy. At the end of 1990, I had sixty-five current files of people who have requested exorcism from the Cardinal's office or from my office directly, coming from many different dioceses and many different places. We were able to dispose of about seven of those cases by sending them to doctors and psychiatrists. But there are about forty that have yet to be looked into. So, the first thing bishops can do is find me some exorcists! The Cardinal said, "help everybody, even if they don't need an exorcism." So, we tried to get them some kind of help in one place or another. If the person allegedly possessed calls, generally they are not possessed. But they may be "oppressed." So, you can't just dismiss them.

I look for four things. First, I look for any extraordinary phenomena that are happening, things moving around, lights flashing on and off without any particular reason. As we go looking a little further, I want to see if there is any super strengths. I want to see if there is any levitation, any speaking in strange languages that the person couldn't possible understand, and if there is any clairvoyance. If I find two or three of those items, then the next thing is to get them to a psychiatrist and a psychologist and sometimes a medical doctor to find out if there are any natural causes for these things.

If the report comes back with nothing pathological, then we would recommend to the bishop that there be a provocation. The exorcist would come and seek to find out if the devil is present. This is done generally by using very familiar symbols, holy water, crucifix, relic of the true cross, relic of St. John Vianny, and the Blessed Sacrament. If the person reacts violently to these items, then we would recommend an exorcism. Let me just give you two examples very quickly.

About two months ago, I got a frantic call from a man in the Archdiocese of San Francisco. He had heard of me through one television program or another, and he told me about his friend. His friend's wife had come reporting this situation. He had been involved in a satanic cult for some period of time and the other day, while he was in his bedroom he started growling, and looked like he was changing forms. So, the wife got a little worried. And I can understand why. She went to the parish priest who very wisely gave her a crucifix and holy water, and told her to put the crucifix in the room and to sprinkle the house with holy water.

She put the crucifix under the mattress rather than prominently on the wall. According to this report they came home that night and he went into bed. He lay on the bed and the next moment the wife found him on the ceiling, growling and yelling and screaming all sort of profanities. "Get that such and such a thing out of here." "What thing?" "I don't know what it is, but whatever it is get it out." So, she took it out from between the mattresses and left. She slept in the other room and he came down. The next morning he went to work and didn't remember a thing that happened. She sprinkled the whole house with holy water, making especially sure to sprinkle the front door area. When he came home from work he couldn't get in. The door was open, but he could not get in. "What did you do to my house? This isn't my house anymore." Finally, he forced himself in, picked up a projection T.V., which has a forty inch screen, with one hand and threw it at her. He missed her, fortunately. She took the child and departed the scene rather quickly. This would be a case where we were ready to go work immediately, but the man fled the scene himself, and we haven't done anymore.

In another case, I visited a sixteen year old girl with the pastor, the assistant, her sister, the girl's mother and three or four other people. This was my first case of investigating something without the exorcist present. So, we sat down and after the pastor said a prayer, I said, "Well, what do we do now?" All of sudden a voice came from somewhere, "You know what to do, stupid. Stop wasting my time." One of the things I learned is you don't converse with the demons. Well, I hadn't determined whether this was a demon or not. I said, "Who is talking?" "I don't have to answer that question." "In the name of Jesus I command you tell me who is talking." "I won't." Notice the change. "If you don't tell me, I will get Father Candido." "Huh, you can't get Father Candido, he's sick." "Then I'll get Father X, my exorcist." "No, no." said a second voice. A third voice, "Don't do that. He'll chase us away."

Now, what had happened? I had been to Rome just prior to this particular meeting, and I had looked for Father Candido who was the exorcist of Rome just recently retired. He was sick, had been in the hospital and sent to Bari, so I wasn't able to see him.

The people in that room, including the young person, had no idea who Father Candido was, and yet that message came out. They had no idea who Father X was, and yet the fear came out. Ultimately, we determined that it was a severe case of oppression, (obsession) where the demons were outside. We found seven of them all together. And we did an exorcism there in October. I do not do exorcisms. But, I do arrange them. I would be happy to help anybody who does have a case, or a situation, but I do recommend that you find two or three priests that can look into the matter. See what you find out, and then call. Then we have eliminated a few steps.

CARDINAL: This is going to be rather dull after all that. But, I want to just say a word about the Universal Catechism. I was looking around to see if Cardinal Ratzinger was here, but I don't see him, because we had talked last evening about the fact that we would say something about this.

He suggested that I might and then he would amplify it. I simply want to report the fact that the Universal Catechism is on track. It should be ready sometime in 1992. The Commission will be meeting in the Spring [1991]. The commission consists of twelve persons. We will be meeting in May to review a draft that is a draft built upon the draft that was sent to all of the bishops, and incorporates changes which we reviewed at our last meeting and now are being put into place by the editor. The response of the bishops to the consultation has been a very good response. The acceptance of that draft which was sent out is an almost universal acceptance in substance. There have been excellent suggestions for its improvement.

I would say that our problem is not that we have been emphasizing perhaps too much the do's and don'ts but that we have not been teaching adequately. I am sure that the evangelicals would emphasize do's and don'ts to a much greater degree than has been the catechetical method generally in the Church in the past twenty years. I think that the task we face collectively is what do we do when this Universal Catechism comes out? The reception of that catechism is something that is really going to be in our hands as Episcopal Conferences, as local bishops and, if that reception of the catechism isn't being prepared for now, I'm afraid that the hope that the Universal Catechism can provide us will be lost. So, I would simply plead that we think about the publication of this catechism as a moment of grace and as an opportunity and attend to the ways in which we can make that a very special tool.

Chapter 17

CONSCIENCE AND THE CORPORATE PERSON

Sister Mary Louise Lyons, D.C.

On the Sunday between Christmas and New Year's, our diocesan paper, THE CATHOLIC REVIEW, carried a front page article about the Holy Father's message for WORLD PEACE DAY, January 1. As I was in the midst of preparing this paper, I was struck by the emphasis Pope John Paul was giving to protection of *freedom of conscience.* He cautioned that conscience "is not an absolute placed above truth and error."

"One of the constant temptations in every age, even among Christians, is to make oneself the norm of truth." the Pope said.

Pope John Paul's warning seems very timely for me and those of us in positions of authority in the health field. We need to be aware of it especially as we try to respond to the moral and ethical challenges we face daily.

Moral and ethical issues have been, and will continue to be, a major focus for us in hospitals, whether we are in management, or in the practice of medicine, nursing or other therapeutic specialties.

Questions surrounding conception and birth; withholding and/or withdrawing treatment or nutrition or hydration; the patient's right of self-determination regarding his health, vs. the right of the caregiver to choose *not* to treat; rationing healthcare; modern technology and its appropriate use; organ transplants; the treatment and care of patients with AIDS—these are the more significant and frequent questions which at times require the involvement of the administrator.

My personal experience has been that in order to respond conscientiously to the moral issues that arise, there has to be in place an effective support system. For me this has included:

1. A close relationship with the *Holy Spirit* whose inspiration and guidance is critical to the wisdom and courage I need.
2. Formulation of *policies* regarding life/death/health issues, approved by the Board of Directors and promulgated throughout the institution. These need to be reviewed at least annually and revised if they are obscure, poorly understood, or not being followed.
3. Seeking *consultation* with a moral theologian whose opinions are consonant with positions of the Church's magisterium.
4. Continuing *education* in moral/ethical matters. (This symposium is a significant resource for those Catholic hospitals who belong to the Pope John XXIII Institute, and receive a copy of the proceedings of the meetings as a resource for updating our knowledge.)
5. Contact with the *local ordinary* of the diocese when the issue under consideration warrants it.
6. Development of a hospital-based medical ethics committee composed of doctors, nurses, a moral theologian, a social worker, a member of the pastoral care team, and administration. Legal advice is sought if needed by the committee. However, the inclusion of

a lawyer as a regular member is discouraged, lest we get too caught up with legalistic aspects to the detriment of sound moral judgment and a Christian approach to the issue.

Because medical ethics committees are of fairly recent origin in individual Catholic hospitals, I would like to spend a few moments commenting on this addition to the support system. They are a mixed blessing. They can be very effective provided the members are willing to devote the time and energy required to become educated, that they accept the role of being *advisory* rather than the decision-makers, and be *available for consultation* not only to other members of the health team, but to families, and to patients themselves on occasion.

On the other hand, the discussions can, at times, generate more heat than light, and result in greater confusion than real clarity. I do support the idea of such a committee, however, as I have witnessed positive growth and greater willingness to listen to each other's opinions, while we struggle together to discern where *truth* lies.

With this somewhat brief background, I should like to present three concrete situations, all of which have occurred or are still ongoing at the hospital in which I work. The principle of *material cooperation* has been basic to the moral stance which I have taken either alone, or in conjunction with staff members, or with the active involvement of the Board of Directors.

I. EARLY INDUCTION OF AN ANENCEPHALIC INFANT

The first of these occurred several years ago, prior to the existence of our ethics committee.

A pregnant woman in her mid-thirties was admitted at sixteen weeks because it was known that her fetus was anencephalic (no brain), and she had a history of mental illness following the birth of her first child. Because she was considered high risk, she was kept for observation. The phone by my bed rang one morning at 2:00 a.m. A senior resident physician wanted to induce the patient as she was becoming quite agitated. He feared some harm could come to the mother, and since the infant would die shortly after birth anyway, he felt the procedure was warranted. (Induction of an infant's birth is quite legitimate if the baby is viable, and the mother is having complications which could result in harm to the infant. However, early induction, before viability, which precipitates delivery, is considered to be a direct abortion.)

The resident had called his chief at home, who agreed that induction could be used, but his advice was to call me first. Meanwhile, the chief prepared to come to the hospital. The mother's consent had been obtained for the procedure.

I told the resident that I would call him back, and proceeded to call Father Tom O'Donnell, S.J. whose advice I have relied on quite a bit over the years. After hearing me out, Father advised that in this instance, he thought the doctor could proceed with the induction. I was comfortable with the decision, and relayed it to the resident who assisted his chief in the delivery.

The next day, a repercussion occurred that not one of the three of us had foreseen. The nursing staff on duty were indignant because they perceived the delivery as a direct abortion. The sister Director of Nursing upheld the nurses; the head nurse came to the office to berate me for changing our hospital from the Catholic one, to one that was no longer Catholic!

The chief regretted that the nurses had not been part of the decision, as he felt sure they would have supported it. I was not so sure, and after talking with Father O'Donnell that afternoon, we both agreed that it would have been better to follow the policy in effect, which was that an anencephalic infant be allowed to deliver at the normal time, and be given comfort measures until it would die. We agreed that the nursing staff would most likely have been able to see the mother through this crisis because of their greater experience in dealing with like situations. Happily that mother has delivered two very normal children in our hospital since!

II. Withdrawal of Treatment

Mrs. P. was an active 69-year old, non-Catholic patient who was hospitalized for back surgery. During the days following the surgery, she was experiencing considerable pain while undergoing physical therapy, but otherwise her progress was normal. One afternoon, her heart stopped beating. She was resuscitated with difficulty and placed in the medical intensive care unit on a respirator. Her brain waves were flat indicating no activity there, but the artificial breathing supported her heart, causing it to continue to beat.

After three days, when no improvement was forthcoming, the family (her two sons and a daughter) asked the physician to remove their mother from the ventilator. However, the physician did not want to discontinue the treatment, even though he admitted it was useless, but suggested that the family and he together ask the administrator for her opinion.

The family presented that their mother would not want to continue this extraordinary life support. The physician expressed concern that they might change their minds later, and accuse him of malpractice. He further indicated to me on the side that he thought she should remain on so that the resident physicians could get some experience in caring for her. I had visited the patient in the hospital several times, and although we never discussed her wishes, I had to agree with the family that she would not want her dying prolonged in this artificial manner. The doctor accepted the opinion, and weaned the patient off the respirator gradually so that she would die as gently as possible.

This is the kind of situation that occurs not just daily, but many times a day in our Catholic hospitals, as in other hospitals, because of a variety of reasons: heart attack (the most common cause of death), stroke, far-advanced illness, etc. Many states have passed living will legislation in the hope that persons will indicate, in writing, what their wishes are, if they are unable to communicate them. However, living wills are not necessarily that helpful. It is impossible for a person to foresee all the situations that might befall them and indicate how they would wish to be cared for in each one.

Before we became such a litigious society, it was usually the family in conjunction with the doctor who made the decision for the patient who was unconscious, as to the continuance or withdrawal of treatment, or indeed whether to start aggressive treatment at all. Now, however, doctors fear being sued if they *don't* treat, and families are divided about what decision to make. The most logical and helpful process which has been determined to be legal in many states is making use of the *durable power of attorney,* which is simply that the person—you or I, for example, would designate in writing a person, usually a family member or a friend, or a superior (someone who knows you or me well), stating that he or she would have the power to make the decision of what is best for us in the event we cannot do so ourselves.

There is a rather large community of religious men whose Provincial Superiors have asked them to complete a form indicating who they wish to act as their personal durable power of attorney, and further indicate if they have any specific wishes about beginning or withholding treatment.

Mrs. P. is living in the next world now, and I must tell you, my brothers, that the knowledge that it was my opinion that resulted in the withdrawal of that ventilator, caused me some deep soul-searching. At that time we still had no ethics committee; I simply did not think of contacting a moral theologian for advice, but I would certainly do so now, and have done so since, in similar situations. However, I have been at peace, because I followed the dictates of my conscience which seemed right then as it still does today.

III. Loss of OB/GYN Accreditation

Our hospital has four residency programs: medicine, surgery, pediatrics, and obstetrics/gynecology. The first three are fully accredited. The fourth, OB/GYN, was fully accredited from 1942 until 1981. In that year it was put on probation. During the survey conducted by the Residency Review Commission (RRC), the accrediting arm of the Accreditation Council for Graduate Medical Education (ACGME) in the years which followed 1982, the RRC acknowledged improvement, but continued to grant probationary status until the survey of October 16, 1984. The RRC recommended to the Council that accreditation be withdrawn.

In its April 30, 1985 letter, nine deficiencies were cited. The hospital asked for reconsideration of the citation as it was felt by the faculty that the deficiencies were not applicable to our program. After reconsideration, the RRC sustained its prior action (withdrawal of accreditation), but rescinded four of the nine deficiencies.

The hospital appealed the decision and was granted appearance before a special Board of Appeals in April 1986. The five deficiencies which were still outstanding were:

1. The resident experience in retropubic surgery is both deficient and uneven.
2. There is little experience with tubal surgery.
3. The experience with brachytherapy is by observation only. (Brachytherapy is the insertion of radium or cesium in the treatment of cancer.)
4. The resident experience with family planning is inadequate. (Artificial contraception, abortion; no mention of natural family planning!)
5. The continuity of education in the sub-specialties is inadequate. The extramural rotations for oncology (cancer) and endocrinology (infertility) do not provide a good ongoing experience in these areas. The parent institution is unable to provide an overall adequate experience.

The purpose of the appeal was to demonstrate:

1. That the hospital offers a residency in Ob/Gyn capable of providing high quality educational, clinical and practical experience to the residents;
2. that it did so at the time of the survey in October 1984; and
3. that the program has, at all times, been in substantial compliance with the ACGME's "Essentials of Accredited Residencies in Graduate Medical Education." ("Essentials")

With legal assistance, the hospital presented its appeal in April 1986 in Chicago to the Appeals Committee which was supposed to be made up of three obstetricians/gynecologists: one physician was designated by the Accreditation Council, one by the hospital, and a third physician was mutually agreed upon by the Council and the hospital. (The third physician did not show up because of illness.)

Information was furnished that brachytherapy is no longer performed by obstetricians, but is in the domain of radiology. The two judges agreed to that.

As for retropubic surgery, additional statistics, which were not available in 1984 because of the illness of the faculty member responsible for putting the data in the computer, were presented and this became a moot question.

The crux of the accreditation denial then was reduced to two: inadequate experience with tubal surgery and with family planning.

In presenting the argument against the citation for inadequate experience with tubal ligation, the brief stated, "The program must also express its feeling that the deficiency is in part directed at the program's refusal to abandon its commitment to obeying the hospital's religious principles. The RRC is aware that the program adheres to the principles set forth in the "Ethical and Religious Directives for Catholic Health Facilities" promulgated by the NCCB which expressly prohibits the performance of sterilization procedures, permanent or temporary, for men or for women, as a means of contraception."

Hence, the residents at St. Agnes are precluded from performing sterilization procedures for contraceptive purposes. However, this does not prevent its resident's ability to learn and perform a full range of tubal surgery procedures done for other purposes: for example, anastamosis (reconstruction of tube which have been tied off), isolation of a diseased uterus, and repairs to the tubes. 108 cases were performed by the residents during the year 1983–1984. This was still considered inadequate by the RRC review during the appeal.

It was against the deficiency regarding family planning experience being inadequate that the appeal made its strongest argument. Very obviously, the inadequacy is in the performance of abortions, that is, "The directly intended termination of pregnancy *before* viability or the directly intended destruction of a viable fetus."

The final deficiency—inadequate experience in oncology and endocrinology—the process by which experience *is* provided, was laboriously explained to the two physician-judges.

212

I might add here that it was very obvious to me during the appeal process that the two judges were unwilling to accept any new information on any of the deficiencies with the exception of the one on brachytherapy.

We left the room feeling that the decision to withdraw accreditation would be sustained. Indeed, it was, and we applied to the Federal District Court for an *injunction* to continue our residency while we prepared to go to court on the matter. Federal District Court Judge Herbert F. Murray granted the injunction on September 19, 1987; the case was heard in Federal Court in Baltimore before Judge Murray during the spring and summer months of 1989. He rendered his opinion in September 1990 that the injunction should be lifted. He based his decision on the rule mandating "hands-on" training in the area of abortion and sterilization for all Ob/Gyn residency programs, stating that it is mandated in the interest of the State.

Our lawyers strongly believe that Judge Murray's opinion is incorrect both factually and legally. On their advice and that of the faculty, and with Board approval, the hospital has filed an appeal with the U.S. Court of Appeals for the Fourth District located in Richmond, Virginia on October 29, 1990. We asked, at that time, for an injunction from Judge Murray, but were refused. We plan to apply to the U.S. Court of Appeals for an injunction, but have not yet done so on the advice of legal counsel.

The new brief was filed December 10, 1990. The hearing is slated for April 1991. Since preparing this paper, we have learned that two groups (The Catholic Health Association and the Catholic League for Religious and Civil Rights) have filed a joint amici curiae brief supporting ours.

You may be wondering at this point how this has affected our hospital to date!

The chairman of the department retired because of severe heart problems; we searched, in vain, for a new chairman for two years, but none wanted to chair a department with such an uncertain residency program. Therefore, the interim chairman who was assistant chairman, became the chairman with the understanding that when the case is settled, he will definitely wish to be replaced, as he wants to retire.

We still have the number of residents, but you can well imagine that we are not attracting the cream of the crop, and therefore, the faculty is having to work that much harder to develop men and women who will practice obstetrics and gynecology with the same excellent quality their predecessors attained.

You may also be wondering why saving an OB residency is so important to St. Agnes?

As a Daughter of Charity hospital located in a city which has the 2nd highest number of teenage pregnancies, we have responded to the need for services to this group, most of whom come from low income to no-income homes.

Our residents enable us to provide them with excellent prenatal care, in-hospital care, and post-natal care.

Because of a lack of insurance, many of these girls are covered by Medicaid, but obstetricians can afford to serve only a few of these at a time. There is a larger number who would be without services.

The experiences the residents have with these pregnant young women are educationally important to the residents because the girls are considered high risk and often have complications.

Now where does *material cooperation* enter here?

When I was missioned to St. Agnes, one of the first questions to be addressed came from the Department of Ob/Gyn: "Sister, is there any way we can allow our residents to do abortions and sterilizations while they are on rotation at University of Maryland?"

"Have you asked that question before?"

"Yes."

"And what were you told?"

"Sister just said no."

"Well, I must say 'no' too, but I'll give you my reason: while those residents are at the University, we continue to pay their salaries. When they complete the residency, my signature goes on the certificate indicating my attesting to their experience. If I were to agree to what you are asking, I would be cooperating materially, as would the Board of Directors, in any abortions or sterilizations performed for the purpose of contraception."

To their credit, the faculty accepted the decision. However, they are as convinced as I am that the removal of our accreditation is due in large part to our stance on these issues.

During an appeal filed by the ACGME against our request for an injunction, their lawyer stated, "St. Agnes is the only Catholic hospital that has not found a way around the requirements of adequate family planning experience and adequate tubal surgery." He further stated "they think they are right and everyone else should march to their step!" At no point in the hearings, or in the voluminous documentation, did St. Agnes indicate that other Catholic hospitals were wrong. We were steadfast in presenting this as *our* position.

Our counsel suggested we assist in seeking information needed to be obtained from Catholic hospitals as to what their practice is, whether they are fully accredited and whether or not they have been cited. We did so, and the results were enlightening! Some hospitals, very few, do as we do. Others do "get around" the directives.

As you can see, this is perhaps the most challenging ethical question I as an administrator of a Catholic hospital have faced.

I am convinced that our residents know what they should know about abortions and sterilizations, and if they wanted to perform either after they leave St. Agnes, they would be able to do so skillfully simply because the techniques are used for other purposes, and they do have adequate experience in applying those skills. They have received didactic information as well, because ignorance is not innocence.

Now, you may ask, have I involved any of the bishops in our diocese in the ongoing process? My answer is negative. My reason? We are one of six Catholic hospitals in our diocese. We can only be concerned with the responsibility for what St. Agnes Hospital does about this matter. We have reason to believe that there would be some division of opinion about the matter, but I also know our hospital does not stand alone in its view, even in our own diocese. However, we are the only one of the six which has its own OB/GYN residency at the present time.

Because there is a difference of opinion in the Catholic community, I am sure that you, too, may have differing opinions on this subject. Let me just say that I respect each of you and your opinions, and earnestly ask that you respect the position my conscience and the corporate conscience of our hospital have dictated us to follow. It is comforting to know that the Board and I have had the support of our Provincial Superiors and the Vincentian priests who have been involved with our hospital during the process of this case.

May I ask you to pray that whatever the outcome is, it will be what *God* wants?

Thank you for listening!

Chapter 18

CONSCIENCE AND THE PUBLIC PERSON

Robert George, Ph.D

I

In modern democratic societies, we rightly prize arrangements that give ample room for individuals to exercise judgment and make choices. One of the great achievements of the West in general and the United States in particular has been the establishment of liberty within the bounds of morally ordered community. Our politics, economics, culture, and religious life have benefited from this respect for human reason and human freedom. By contrast, the experiences of peoples subjected to totalitarian rule in this century make it plain that the failure of governments to respect individual judgment and freedom of choice impoverishes human existence in all of its manifold dimensions. As a result, our inclination to defer to individuals in matters that directly affect their lives has been significantly enhanced. The notion of individual choice has come to enjoy tremendous prestige among us. And yet, when we speak of choice, at least as American Catholics, clarifications are needed and distinctions must be drawn, especially when we examine choice in relation to abortion.

It is my goal in these remarks to offer some clarifications and draw some distinctions that I hope will be useful to you in thinking about the choices that Catholic voters and politicians are being asked to make in connection with abortion and the rights of the unborn. The prestige enjoyed by the notion of freedom of choice has been exploited to great advantage by advocates of what the elite media has taken to calling "abortion rights." Many Catholics—including a large majority of nationally prominent Catholic politicians and a significant number of notable Catholic theologians—now say that respect for freedom of choice requires Catholics to refrain from acting on their conscientious opposition to abortion in the public forum. In my judgment, this position is philosophically and morally untenable. A choice to give someone else the choice as to whether an innocent third party shall live or die is a choice that no one concerned for basic human rights should be willing to make. Moreover, a proper understanding of the moral significance of human choosing makes it plain that such a choice is one that no Catholic whose conscience is properly formed regarding the injustice of abortion can afford to make.

II

Some of the choices people make are quite unlike the "choices" made by non-rational animals. A mule may hesitate when faced with the possibilities of drinking from a pail of water or eating from a bale of hay. In the end, it will do one or the other first. Now, let us suppose that on this occasion the mule drinks the water before eating the hay. In a loose sense, the animal can be said to have "chosen" to drink before eating. Nothing *external* to the mule determined that it would drink first; what settled the matter in the end was something *internal* to the mule, namely, the mule's own desires or preferences. The animal hesitated between the pail and the bale because it was experiencing a conflict of felt desires: it felt a desire for the water and, at the same time, a desire for the hay. Eventually, the desire for the water prevailed and the mule drank.

Like mules, people can be motivated by hunger, thirst, and other felt desires. They can experience conflicts of felt desires and make "choices" in the loose sense in which mules and other animals can be said to make choices. Unlike mules and other animals, however, people can "choose" in a stricter and philosophically more interesting sense. The choices that people can make that are quite unlike the "choices" made by other animals are what philosophers mean by "free choices."

A free choice is a choice between two or more open practical possibilities in which no factor but the choosing itself settles which possibility is chosen.[1] Inasmuch as the mule's choice to drink before eating was *determined* (albeit by its own desires) it was not a *free* choice. Insofar as similar choices made by human beings are similarly determined they are not free choices. Free choices are choices that are not determined by desire. Free choices are not determined by anything. They are, in short, not determined.

Choice in any sense is possible only where someone has motives for incompatible actions. *Free* choice is only possible where these motives are reasons for action or, at least, where reasons for action are among these motives. There can be no free choice where the *only* possible motives for action are *subrational,* e.g., feelings, desires, preferences, habits, emotional inertia.

Because mules can be motivated by possibilities that appeal to feelings, desires, preferences, habits, emotional inertia, etc., they sometimes *hesitate* between incompatible possibilities and "choose" in the looser sense of the term. Because mules cannot, we must suppose, appreciate the *rational* appeal of some possibilities for choice, they cannot *deliberate* between incompatible possibilities that provide reasons for action and make free choices between or among them. People and other rational beings, precisely insofar as they can understand certain possibilities as

219

providing reasons for action, *can* deliberate between incompatible possibilities and make free choices.

It is important to notice that reasons for action, though they are conditions of free choice, are not causes (in any modern sense of "cause") of the actions they are capable of motivating. One can choose not to perform a certain act that one has a reason (and, thus, a rational motive) to perform or one can choose to perform a certain act that one has a reason (and, thus, a rational motive) not to perform. In the simplest case, one may have a reason to perform an act yet have a strong aversion to performing it (and, thus, an emotional motive for not performing it). One's failure to perform it may be due to weakness of the will.

In a more interesting case, one may have a reason to perform a certain act and, at the same time, a reason not to perform it. One may freely choose to act on the latter reason. In a case of this sort where one has a conflict of reasons and no conclusive reason to act on one reason rather than the other, the choice between the two is rationally underdetermined. Nevertheless, a choice either way remains rationally grounded.[2] If one performs the act, one does so for a reason; if one refrains from performing the act, one also does so for a reason.

Let us consider an example. Suppose that Ferdinand is a bright young college senior who is trying to decide on a career. He has talent and interest in anthropology and could, no doubt, contribute to the advancement of knowledge in that field. Thus, he has a reason to pursue a Ph.D. in anthropology. At the same time, however, he has talent and interest in medicine. Thus, he has a reason to forego graduate work in anthropology and go to medical school. A choice either way would be "for a reason" and, thus, rationally based; yet Ferdinand has no conclusive reason for making it one way rather than the other. A choice in favor of either possibility would be consistent with those principles of reasonableness in practical affairs that we usually refer to as moral norms. Hence, no such norm provides a reason for action which defeats one or the other of the conflicting reasons and dictates a choice one way rather than the other.

There are cases of conflicting reasons, however, in which moral norms do provide conclusive reasons to do something that one has a reason not to do or not to do something that one has a reason to do. Nevertheless, one may freely choose to defy a conclusive reason. In such a case, one's action, while not utterly irrational, is not fully reasonable. An act in defiance of a conclusive reason remains rationally grounded insofar as one performs it for a reason. Yet inasmuch as one's reason for performing it has been defeated, one's nevertheless choosing to act in this way is practically unreasonable.

Let us suppose that Ferdinand has opted for medical school. Suppose, further, that two years into his medical education, he learns that students in all medical schools are required to perform abortions as part of their training.[3] He requests an exemption from this requirement on moral and religious grounds, but his request is denied. Thus, he faces the alternatives of performing abortions or dropping out of medical school. Like his earlier choice between going to graduate school in anthropology or going to medical school, Ferdinand's choice between performing abortions and dropping out of medical school is a choice between rationally grounded possibilities. He has reasons for a choice either way. Here however, he has a conclusive reason for making the choice one way rather than the other, namely, the moral norm that forbids him from taking innocent human lives.

Moral norms are norms for free choice; they are principles of practical reasonableness that guide choices between incompatible possibilities in which one has a reason, or reasons, for action. As action-guiding principles, moral norms are, moreover, themselves reasons for action. They are not the most basic reasons for action, however; for the most basic reasons are principles that guide action by directing choice toward rational possibilities and away from what is utterly irrational. And certain possibilities, while holding some rational appeal (and therefore available for choice in the strong sense of the term) are, nevertheless, not fully reasonable (i.e., the reasons for choosing them are defeated). Moral norms guide action by directing choice toward *fully reasonable* possibilities and away from possibilities that, while not utterly irrational, are practically unreasonable.

Moral norms (such as the norm that absolutely forbids the direct killing of innocent human beings) are conclusive reasons for action that exclude certain possibilities despite the fact that one has (non-moral) reasons to choose these possibilities. Where a moral norm excludes a possibility, one's reason for choosing that possibility (assuming that one had a reason and not merely an emotional motive for it) has been defeated. Defeated reasons are reasons on which it is unreasonable to act. Nevertheless, such reasons retain some rational appeal. In declining to act on them, one forgoes some real benefit. By declining to perform abortions, Ferdinand, for example, forgoes a genuine good, namely, a career in medicine.

Let us suppose, though, that Ferdinand chooses to preserve his medical career by agreeing, however reluctantly, to perform abortions. Perhaps he has been reading the works of some contemporary Catholic moral theologians of the "proportionalist" school and has decided that the evil of performing the abortions would be outweighed by all the good he could go on to do as a physician. In accounting for his choice, we might take note of the irrationality of supposing that the goods and evils at stake here can be commensurated in a way that would enable someone to identify a choice one way or the other as promising a greater net proportion of good to evil. We would not conclude, however, that Ferdinand's choice to perform abortions (and, thus, to save his medical career) was utterly irrational. His reason for making it, namely, the good to be done as a physician, while defeated here by the absolute norm against directly killing the innocent, remains a reason. In view of the conclusive reason for action provided by the norm, however, his choice would fall short of what reason requires: it would thus be unreasonable, irresponsible, immoral.

III

I have subjected you to this long and, I fear, tedious disquisition on the phenomenon of free choice in order to make two points about the significance of free choice that are, I think, relevant to the question of Catholic conscience in the public forum. Free choices are events or states of affairs in the world; they are, however, not *merely* events or states of affairs like the events and states of affairs that they bring about. In addition to their significance as events that shape the world external to the chooser they have an additional and profound significance.

First, free choices reflexively shape the personality and character of the chooser. In freely choosing we integrate ourselves around the principles of our choices. Thus, we constitute (or re-constitute) ourselves as particular sorts of persons. We construct (or re-construct) our moral selves. Typically, this self-constitution or moral self-construction is not the precise reason for our choosing; nevertheless, it is an unavoidable side effect of that choosing.

The second point I wish to make about the intransitive (i.e., self-shaping) significance of free choice is that precisely insofar as our choices are self-constituting they last beyond the behavior that carries them out. Indeed, they last in the personality and character of the chooser until, for better or worse, he repents of his prior choice and either makes a new choice that is incompatible with that prior choice or genuinely resolves not to repeat the choice he has now repudiated.[4]

In the light of faith, the self-shaping quality of human choice and action has still more profound significance. Our free choices can be understood to last into eternity and to contribute here on earth, insofar as they are morally upright, to the building up of the heavenly kingdom as described in *Gaudium et Spes* 38–39. By our free choices we can cooperate with God, humbly accepting his offer of friendship, or refuse to cooperate, thus (usually implicitly) repudiating his friendship. The immoral choices by which we repudiate God's friendship persist in our personalities and characters no less than do those upright choices by which we accept God's friendship and contribute to the building up of His kingdom.

The possibility of repentance of an immoral choice manifests a lack of complete integration in the human personality, at least in this life. Someone who has by his immoral choices constituted a wicked character can, with difficulty, re-constitute himself. Fiction and even biography are replete with examples. So long as this lack of complete integration continues, the constitution of a wicked character does not preclude the possibility of repentance and re-constitution around upright principles of action. Nor, of course, does the constitution of a good character eliminate the possibility of evil choices and the re-constitution of one's character around immoral principles. Life and imagination provide plenty of examples here too.

Will this lack of complete integration of the human character continue beyond death? If not, then each of us will enter upon eternity with the character he has constituted at the time of his death. The possibility of having constituted a character that is incompatible with a sharing in divine friendship is the possibility of hell.

Of course, it is unlikely that someone would formally and explicitly choose hell. Someone who knows that he has done wrong and fears eternal damnation will constantly resolve to repent, though, alas, the resolution to repent can fall short of the resolution required to effect repentance. Even more chilling, of course, is the possibility of rationalizing the evil-doing by which one, in fact, corrupts one's character and repudiates God's friendship. This possibility has been significantly enhanced in our own time, even within the Church, by the influence of philosophical methodologies of moral judgment which, in reality, can be nothing more that techniques of rationalization. I speak, of course, of utilitarian, consequentialist, or proportionalist methods by which people (formally or, more commonly, informally) attempt to justify actions (usually as putatively "lesser evils") that have been firmly and constantly condemned by the *magisterium* as always and in every circumstance incompatible with a sharing in divine life.[5]

IV

One of these actions is direct abortion. In direct abortion one adopts by choice a proposal to destroy the life of an unborn human being either as an end-in-itself or, more commonly, as a means to another end. One who requests or performs or formally cooperates in a direct abortion integrates the evil of abortion into his or her own will, thus quite possibly constituting a character that can only be described as repudiating all friendship with God. This, I take it, is what the Church means in her firm and constant teaching that direct abortion is always grave matter. Until one repents of one's participation in an abortion, the evil of that abortion lasts in one's character, in one's soul. To die with a character thus constituted is to face the real possibility of hell.

Now, the question of Catholic conscience and the public forum becomes most acute over the issue of how Catholic voters and politicians ought to act in respect to the public regulation and funding of abortions. A related, though less acute, question has to do with the proper role of bishops and other ecclesiastical officials in the debate over abortion. I will briefly treat the latter question in the final section of these remarks. I will say nothing more, however, about whether direct abortion is ever morally permissible. From the point of view of Catholic faith, *that* question has, in my judgment, been definitively settled: a properly formed Catholic conscience will judge direct abortion always to be intrinsically evil. The position I wish to consider here, therefore, is the increasingly familiar one that claims that Catholics who have properly formed their consciences with regard to the moral status of abortion may nevertheless act to make or keep abortion legal or to fund abortions for poor women.

Morality is primarily a matter of rectitude in willing; and as a matter of Catholic conscience no one can rightly will a direct abortion. The legitimacy of the "personally opposed, but pro-choice" position hinges, therefore, on the possibility of someone who supports legal abortion and abortion funding willing not that someone have an abortion, but only that someone have the choice as to whether to have an abortion. Now, it *is* possible to will that someone have the choice as to whether to have an abortion while, at the same time, *hoping* that they will choose not to have it. But it is *not* possible to will that someone have the choice as to whether to have an abortion without *willing the injustice of abortion.*

One who wills that someone have the choice as to whether to destroy an unborn child necessarily wills that the child be denied the legal protections against direct killing that one wills for oneself and others whom one considers worthy of the equal protection of the laws. Someone who supports legislation or public policies that exclude the unborn from these basic protections violates the Golden Rule. Someone who acts on a proposal to deprive the unborn of legal protection against abortion unavoidably renders himself complicit in the injustice of abortions that his actions help to make possible. Someone who by free choice renders himself complicit in the evil of abortion corrupts his own character thus placing his soul in dire jeopardy.

A year or so ago, when Bishop Austin Vaughan warned Governor Mario Cuomo of New York that he was in danger of going to hell for supporting legal abortion and abortion funding, sophisticates scoffed. Bishop Vaughan's reasoning, however, was impeccable. To will the injustice of abortion, however reluctantly, is gravely immoral. Gravely immoral choices corrupt souls and seriously damage the possibility of sharing in divine life. We have no reason to suppose that after death it will be possible for us to repent of such choices and reconstitute our characters to accept God's offer of friendship.

It will be urged against the position I am defending that Catholic voters and public officials can reasonably disagree as to *strategies* for protecting the unborn, and that the question of whether to support or oppose legal abortion and abortion funding can be a question of strategy on which people who recognize the immorality of abortion may legitimately disagree. Thus, someone might say, one may be personally opposed to abortion, but favor a strategy for protecting the unborn that does not include legal restrictions on the practice of abortion.

An argument along these lines has recently been made by defenders of Vincent Schoemehl, the Mayor of St. Louis. Schoemehl is a young Catholic politician who had supported a constitutional amendment to outlaw most abortions. A couple of months ago, however, he changed his mind and promised that if he is elected Governor of Missouri, the office to which he now aspires, he will veto any new restrictions on abortion that should pass the state legislature. He remains "personally opposed to abortion" but has adopted the pro-choice position on abortion regulation. Rather than try to restrict access to abortion, he now argues, we should work toward "a comprehensive program" of education and health and family support services to reduce the incidence of abortion.

Schoemehl, and his principal theological adviser on the abortion issue, Fr. Kevin O'Rourke, claim that Schoemehl's about face is nothing more than a legitimate change in pro-life strategy. "If I have any disagreement with any person who is against abortion,"

Schoemehl has been quoted as saying, "it is a difference of strategy." According to O'Rourke, by combining a pro-choice position on abortion legalization with advocacy of initiatives to reduce the *number* of abortions Schoemehl "is trying to . . . develop a more effective relationship between conscience and public policy."

Let us give Schoemehl the benefit of the doubt here and assume that his turn around on abortion is not motivated merely by his desire to be elected Governor. Does his position represent a legitimate way of translating conscientious belief in the wrongfulness of abortion into public policy? I cannot but conclude that it does not.

It is true that people who perceive the injustice of abortion may legitimately differ as to strategies for combating that injustice. It is also true that sometimes one may support legislation or policies that fall short of the equal protection of the laws to which the unborn are morally entitled. Support for such legislation or policies is permissible, however, *only* in circumstances in which a voter or public official prudently judges that the only realistic alternative to the legislation or policy in question is a scheme of abortion regulation that would leave the unborn with even less legal protection and therefore even more vulnerable to unjust attack.

So, for example, a pro-life legislator who reasonably believes that in the prevailing political circumstances there is little hope of enacting legislation that would fully protect the unborn may in good conscience vote for legislation that would prohibit abortions after twelve weeks gestation in preference to a public policy that would permit abortions to be performed up to the point of fetal viability or all the way until birth. Or again, a legislator who is working for the protection of all unborn children may nevertheless vote for legislation that would leave unborn children conceived in acts of rape or incest unprotected in preference to a public policy that would leave all unborn children vulnerable to abortion.

In other words, one may legitimately vote for less than fully protective legislation when (and only when) one's *reason* for voting for the legislation is precisely to win (or maintain) the protections for the unborn contained in the legislation. Where one's reason for action is precisely to protect the unborn, one *intends* only those aspects of the legislation that are protective and merely *accepts as a side effect* those aspects of the legislation that are unfair. Thus, one's intention is free of injustice towards the unborn: one treats them no differently than one would wish to be treated were one's own life among the lives that the legislation leaves unprotected.

Where, however, one votes for less than fully protective legislation, not (or not merely) for the sake of the protections contained in the legislation, but rather (or also) for, say, increasing the freedom of women, fighting overpopulation, or improving one's own prospects for reelection, one seeks to impose risks on the unborn that one would not be willing to have imposed on oneself and deprives them of rights that one cherishes for oneself and those whom one favors. By *intending* the not-fully-protective aspects of the legislation, albeit not as an end-in-itself but rather as a means to another end (e.g., enhancing women's freedom), one acts unfairly towards the unborn by treating their lives as less worthy of protection than one's own.[6]

"Intending" and "accepting side effects" are distinct modes of voluntariness. In intending something, whether as end or means, one effects a sort of synthesis between oneself and what one chooses. If the choice is morally upright, its contribution to one's moral character is positive; if wicked, one integrates the evil of the choice into one's will, thus corrupting, or further corrupting one's character. Now, I do not mean to suggest that in accepting side effects one is not subject to moral norms. One may be under an obligation not to accept a certain side effect and therefore not to perform an action that would produce that side effect. Typically, one's obligation not to accept a certain side effect is an obligation in fairness or justice. And where one fails in this obligation, one intends the injustice involved in accepting the side effect and thus integrates that injustice into one's will. One is not morally responsible for bad side effects that one may legitimately accept; but one *is* morally responsible for whatever one intends, including the injustice one intends in *unjustly* accepting bad side effects.

It is in the area of accepting injustices that one does not intend that people may *legitimately* differ as to strategies to protect the unborn. The question here is how far one may go in preferring long-range strategic advantages to the more immediate protection of lives that are at risk. A *merely* strategic pro-life allegiance could be used to surrender in every battle for the sake of winning a war that, without individual battles, will never be fought. A particular piece of protective legislation could be discarded because of fears that its enactment would create a pro-abortion backlash. A certain act of solidarity with the pro-life cause could be side-stepped in order to ensure reelection and the consequent ability to participate in the process of governance at a later date. Even if one is not hewing to the "strategic" line as a ploy to delude the electorate, one is probably merely deluding oneself. [This "strategic" approach has no more rigor than proportionalism has as an ethical theory. Indeed, like proportionalist rationalizations, it purports to justify acting badly or weakly now in the hope that greater good will eventually result from what only seems to be treachery or cowardice.]

In the final analysis, one can proceed towards greater justice for the unborn (and other victims of injustice) in steps and by stages, but one must always be striving in the right direction. The moral landscape has no room for the strategic retreat, for taking one step backward in order to leap further forward, for doing evil that good may come of it. One cannot *intend* the injustice of abortion even as a temporary expedient or a means to some hoped for greater good.

In making political choices, no less than in making other sorts of choices, one forms intentions and accepts side effects. One is subject in the public forum, therefore, to the same norms of morality that govern the forming of intentions and accepting of side effects in all other aspects of one's life. In adopting by choice a proposal to deprive unborn human beings of the equal protection of the laws, one necessarily integrates injustice into one's own will. That choice, no less than any other morally significant choice, lasts in one's character and personality until one repents of it. Its status as a political choice, a choice in the "public forum," in no way diminishes its self-shaping impact on the character and personality of one who makes it.

Nor can an advocate of legal abortion negate his complicity in injustice towards the unborn by supporting educational policies or family support programs designed to reduce the number of abortions. After all, no voter or legislator would support a public policy that placed into the hands of others the arbitrary power of life and death over himself and those he holds dear. Indeed, few of us would be willing to rely on mere programs of education to protect ourselves against, say, racial or ethnic discrimination in housing and employment; much less would we rely on such programs in place of the protections we currently enjoy by virtue of the legal prohibition of homicide. Furthermore, it is hardly plausible for someone who promises to *veto* pro-life legislation (which, but for that veto, would become operative law) to claim that he is prudently working within the limits of what is possible in the prevailing political circumstances to maximize the protection of the unborn.

V

I now wish to turn to the question of the proper role of bishops and other ecclesiastical officials in the debate over abortion. In view of the self-shaping significance of choices made by voters and public officials concerning abortion and the rights of unborn children, those whose primary responsibility is the care of souls have no choice but to vigorously remind the faithful that "no Catholic can responsibly take a pro-choice stand when the choice in question involves the taking of innocent life."

The gravity of the matter of complicity in the injustice of abortion places the salvation of souls at stake. In fact, although concern for the lives of unborn children whose rights are denied in unjust political choices to permit and pay for abortions is the primary reason that *voters and public officials* should oppose legal abortion and abortion funding, this concern is only a secondary reason for teachers of the faith to insist that Catholic voters and public officials act on authentically pro-life principles. To be sure, bishops are obliged to speak out in defense of the unborn, just as they must speak out in defense of all victims of injustice. The *primary* concern of bishops, however, is the saving of souls; and the souls that are at stake in the political controversy over abortion are the souls of those who would fail in their obligations in justice to the unborn.

Moreover, bishops may find it necessary publicly or privately to instruct Catholics who publicly persist in the advocacy of legal abortion and abortion funding to refrain from receiving Holy Communion. Firstly, a Catholic who integrates the injustice of abortion into his will, thus constituting himself around the principles of that injustice, compounds the gravity of his situation by reception of the sacrament prior to repentance and absolution. Secondly, the public reception of the sacrament by Catholics who publicly advocate abortion is increasingly a source of grave scandal in the Church. The consequences of this scandal are profound: by calling into question the Church's firm, constant, and, I would say, infallibly proposed teaching on the sanctity of innocent human life, publicly pro-choice Catholics weaken the resolve of other Catholics to avoid complicity in abortion.

It is not merely that "pro-choice" Catholics encourage others to suppose that the promotion of legal abortion and abortion funding is consistent with Catholic faith, though that by itself would be serious enough to warrant concern and action; even more insidious is the tendency of the scandal they create to weaken the resolve of Catholic women and girls not to request abortions and of Catholic boyfriends, husbands, parents, other relatives and friends not to co-operate in abortions by, for example, counseling, facilitating, or paying for them. The toleration of publicity "pro-choice" activities by Catholics—especially prominent Catholics, and most especially prominent Catholic theologians—can send a message to the faithful that the Church's historic teaching on the sanctity of innocent life and the evil of abortion need not be taken too seriously. In the stressful (and sometimes quite desperate) circumstances of an unwanted pregnancy, the consequences of sending that message can be tragic.

What I have to say in conclusion, I offer with the greatest humility, and without the slightest intention to instruct those from whom I should (and do) seek instruction. Resolute persistence in spreading the difficult, but ultimately liberating, moral teachings of the Catholic Church is no recipe for easy popularity. Those prominent in society who have no friendship for the Church or her teachings will seize on any pretext to criticize you. They, who profess to prize tolerance above all things, will warn you against inciting bigotry against yourselves and other Catholics.

231

The more you compromise or temporize or just stay silent, the more they will praise you for your broad-mindedness and compassion. These self-proclaimed enemies of censorship will congratulate you for censoring yourselves.

Approval by such men and women is to be feared, not coveted. If they applaud your approach to issues of sex and marriage, abortion, infanticide, suicide, and euthanasia, you are almost certainly doing something wrong. Remember the words of Our Lord: "Woe to you when all men speak well of you!" But, at the same time, you may have the comfort of Our Lord's words when you suffer condemnation and reproach for boldly proclaiming His teachings:

> Blessed shall you be when men hate you and when they shut you out and reproach you and reject your name as evil because of the Son of Man. Rejoice on that day and exult, for behold your reward is great in Heaven. (Luke 6:20–26)

NOTES

*The author is grateful to James R. Kurth, William C. Porth, and Robert Royal, all of whom carefully reviewed early drafts and offered helpful criticisms and suggestions.

1. For a full defense of the possibility of free choice as here defined see Joseph M. Boyle, Jr., Germain Grisez, and Olaf Tollefsen, *Free Choice: A Self-Referential Argument* (Notre Dame: University of Notre Dame Press, 1976).

2. For a useful explanation of how choices between rationally grounded possibilities can be rationally underdetermined see Joseph Raz, *The Morality of Freedom* (Oxford: Clarendon Press, 1986).

3. I do not know whether some medical schools in fact require students to perform abortions. Certainly not all medical schools currently have such a requirement. Imagine, however, for the purposes of my hypothetical case that they do.

4. The resolution required to effect a reconstitution of one's character based upon repentance of one's earlier choice cannot be merely the resolution to avoid the circumstances in which one would feel it necessary to make the choice one now regrets. It can be nothing short of the resolution to choose differently even in the identical circumstance.

5. For compelling critiques of proportionalism by Catholic moralists, see Germain Grisez, "Against Consequentialism," *American Journal of Jurisprudence,* Vol. 23 (1978); John Finnis, *Fundamentals of Ethics,* chs. 4–5; and John Finnis, Germain Grisez, and Joseph M. Boyle, Jr., *Nuclear Deterrence, Morality and Realism* (Oxford: Clarendon Press, 1987), pp. 245–267. Many non-Catholic philosophers have also presented powerful arguments against proportionalism, see, for example, Alan Donagan, *The Theory of Morality* (Chicago: University of Chicago Press, 1977), especially pp. 149–157; Joseph Raz, *The*

Morality of Freedom (Oxford: Clarendon Press, 1986), ch. 13; and Philippa Foot "Utilitarianism and the Virtues," *Mind,* Vol. 94 (1985).

6. As many commentators have observed, Governor Cuomo understands these principles and acts accordingly when it comes to capital punishment. When it comes to abortion, however, which he also says he personally opposes, he staunchly supports the legalization and even the public funding of manifestly unjust acts.

Chapter 19

PASTORAL CONCERNS
CORPORATE PERSONS,
PUBLIC PERSONS AND CONSCIENCE

PROFESSOR GEORGE: After my talk, Father Benedict Ashley kindly pointed out to me that while Father O'Rourke did endorse the statement that was put out by Vincent Schoemehl of St. Louis, the statement did not contain Schoemehl's promise to veto legislation. That promise to veto apparently came very shortly thereafter at a press conference.

BISHOP: Sister, I understand your reluctance and sensitivity in not wanting to make judgments on other hospitals and their approach to the problems that you have described, and which you are facing so forthrightly. Perhaps you can describe or explain what other alternatives these other hospitals might be using in getting around the problem.

SISTER MARY LYONS: Right after I finished the talk today, Father Albert said that he knew of at least one hospital that seemed to be doing something that was an acceptable way to get around the problem. The hospital gave a free period (of time) to the residents for them to contract with another hospital to get the experience and then they would return and finish their residency.

We did look into something like that to see if the university of Maryland would pay for the salaries of the residents while they are there, because we do have that kind of an affiliation.

But, at the same time, the intention for letting them do that is to let them do abortions and sterilizations and I would have a problem with that. Plus, I certainly would have a problem signing that bottom line that I approved of everything that they had learned in order to earn a certificate. To me that's not just a blank piece of paper saying that the man is qualified to do everything. It's an attesting to the education he had had, particularly the experience.

One of the things I learned was that some of the administrators didn't know what's going on in their own hospitals. And they don't ask questions. I can understand that. You know, hospital administration has a lot of other problems that have to be taken care of besides the ethical ones. The actual situation is that some people just don't know, and we are not talking just about Sisters now. I am talking about lay administrators as well. They really don't know that when the people go out from their hospital to another hospital they do abortions and sterilizations there. We did have the difficulty right in our own city of one Catholic hospital being advised by a moral theologian that it was okay to do sterilizations at their hospital.

Well, that was a bit of a contention at our hospital for some time. In fact, at a Board meeting I was told by a physician who came to present the case of the attending OB-GYN: "Sister, you are more Catholic than the Catholic Church." I said, "Well, be that as it may, that's a compliment, not a criticism." I was very comfortable with it, because I felt that we were doing the right thing.

BISHOP: How would you deal with the advice that we often hear during electoral campaigns, "Beware of being a one issue person?"

PROFESSOR GEORGE: I would deal with that first by pointing out that where there are grave injustices the most important political issue will be the gravest of these injustices.

236

Secondly, I would observe that what we are most interested in, or should be most interested in, is the *character* of those who will serve us in public office. We want to have people who are zealous for justice above all. We can absorb the cost in terms of efficiency or other values. We cannot absorb injustice.

Nothing could be more fundamental a mark of injustice than the willingness of someone who would serve us in public office to expose some among us to the grave injustice of putting their lives at stake, treating their lives as unworthy of equal protection.

When the most important issue in the United States was one of racial justice, the issue of character came most to the fore over the particular candidate's position on, say, the segregation or integration of public schools. That, thank God, has largely been solved. While we continue to have de facto segregation in many parts of our country, we have eliminated de jure segregation.

Today the gravest issue and the one on which characters are tested with respect to the virtue of justice is the issue of abortion. There are other issues, but that one is central. It shouldn't be a single issue, but it has a peculiarly significant role in our public life.

BISHOP: Professor George, to form and bind the conscience of the faithful, the Church canon law states that the absolution of the sin of abortion, and the remission of the subsequent excommunication are reserved to the Bishop. Practically, many, many bishops delegate this faculty to their priest-confessors. What do you think of that policy?

PROFESSOR GEORGE: Bishop, I can pretend to no expertise in the area of canon law. But, I was very impressed by an article that I had the opportunity to review in advance of its publication in the *Homiletic and Pastoral Review* by a young canon lawyer who is also trained in the civil law named Ed Peters, from the Catholic University of America.

I believe after reading Peters' very lucid article that it is possible canonically to prevent sacrilege not under canons having to do with excommunication, but rather under the canon, I believe it's 911, which allows for the withholding of the Sacrament of Communion in cases of obstinate persistence in manifest grave sin.

If what I have said about abortion is true, then I think frequently in our public life we are confronted with Catholics who are obstinately persisting in grave sin. For their sakes, in terms of sacrilege, and for the sakes of others those whom their actions would scandalize, the problem might appropriately be dealt with under that canon.

BISHOP: Professor George, it was a delight to listen to you and to the well reasoned presentation that you made. Have you ever had any personal occasion to discuss the reasoning that you have given to us with one of these men in public life who are so obviously in favor of abortion while at the same time trying to say they are Catholic and that they are personally opposed?

PROFESSOR GEORGE: Yes, I have had some experiences, curiously with an Episcopalian politician who was personally, strongly, sincerely opposed to abortion, but running in a heavily Democratic and liberal state, and needing room politically to maneuver.

His attitude was, I'm afraid, a kind of consequentialist reasoning that said: look, I can do a lot of good outside the area of abortion. I have to do a little evil here. I can't stop abortion anyway. So, I'll go along. I know it's wrong, but I'll go along.

On another occasion, I spoke with the chief of staff of a very prominent Republican politician. That person is a Catholic, although the Congressman he serves is not a Catholic. The Congressman has taken a moderately pro-choice position in politics. The Catholic chief of staff, who himself aspires to public office, had a very interesting perspective. He said, "Well, you guys"—I think he meant, you philosophers—"are laying a rather heavy burden on us. It might mean that we are going to lose, but we care for truth and justice more than we care for public office. We'll do what is right even at the risk of losing elections. Give us all the room you can, but we don't expect you to give any more room than the truth will bear."

Now, of course there was a slight defect in his attitude. Firstly, philosophers and theologians are not teachers of the faithful, not in the formal and important sense in which you bishops are. Secondly, of course, moral teaching is not a matter of legislating, nor as moral teachers are you in the business of legislating. In proclaiming the constant teaching of the Church on the sanctity of human life, you are articulating truths of the faith over which you have no control. You can't change them.

So, you can't "give room to maneuver" in that sense. But, I think what you can do is try to be very, very clear with our faithful Catholic politicians and others of good will who sincerely oppose abortion and wonder what they should do about it. Say firmly that support for legal abortion and abortion funding is unjust. But remind them that they—and not you—must make the prudential judgments necessary to serve maximum protection for the unborn in a political climate that makes true "equal protection" for the unborn unattainable for now.

So, clarity is what faithful Catholic politicians need. Now, of course, those politicians who are Catholic in name only are not going to care about what you say. They have chosen to follow other teachers. But, I am certain that there are many faithful Catholic politicians and many more faithful Catholic voters who want guidance, but they want it to be clear.

BISHOP: Sister Mary Louise, the problem you raised from obstetrics and gynecology, it would seem to me that Catholic medical schools would probably run into the same problem on accreditation. I am just wondering if you have any idea what they do about it? Also, I have been told that it is hard for a pro-life medical student to get through in obstetrics and gynecology in our country at the present time. Would you have any reaction to that?

SISTER MARY LYONS: In my phoning around, I did contact at least one university program. And although they do not do them (sterilization) at the university hospital, they do send their residents out for experience to hospitals that do them, and leave it up to the resident whether he does them or not.

The resident has the constitutional right to not do abortions, and they cannot penalize him or keep him from taking his boards simply because he did that. But, you are perfectly right in the comment that the resident has a tough time in any program that requires abortions and sterilizations. He is given the least experience and made to feel that he is somewhat of a traitor in the group.

I have kept all the correspondence I have received since 1984 from doctors I have never heard of before, from all over the country. Not in great number, but enough to give you an indication that they were so glad somebody was taking a position because of what they went through in trying to get their status in O.B. even though refusing to do abortions and sterilizations.

ARCHBISHOP: Sister, since you mentioned the constitutional right to refuse to perform an abortion, would there be possibly, by extension, a type of corporate constitutional right on the part of the hospital not only *not* to perform abortions, but also not to offer this service to those whom it is forming in the practice of medicine?

SISTER LYONS: That was our argument, but unfortunately, the corporate person is not protected by that constitutional right. The reason given by Judge Murray was that the state has a mandate and it really does not. There is no such mandate that everybody who gets a license to practice or gets board certified has the ability to do all of those things.

What they said in court was that the resident might not do them while he was with us, but when he left he could do them if he wished to do them, and that in so doing we could maybe do harm to the public, and that the state had the right to prevent that from happening and therefore, the residents would have to do them in order to know how.

Not only do most of the residents not do them when they leave, but if they did do them, our argument was they would be able to do them, *because many of the same procedures that are used for abortion* and *sterilization are used for other reasons legitimately*. And therefore, they know how to do them, because the procedure would have been learned.

ARCHBISHOP: The Ethical (and Religious) Directives are very important for the hospital. We must make sure that the hospital board make a formal resolution adopting those ethical norms as its policy, because if the court were to determine that there were no such ethical norms or that in some cases they were not observed, then the court would have an entré to insist that abortions must be done in that hospital.

SISTER MARY LYONS: And you may be sure our Board did just that many years ago. They reaffirm (that board action) every year.

PART THREE

THE CHURCH AND THE MEDIA

Introduction by Archbishop William J. Levada
Chairman of the Board
Pope John XXIII Center

We look forward to this panel presentation with great anticipation. The Church and the Media. We have approached the question of conscience and the formation of the conscience from many aspects, and we thought it important to have the opportunity to address the interaction of the formation of conscience and our responsibilities for teaching conscience where they intersect so directly with modern culture, and especially in the media.

We are delighted to have a distinguished panel with us today. And I want to introduce them to you briefly and then let them make a brief presentation:

Archbishop John Foley needs no further introduction to us. He was a priest of the Archdiocese of Philadelphia, a former professor at St. Charles Borromeo Seminary, and former editor of the Catholic newspaper *The Catholic Standard and Times*. He presently serves as president of the Pontifical Commission for Social Communications at the Vatican.

On my far left, Ambassador Frank Shakespeare comes to us from a rich background of responsibility in the media of the United States as president of CBS television services. At the end of a distinguished career with CBS, he was president of RKO General from 1975 to 1985, director during the Nixon administration of the United States Information Agency and United States ambassador to Portugal, and United States ambassador to the Holy See.

Father John Catoir is a well-known personage to all of us in the Catholic Church in the United States and beyond. A priest of the diocese of Patterson, New Jersey, he is the Director of the Christophers since 1978, and has had in that position an extremely responsible role in developing the Christophers in various aspects of the media. He is past president of the Catholic Press Association, and has received numerous prestigious awards for his involvement in various media.

Mr. Paul Lauer, at my far right, is the editor of *Veritas* magazine, and, as you see, his hair is not even beginning to gray. He represents a youthful dimension which is unusual in our gatherings here at the Pope John Center, at least as far as the participants are concerned. He is very active in magazine production and in producing videos for cable T.V.

Mr. Bill Plante is with CBS News in Washington, D.C. He has been the State Department correspondent since January 1989 and has been anchor of CBS Sunday night news. We are particularly pleased to have the opportunity to have someone with your experience in the kind of media that most of us watch on such a regular basis and to hear your presentation and your views on the issues of conscience, Church and the mass media.

Chapter 20

A VIEW FROM THE VATICAN

The Most Reverend John P. Foley, Ph.D.

My brother bishops and fellow communicators:

It is certainly a delight to be at this world renowned workshop in moral theology for the first time, to be with so many bishops from the Western Hemisphere and to preside at a panel which includes such distinguished communicators. You have the biographies of all of us on the panel, but I would like to note that I already know three of the panel members personally and the other, Bill Plante, through his distinguished reputation as White House and State Department correspondent for CBS, a delicate task he performs very well.

To go in alphabetical order, I've known Father John Catoir for more years than either of us cares to remember through the Catholic Press Association and other Catholic communications initiatives. Also, it was because of Father Catoir's predecessor,

Father James Keller, founder of the Christophers, that I became involved in communications. When I was in eighth grade, my parents gave me Father Keller's book, "You Can Change the World," about what one person can do to improve the world through work in politics, education and communications, and I took it seriously. At the age of 13, I began to write radio plays on the lives of the saints, which were produced on a local station on which I became a part-time announcer at the age of 14, I became active in local television while I was in college—and I ironically thought that my communication days were over when I entered the seminary, but I was asked to take a summer job at the diocesan newspaper—and, one year after my ordination, Cardinal Krol sent me for my doctorate in philosophy to Rome, where I also wrote six articles a week for our paper during the sessions of the Second Vatican Council. Then I was sent to Columbia University in New York for journalism studies—and I've been in media work ever since, including serving the bishop's conference for fifteen years as a news secretary during the semi-annual meetings.

Paul Lauer and I met for the first time after I was a bishop at a convention of the Catholic Press Association. I was and am impressed by his dynamism, imagination and inability to be discouraged—and, of course, by his love of the Lord. He puts out a great magazine for young people, and he produces interesting and fast-paced religious videos.

Ambassador Frank Shakespeare and I have known one another for the past five years, and I am proud to count him among my friends. He was a most effective ambassador of the United States to the Holy See. As a former president of CBS Television, he has been most helpful to me. Of particular importance, however, is the example he gave and continues to give. Alone among the ambassadors to the Holy See, Frank Shakespeare was at Mass every morning at St. Peter's Basilica, and—unknown to him, possibly until this moment—the employees of the basilica and of the Vatican in general were profoundly edified by his example and, because of him, expressed renewed respect for the nation which named him its ambassador.

Before I give the floor to the other panel members, however, I would like to offer some of my own reflections on the influence of the media in the formation of conscience.

246

The formation of conscience is obviously influenced by what appears in the public eye to be normative or at least acceptable, by what other apparently respectable people are doing, by what seems to be the accepted wisdom.

Thus, if—for example—the daily soap operas portray divorce as the way normal people solve their marriage difficulties; if they depict fornication and adultery not as lust but as the natural and expected expression of emotional attraction; if contraception is virtually presupposed in any sexual relationship and if abortion is presumed to be the only alternative if contraception fails in an extra-marital relationship; if lying is shown as acceptable in the service of what is seen as a good purpose—such as to deceive one's spouse or parents, who are presumed to lack understanding, then is it any wonder that what is said on Sunday from the pulpit—if indeed it is said on Sunday from the pulpit—seems restrictive and almost irrelevant.

Certainly the soap operas and other series provide a cast which includes the obviously evil characters—the people you love to hate, but the truly insidious influence is exercised by those who are depicted as good people and who are portrayed in a sympathetic light as they engage in activity certain to erode the moral fibre of our people.

As I personally was inspired by the book written by Father Catoir's predecessor to write material for radio and television, I am convinced that we must seek to inspire young people to take up careers as writers—of novels, of movie scripts, of television scripts which will have artistic value, commercial appeal and moral integrity. This does not mean that evil cannot be depicted—but as evil. It should not be canonized as good.

That is, I would hope that the dramatic programming we see on television would reflect not only the religious and spiritual values of our society but also the validity of the Judaeo-Christian heritage which has been our public philosophy and which has contributed so much to the development of a society based on family values.

I recall "The Waltons," "Little House on the Prairie" and even the "Loretta Young Show" of forty years ago, together with with "Bill Cosby Show" today. These were programs which left you with a good feeling, which affirmed sound values and which

247

even provided some good ideas for coping with some of the same difficulties. Such programs are part of the solution, not part of the problem—and we need more of them, more writers capable of preparing them and more companies willing to produce them.

Thus, in addition to encouraging young people to become involved in the entertainment media, especially as writers, we must affirm the good that already exists and provide special pastoral care for those in the communications and entertainment industries. If the media can influence the consciences of those who come into contact with them, do not the consciences of those responsible for the media need special and sensitive care and attention, so that moral integrity and artistic quality might survive and flourish in a very competitive environment?

The same competitive environment exists in the news media, an area filled with moral dilemmas for those reporting the news. We must face the fact that we will never see, hear or read completely objective reports—but we must encourage such objectivity and the continuing examination of conscience by publishers, producers, editors and reporters which is necessary to strive for such objectivity.

Individuals and groups seek to use the news media and to influence consciences to embrace their positions through press conferences, demonstrations and staged events which are easy and tempting to cover but which are not necessarily the real news.

How is news reported?

Are those who are concerned for life depicted as crazies who seek to deprive women of what is perceived as a fundamental right?

Are those who raise questions about euthanasia depicted as heartless legalists who wish to see old people suffer and their families reduced to penury?

Are those who object to the distribution of condoms in schools depicted as unrealistic dreamers who actually think that teenagers should be encouraged to practice chastity?

Consciences are formed through the words which are used, the scenes which are depicted and the people who are chosen to be interviewed.

While I am not suggesting that the news media can shrink from treating of any of the problems I have just mentioned, I am suggesting that the media themselves must always be engaged in an examination of conscience—media semper reformanda.

Also, I would hope that there might be some investigative reporting about the hidden saints in our society—about the people who sacrifice themselves to make a difference, to serve the poor and the sick, to work for justice for the oppressed. Such media profiles can have the effect of good example, of stimulating imitation, of helping to resolve problems by showing the public how others are resolving them or at least responding to them.

In his occasional feature, "On the Road," Charles Kuralt of CBS talks with people who make a difference in some small way. One can savor the simplicity, the integrity, the common sense of good people doing good things and making good news.

I started in the media by writing about saints. I'm convinced that people need good role models. The Church can and should canonize saints—but the media in a sense canonize people when they focus on them. The people to whom the media pay attention often become the people others want to imitate. I would hope the media would go "On the Road" to find more hidden saints whose lives make a difference. The Church can help in this search, and its public relations efforts should focus not only on what bishops are doing but especially on what individual Catholics are doing in a positive way to help others in the name of the Lord and to make the good news of Jesus Christ a reality in a wounded world.

Chapter 21

A VIEW FROM MULTI-MEDIA EXPERIENCE

The Reverend John Catoir, J.C.D.

My brothers in Christ, I owe you a debt of respect and gratitude for inviting me here today. Speaking to all these bishops, I feel a little bit like the valedictorian who opened his speech with these memorable lines: "Washington is dead, Lincoln is dead, and I don't feel too well myself."

The Christopher motto is: It's better to light one candle than curse the darkness. With this in mind I would like to discuss the print and electronic media today, not in terms of its bias against the Church and all institutional religion for that matter, but in terms of the opportunities available to us in our efforts to show forth the Church in its splendor as the People of God.

My talk will have two parts: the first has to do with a principle in the TV industry that governs all television production, "marketing decisions must always precede production decisions." This is a basic law in the commercial television industry and those who fail to observe it usually do not last long in their jobs.

My second point will be a brief report on an initiative of Cardinal Suenens which links up prayer and evangelization. With the cooperation of Cardinal Daneels of Belgium, Cardinal Suenens began a new grass roots apostolic association called FIAT which is a network of prayer groups throughout the world directed toward the goal of uniting prayer-groups and evangelization. If we look at the word media in its broadest possible meaning, we can see that our means of communication is not limited to radio, television and the printed word, we have that precious person-to-person network of Catholics who can serve as the Church's link to the world.

The entertainment industry knows well that word of mouth promotion is more powerful than paid advertising. Imagine what a network of spirit-filled lay people can do to spread the faith. I'll return to FIAT in a moment, but first the marketing principle: marketing decisions must always precede production decisions.

The U.S. Catholic Conference of Bishops, in the late 1970's decided to enter the world of electronic media by creating a TV network called CTNA, the Catholic Television Network of America. It cost them millions of dollars and though their intentions were noble, ten years later they have little to show for their investment, in terms of visibility and audience recognition. Only a small percentage of the laity even know of the existence of CTNA, and fewer still have ever seen it's signal on their home TV sets.

There's not much sense in owning a TV station if you do not have quality programming and even if you do, you must have a delivery system to bring your programming into the homes of viewers. Had the U.S. bishops made the necessary marketing decisions before proceeding with their plan to purchase expensive electronic hardware, they would have been in a better position than they are today.

Since nearly all the available money was spent on hardware, there was little left to finance the production of quality programming, and without quality programs the whole venture began to fail.

I wish that those millions had been spent on inspirational, consciousness-raising, value-oriented, and instructional video tapes to be made available at reasonable rates to pastors, teachers on all levels: universities, high schools, grammar schools; to the leaders of prayer groups and to individuals and families all over the English speaking world. Topics ranging from religious instruction, to the moral ethics of ministering to the dying, to the art of contemplation could be available at Catholic video libraries all over the world. We do not have to depend on the mercy of commercial television to gain access to the public. We have our own delivery system, our people, and we have the technology to deliver the highest quality inspirational programming the world has ever seen.

Marketing decisions are concerned with delivering the message to the audience. When the Church produces a 50,000 word document for the faithful, chances are most of them will never read it. The Catholic press will print it for us, and the secular press will allude to it briefly, but the delivery of the message will be muted. We do a poor job of marketing our teachings.

Marketing decisions have to be faced before production begins in any use of the media. When they are, success is at least possible, when they are ignored, failure at communication is assured.

At the Christophers, we have been producing a continuous weekly television program for over 37 years, reaching millions of viewers and listeners on radio and TV. In all that time we never purchased one microphone, or a TV camera. We specialized in the production of programming, and we rented the professional equipment, the studio facilities as needed, thus avoiding the endless expense of maintenance. Keeping equipment at the state of the art level is costly. Expensive cameras for instance are virtually obsolete in four or five years due to the rapid improvement of the technology. This formula of renting rather than buying seems expensive at first, but it has saved us millions of dollars over the years.

The important thing in broadcasting is quality programming. Our people are becoming more and more sophisticated in their video viewing. As a result they do not have much patience with amateurish productions. One can hear the teen-age viewer reacting to some religious programming with the word: boring!

At the Christophers we have experimented with various approaches for years, and we are still far from perfect in the art of TV production, but we keep trying. Recently we have produced a series called THE CHURCH ALIVE. Three segments have been completed so far on topics such as: the Eucharist, the Forgiveness of Sins, and the Communion of Saints. A fourth video on Creation and Redemption is now in production.

The first three parts aired nationally in the U.S. within our weekly TV program Christopher Closeup. One viewer wrote to me and said she cried when she watched the one on the Eucharist, and afterward took her three children to be baptized. Many touching letters came to our offices after the series aired, the most popular one was on forgiveness.

For the first time in our history we are going to buy air time to broadcast "The Forgiveness of Sins" during Holy Week this year in 20 major cities throughout the U.S. This program was funded in part by the bishop's Communication Campaign. If any of you would like a free copy of it I'll be happy to send it to you.

We are also beginning a project to send inspirational videos free of charge to third world bishops. If you're interested in participating, write to me at the Christophers, our address is a simple one, The Christophers New York, N.Y. 10017.

Returning to the question of how to mount a credible media campaign, I thought it might be useful to look at the study the U.S. bishops commissioned ten years ago. The document challenged the Catholic Church to preach the Gospel more effectively in the 1980's. I wish they had followed their own research. Nine essays were written and the one I think was most important for our purposes was written by John Seigenthaler, the man who helped found the national newspaper USA TODAY. In his chapter entitled, "A Secular Print Journalist's View" he wrote a list of tough marketing questions which managers in any field must answer before they undertake any ambitious media program.

After deciding what the problem is that they are attempting to solve, they set out to analyze the various options. Let's take a test case. Suppose you are losing many Catholics to the Fundamentalist sects in your area, and you wanted to do something to stop the leakage. Here are the questions John Seigenthaler presents for your consideration:

1. What audience are you trying to reach?
2. What message do you want to convey? (This question needs careful analysis, lest you spend a great amount of time and energy on a project that may turn out to be counter-productive. Test your theory first and analyze the reactions to assess your effectiveness. If possible get an outside professional to guide you. This is what major marketing campaigns do in the commercial world.)
3. What agencies and outlets of the Church media are to be assigned specific responsibilities in communicating the message? (Don't overlook the power of posters, leaflets, and newspaper ads in your effort to communicate your message. A multi-media campaign will have to include the pulpit. If the priests are motivated properly their impact can be significant.)
4. Should the secular media be utilized? What if anything is available to you?
5. How should Church agencies and personnel interact in the campaign you are undertaking? (A team spirit is necessary for the success of any venture.)
6. How should the needed funding be allocated?

Hopefully future projects will be answer these marketing questions before undertaking actual production.

The bishops of Africa are holding preliminary meetings to prepare for the pan-African synod of bishops to be held in 1993. Although they meet regularly on a regional basis, this will be the first continent-wide meeting of some 400 dioceses. Pope John Paul II called it "an event that demands the participation of all." To guide the synod preparations, the Holy Father appointed an 18 member secretariat, composed entirely of members of the heirarchy. The synod will deal with five major topics: evangelization, inculturation, dialogue, social communications, and justice and peace.

Although the word communications is used only once in the five topics, all five are related to the art of communications: evangelization, inculturation, dialogue, social communications and justice and peace. All involve a message, and we are living in an age where people read less and less. Will a 20,000 word document be the fruit of their labors. If so, who will read it?

Bishop Peter Sarpong of Ghana said recently that the main question behind the whole five topics is this: "What has the Word of God to say to the African people in this moment?" Indeed! How would you answer that question for your own people? How to deliver the message is essentially a marketing problem. I do not pretend to know all the answers to these difficult questions, but I do urge you to follow the best tactics for arriving at some reasonable answers.

Part two of my paper concerns Cardinal Suenens, and FIAT. With the approval of Pope Paul VI and Pope John Paul II, Cardinal Suenens, the retired Primate of Belgium, created a new spiritual initiative called FIAT, taken from the Latin, "Fiat mihi secundum verbum tuum."

The idea is to encourage people to say "yes" to God's call as Mary did. The goal is to pray with Mary to the Holy Spirit, not necessarily to her directly. Her "Yes" to the Spirit brought Christ into the world, and again at Pentecost, when she prayed with the twelve frightened Apostles to the Holy Spirit another great miracle occurred, the birthday of the Church. The Apostles left that room as new men, emboldened to speak out fearlessly and preach the Good News of the Gospel.

FIAT is a loose federation of individuals and prayer groups who pray in union with Mary to the Holy Spirit for the grace to bring Christ to the world. Each group develops its own style and character, each individual is free to go at his or her own pace, but the overall purpose is clear: evangelization. FIAT Chapters are now operating in the US, France, Spain, England, Holland and Belgium, but we are still at the fledgling stage of development.

Here are the Seven Pillars of FIAT Spirituality:

1. Pray for the grace to overcome all sin.
2. As you awaken each morning, make a solemn sign of the cross and recite one Our Father. Offer the Lord all the joys and sufferings of the day.
3. Attend daily mass, and if this is not possible, review the scripture readings of the Mass of the Day.

4. Create a prayer corner in your home with your favorite picture of Jesus on display. Spend some quiet time there each day in prayer and spiritual reading.
5. Recite the FIAT rosary daily, uniting with Mary before the Holy Spirit, recalling the story of Christ's mission on earth: to save souls and proclaim God's love to the world.
6. Join a few other friends of like mind and meet together at least once a month to encourage one another to be modern day apostles. Rely on the Holy Spirit as the Apostles did, He will guide you.
7. Witness to the Good News of God's love and mercy by living gladly because of the knowledge of His love.

We are living in an age of individualism, where the level of commitment to the community, is steadily weakening. The priests and bishops cannot do it alone. We must awaken the sleeping giant, the laity, and galvanize them to help make Christ known and loved more in this world. If we can succeed in bringing people together in groups to support and encourage one another, we won't need the broadcast media to get our message to the world.

We can't afford to buy air time, and even if we could, there are limits to what we can hope to achieve through the media, but we can ask our people to be our link with the world. Under the inspiration of the Holy Spirit we can produce home videos to form them to be lay leaders. With the help of God we can inspire our people to be modern day apostles.

The media can serve us well if we use it intelligently, by following the basic communications principles, making sure all marketing decisions are made before the script is written we can make great strides forward.

The question raised by the African bishops in preparation for their 1993 pan-African Synod, is a good one: "What has the Word of God to say to the people in this moment of history?" The four words of Jesus are there for all of us to see: LOVE, PRAY, GO, TEACH. May the Lord be your strength and your joy as you lead your people, and may Mary be your guide and inspiration.

Mary, Queen of Apostles, pray for us.

Thank you and God bless you.

Chapter 22

A VIEW FROM ADMINISTRATION AND GOVERNMENT

Frank Shakespeare

May I say, regarding the introduction of this panel, that it's the first time I have ever been identified as being to the far left of Archbishop Levada.

Father Catoir referred to diverse ways of looking at things. That reminds me of a remark by Duff Cooper, a buddy of Churchill's. He said that "For the English there are only two kinds of religion— the Roman Catholic, which is wrong, and the rest, which don't matter."

When I phoned Father Russell Smith about my participation here, I said "Father, what shall I talk about?" He said "About ten minutes."

I propose to make observations about the change that has taken place in our country in the acceptability of references by our political leaders to religion and Christianity.

I realize that non-U.S. Bishops are present and ask their indulgence for citing examples from our country only. I do so because it is that with which I am familiar.

I will cite three American presidents. . . . one from the nineteenth century, Lincoln. . . . and two from the mid-twentieth century, Roosevelt and Truman.

Abraham Lincoln used the occasion of his second inaugural in 1865 to talk to his fellow countrymen about the Civil War, just then ending. He reflected on what had happened and why it had happened. It was the shortest inaugural address in our history . . . and many think the greatest.

Listen to Lincoln's words as he refers to the two sides in the war. . . .

> Both read the same Bible, and pray to the same God, and each invokes His aid against the other. It may seem strange that any man should dare to ask a just God's assistance in wringing their bread from the sweat of other men's faces; but let us judge not that we be not judged. The prayers of both could not be answered; That of neither has been answered fully. The Almighty has His own purposes. "Woe unto the world because of offenses! For it must needs be that offenses come; but woe to that man by whom the offense cometh." If we shall suppose that American Slavery is one of those offenses which in the Providence of God must needs come, but which, having continued through His appointed time, He now wills to remove, and that He gives to both North and South this terrible war, as the woe due to those by whom the offense came, shall we discern therein any departure from those divine attributes which the believers in a Living God always ascribe to Him?

> "Fondly do we hope, fervently do we pray, that this mighty scourge of war may speedily pass away. Yet, if God wills that it continue, until all the wealth piled by the bondman's two hundred and fifty years of unrequited

toil shall be sunk, and until every drop of blood drawn with the lash shall be paid by another drawn with the sword, as was said three thousand years ago, so still it must be said the "judgements of the Lord are true and righteous altogether."

Such words, of course, are near to a prayer. No church sermon could be more profoundly spiritual. Clearly Lincoln understood himself to be a Christian leader addressing a Christian nation.

75 years later, in the mid-20th century, the climate of acceptability for religious references by our political leaders had so changed that public remarks cast in such a spiritual framework as Lincoln's would have been considered politically awkward and insensitive.

It may astonish you to know, however, that it was then still possible for presidents . . . *in official correspondence* . . . to root their observations in the most explicitly Christian principles.

I learned this during my service as U.S. Ambassador to the Holy See when reviewing the exchanges of letters between Roosevelt and Truman with Pope Pius XII during and following World War II.

As a first illustration, let me cite words from a letter which Franklin Roosevelt wrote to Pius XII in December 1939, As a world crisis threatened:

"I take heart in remembering that in a similar time Isaiah first prophesied the birth of Christ. Then, several centuries before His coming, the condition of the world was not unlike that which we see today. Then, as now, a conflagration had been set. But, in that very moment, a spiritual rebirth was foreseen, I believe that while statesmen are considering a new order of things it is even now being built silently but inevitably in the hearts of the masses whose voices are not heard, but whose common faith will write the final history of our time. They know that unless there is belief in some guiding principle, and some trust in a divine plan, nations are without light and peoples perish. They know that the civilization handed down to us by our fathers was built by men and women who knew in their hearts that all were brothers because they were children of God. They believe that by His will enmities can be healed, that in His mercy the weak find the deliverance and the strong can find grace in helping the weak."

In two 1941 letters, Roosevelt wrote . . .

March

"Only when the principles of Christianity are established can that peace which we so ardently desire be found."

September

"We desire that a firm basis for the lasting concord between men and nations founded on the principles of Christianity again be established."

Just after the war had ended, President Harry Truman wrote Pius in a similar vein (April 1946). . . .

"Although hostilities have ceased, peace has not yet been achieved. We must employ every resource at our command to bring an enduring peace. And no peace can be permanent which is not based on Christian principles."

With the west in a hard struggle to reconstruct civil society after the ravages of the war, Truman wrote Pius in 1947. . . .

"As the chosen leader of the people of the United States, I pledge full faith to work for an enduring peace. And enduring peace can be built only upon Christian principles. To such a consummation we dedicate all our resources both spiritual and material, remembering always that "except the Lord build the house they labor in vain who build it"".

"Your Holiness, this is a Christian nation. More than half century ago that declaration was written into the decrees of the highest court in this land. It is not without significance that the valiant pioneers who left Europe to establish settlements here at the very beginning of their colonial enterprises declared their faith in the Christian religion and made ample provision for its practice and for its support.

"The story of the Christian missionaries who in earliest days endured perils, hardship, even death itself in carrying the message of Jesus Christ to untutored savages is one that still moves the hearts of men.

"As a Christian nation, our earnest desire is to work with men of good will everywhere to banish war and the causes of war from the world whose Creator desired that men should live together in peace, good will and mutual trust."

By 1948, the Soviet threat was looming in the east. Peace seemed elusive. A discouraged Truman holds tightly to his faith in these words to Pius. . . .

"The years immediately behind us have been fraught with difficulties. Although hostilities came to an end, our hopes for an enduring peace have been deferred. But, we do not despair. Rather, in a spirit of rededication should we renew our labors to achieve the peace of Christ in a world too long divided by enmity, jealousy and ill will. This nation holds out the hand of fellowship to all who would seek world unity under God, the Lord and Father of us all. We can not, God forbid that we ever could, accept the teaching that religion is unnecessary, that Christianity is untrue."

In a last illustration, consider these words from Truman in December, 1949, as he makes clear his understanding of the deepest philosophical premises of then United States foreign policy . . .

"The significance of the divine call personified in the birth and mission of the savior is increasingly visible in the record of history despite the viscidities oftentimes encountered on the long path of the century.

. . . mindful of its Christian heritage, the United States gladly rededicates its efforts to the creation of a peaceful and, lasting world order."

Let me emphasize that these were official letters from American presidents to a foreign chief-of-state.

Everyone in this room knows that an American president who today expressed such thoughts as those you have heard by Lincoln, Roosevelt and Truman would be subjected to intense criticism. Our political leaders have become psychologically circumscribed by the secular humanist ethos which has risen in our nation. The extent of this conditioning becomes evident only when we focus on how our leaders once referred to the nations' spiritual premises.

It would be presumptious of me to dwell on the meaning of this change in front of men dedicating their lives to God.

May I simply observe that in the vacuum which now exists, the importance of your voice rises. You become more than ever the sign of contradiction. You are now all that we have.

Chapter 23

A VIEW FROM CATHOLIC YOUTH

Paul Lauer

With all due respect, Archbishop, I do have a few gray hairs. I got them when Father Russell called me and asked me to do this.

I'm here because I'm a miracle incarnate. I really shouldn't be here. I should be out on the streets with the rest of the young people who are lost. I was out there. I was baptized a Catholic and raised Catholic until I was about eleven. The last thing I remember is my first Holy Communion. In most of my teen years and years in college, I had no religion and I certainly didn't live with any Christian morals. But, God has His ways and I think the fact that I am standing here can be a source of hope to all of you that the Holy Spirit is working, and the Holy Spirit is calling young people, in very strange ways. So, your work is not in vain.

I was in a rock band. That was my career. At that time, I had a major conversion in my life, which I won't get into now. Maybe you can invite me to your dioceses sometime and I'll tell it to your youth there. I quit my band and I moved into the desert for two years, and learned about God, and the Catholic Church, and read a lot of books. And when I came out of the desert, God gave me an apostolate to youth, an apostolate through communications.

I started a magazine in my parent's garage with $3000 from my Jewish grandfather's will. He left it for religious purposes. He was an orthodox Jew. I think he's rolling in his grave now. But he was an excellent man. I called the magazine *Veritas Catholic Youth magazine,* and I recently changed the title to *YOU!* magazine. That was three years ago and I've since gotten into other areas of the media, like video producing, and I have my eyes on television and radio—you name it, I want to do it.

At any rate, thanks be to God, this stuff is working. And a lot of people ask why. Just prior to *Veritas Catholic Youth Magazine* there was a magazine put out called *Catholic Teen.* It didn't work. So people wonder why mine is. And bouncing off of something Father Catoir said, one of the reasons it's working is because is goes to the heart. And the reason it goes to the heart is because it's coming from my heart. This isn't a set of rules and regulations or theories that you would read in a book. This is based on my own experience, what brought me back to the Church, what totally changed my life.

We try to see pop culture through the eyes of faith. It's very important for the Church not to turn its back on pop culture, which is having the greatest influence on young people and the world as a whole. But, rather, we must look at pop culture, all of it—the music, dancing, the fashions, the movies, the language—and put it into perspective through the eyes of faith. Youth need us to do that.

And we must challenge young people. At Veritas, we never look at young people as being incapable of rising to the occasion of following Jesus Christ, of making a radical commitment. We believe they can because we have done it ourselves and because God has given us the grace and he will give it to others. So, we challenge other young people to that radical commitment. Young people have guts. It takes a lot of guts to paint your hair pink, put an earring through your nose, and show up to Grandma's Christmas Eve party! These are things only young people would do!

Our Lady was a young person. She was a teenager. And that which was asked of her was even more radical than the things teenagers do today. An maybe that's why God asked it of a teenager.

We offer alternatives. Instead of just telling people what they are doing is wrong—which I realize is important—we offer alternatives to say "yes" to. Instead of always saying this is what we say "no" to, we build up what we say "yes" to. Instead of talking about how premarital sex is wrong, we talk about how chastity is right. That had profound effect in my life. Because when my friend called me and started telling me about the Church, I was far away from it. He could have condemned me for all the things I was doing, But instead, he said, "Listen Paul, what you're doing is interesting and everything, but you should check this out. This is even more radical. This is even more exciting."

And as I said, it's working. The youth are responding. There are miracles going on right now. The miracle of my own conversion and the miracles of the conversions of the letters we get from young people. Why right now? I think five years ago this magazine would not have done as well. Why is it doing well right now? Because the world is ready, especially the Western World. Our sins are catching up to us. We young people are inheriting the results of our parents' sins of the '60's where we left all our traditions and our Judeo-Christian beliefs. The results are abortion, AIDS, suicide, gangs, drug abuse.

Young people want a way out. People want a way out. They're searching for alternatives. And I believe this is a profound point we have to look at in terms of the media. I live in L.A. I grew up in L.A. I have a lot of young friends who are in the media, in music, in television, in motion pictures. And I am seeing more and more that in the media there will be a demand for good, moral material, because society is hungry for it. And it will sell!

Who can give us that good moral media? Who else but the Christians, the God-fearing people who have it in them. Why is Veritas working? Because it comes from the heart. It comes from me. And when these studio executives go looking for somebody who can give them a good television show, a good movie, they're not going to find those people in their ranks. Because they don't have it in them. But we do! We young Christians, we young Catholics, we have it in us provided it's given to us, and provided we are well formed. And that's why its so important now to form young Catholics, to encourage them to go out into the world and take their faith and apply it to bring God and His truth out of the Church and into society.

The Church needs to be more involved in the media. In the Middle Ages, the Church was responsible for building huge cathedrals that people marvel at today. Where are the cathedrals today? What cathedrals are we building? I believe we could build some beautiful cathedrals in the media. Some beautiful movies. But is it your job as Bishops? Are you called to go and produce and direct and write a movie? Maybe a few of you. But more often than not, it's the mission of lay people, and that's the miracle of the age we are living in today—that the lay people in the Church are coming to action.

Your responsibility, I believe, is to call them to action. I guarantee everybody in this room knows somebody important in the media, someone who has influence. Have you had dinner with that person? Have you sat down and said, "Hey, you know, you are really in an important position, are you using it the way God would have you use it?"

I believe you, as bishops, like no one else can call upon these people. Befriend these people and encourage them. Because just as my speaking here will encourage you, which in turn will encourage perhaps millions of other people, so your invitation to one person in the media to use his or her talents more directly for God will influence tens of millions of people! So, I beg you to help people like myself and other young people who are trying to work in the media, we who are professionals, who are trained, who have the talents, and can apply them with your support.

I want to tell you a little experience I had that I really feel my apostolate stemmed from. I was praying in church one day before the Blessed Sacrament and I imagined Jesus was a king sitting on this throne. And I went before the King and I thought of myself as his soldier. I said Lord, King, I know there is a battle going on out there, and I want to fight on your side. I want to be on your team. What shall I fight with? And I imagined that Jesus held up a huge blazing sword with all this light coming off of it. And I thought, "What the heck is that?" I went home and I thought about it some more, and I realized that that sword is the sword of truth. What's important today is not that that sword cuts off heads, but rather that it is seen, that it's presented, that the truth is given.

And so, as other Christs you present that sword of truth like St. Paul did. That is your most important role. That's what affected me the most, and that's what affects my peers, the young people. It's not how you do business. It's not how you play golf or how you do anything. It's how much like Christ you are.

Chapter 24

A VIEW FROM IN FRONT OF THE CAMERA

Bill Plante

As the final speaker, it may well be that the greatest contribution I can make is to be brief. That comes naturally enough to those of us in television. We do everything briefly. There is an old joke which has gone around Washington for years, which has it that if television had existed at the time the ten commandments were delivered, the report probably would have gone something like this.

"Good evening. At Mt. Sinai today, God gave Moses ten commandments. Here are the three most important."

So, in that spirit, let me make a few observations.

We know that radio and television are pervasive in the daily lives of people in this country and of most western nations. In many a household, the television is on six to seven hours a day. About seventy to eighty percent of the people in this country get their news primarily from television.

Broadcasting, I think—particularly news broadcasting—*reflects* society's concerns and values more than it shapes them, which may have something to do with what we're talking about. I can talk to you about news broadcasting. It's what I know best. And I would suggest to you that if you would communicate Catholic values through journalists, then you have to take into account a number of things, some of which may seem obvious, but may be worth restating.

First of all, in a pluralistic society such as we have, the truth is regarded not as revealed, but as objective—demonstrable to those who seek it. And all things which cannot be proved according to the rigors of the scientific method are deemed matters of opinion, about which people may differ. Society accepts few absolutes. Truth is believed in this society to emerge from diversity of voices or points of view. Thus, conflict becomes essential to ascertaining truth.

Second, journalists tend to be skeptical and adversarial. We are often accused of being liberal, in the sense that we are thought to be left of center on the political spectrum. The fact is, I think, that most reporters are not ideological, but are anti-authoritarian and iconoclastic—challengers of the status quo. They usually view power, whether it is secular or ecclesiastical, as corrupt and self-serving, more likely than not.

Finally, there is one other thing to take into account: the public—by and large—is smarter than it is generally given credit for being. The public is not easily fooled, particularly over the longer term. Nor is it anywhere as easy to manipulate as some imagine.

So the Church can, I think, communicate through the news media, but only if it understands some of the things we are discussing and is willing to mingle in the marketplace of ideas. This is not, I think you will agree, a natural concept for most people in the Church.

272

The thoughts or actions of a Bishop may carry some special weight if the message is seen on television—but those thoughts will not be stamped with the magisterium. And that, I think has created a problem for the Church and its members in the past.

Does getting the message across become a question of technique or charisma—the former being more easily acquired than the latter? A brief look at he political contest may be helpful.

Take the case of Ronald Reagan, who was unlike most politicians and pretended not to be one—and did not boast a particularly fine grasp of detail. He was a delegator, who often did not know—nor particularly care—what was going on. He used to take great delight in his response when we yelled at him: "Mr. President, Mr. President, what are you going to do about such and such?" He would stop for a minute—the pause was always timed perfectly—and look back over his shoulder with a wink and a grin. Then he'd say, "Well, I don't know. They haven't told me yet."

Ronald Reagan could convince himself of anything, as he once told us. He was successful despite his lack of experience and detail, because he understood very well that his strongest point was his ability to articulate a vision and deliver a message. The message was always consistent through his twenty years of active political life: lower taxes, less government, a strong military. The moral message was consistent as well.

Now George Bush, by contrast, as active as he is personally, seems mostly reactive when it come to things like decision making or expressing a vision. He appears to have no domestic policy. He has a difficult time explaining his goals to the public. I would include in that the present conflict. [The war in Kuwait]

The point I am trying to make is simply this: it is far easier to communicate something if you believe it.

No problem—unless of course what you believe is not generally accepted in the larger society. From abortion to human sexuality, to womens' issues to academic freedom, the Church—and I think specifically the Bishops—are often at odds with the majority. (They are often at odds as well with many of the faithful—but that is not my province or my point.)

Abortion is an example. I think you are probably sick of hearing this, but here's a situation in which you have U.S. Catholics believing in roughly the same proportion as the general population (approximately 60–35) that abortion should be legal, regardless of their personal beliefs.

The Bishops had very little luck last fall pressuring Catholic politicians and voters. Abortion was not a defining issue in any Congressional race. Talk of excommunication in one instance didn't help. Neither, as far as I can tell, did spending a fair amount of money on a public relations firm.

Confrontation did not work where politicians and voters were concerned. It was one more example of the failure to make human behavior fit dogma—whether it is Christian dogma or Marxist dogma, civil or ecclesiastic law.

Issues of conscience can certainly be brought before the public, but probably not forced upon them in this society. A significant portion of the broad public we serve simply does not understand the teaching of the Church. There is hostility from some members of the media as well as from some members of the public. This is to be expected. You must expect the teaching of the Church to be challenged as sexist, medieval and worse. You have heard the litany.

I can only suggest that in responding, the soft answer turns away wrath much more effectively than the Jeremiad. I don't envy you your obligation as teachers and shepherds. I do suggest to you that it is possible to work through the media, but only if you labor to understand the conventions of the media and of the larger society—where hostility or indifference will often be expressed.

Finally, I cannot leave this lectern without voicing to you the concerns of some people, concerns which I have heard in both a professional and personal context. People who knew that I would be here today implored me to communicate to you concerns they have which they believe to be formed in conscience. I make no judgements. I am the messenger.

Women particularly anguish over what they perceive to be their exclusion from positions of authority and influence in the Church. They have many other problems with Church teaching which, in their view, flow from that. I don't need to take you through it. Many who grew up in the Church are alienated—or worse yet, indifferent—because they see no home. I can only conclude from that that your message is not getting through. There are ways to assure that it does.

Postscript

Dialogue with Cardinal Ratzinger

BISHOP: It surprised me somewhat in reflecting back on it that Father Gill in his presentation about conscience and psychology seemed to indicate that from the discipline of modern psychology there is no consideration of conscience as such. I wonder if you have any thoughts from your perspective whether this is psychology from a too narrowly conceived modern experimental idea, or whether it's simply an American look at psychology?

CARDINAL RATZINGER: I think this is a special aspect of the more general problem of the relation between modern sciences and the level and method of theology and philosophy.

In psychology we have the classical approach of the modern sciences and this is an empirical and phenomenological approach. Science can study only those things which are empirically verifiable. It can not study the question of being as such, or the question of God, because God does not appear.

The level of modern science is the level of what is an empirical matter and verifiable. The consequence for psychology is that here we can study the function of realizing and preparing moral judgements. I think the level of psychology is the level of function.

The question of psychology is how does the formation of moral judgements function? This is a very important thing for pedagogy and for healing ill consciences. But the theological level is, what is conscience?

In correspondence to the two levels you could see the study of values, since values are a concrete reality. Even eating is a value, having a good dinner is a value. We have many values and we must find priorities between the values. But you can not have a final decision between these values, only a balance between different values.

The key word of theology is not value, it's truth. Truth does not appear in the sciences. In sciences about conscience we have the function, but not the truth. But only truth can give us the final decision between values, and can give us what to choose in the given situation from the values offered.

In this sense, I think theology is broad and open since psychology is limited to what I can observe and realize and verify with empirical methods. Theology can integrate this. I think it's very important to take account of all these concrete observations to be a real good pastor and educator. Theology can integrate them and must integrate them. It must take account of all concrete experiences, but it is broad and, seeing God, seeing the last foundation of our being, it can give also the last ultimate appreciation of values.

Perhaps another example could clarify this more from guilt feelings. We heard some things in the different papers about guilt feelings. I think it was very illuminating to hear what Father Mulligan said to a person with guilt complexes. He, as a priest, and as a Christian theologian, finally after hearing the report of this person could say, "I have good news, you do not have guilt complex, you are guilty." This was redemptive, because if you are guilty, you can convert and there is pardon in the grace of Christ.

The psychologist can not say this. He can give analysis, knowledge, and ideas about behavior. He cannot give a new reality and, in effect, pardon. So conversion and a new beginning is only given where we have the reality of a speaking and revealing God.

Perhaps thus you can see what are the different levels, how synthesis and integration in theology is possible and in what sense theology possibly needs the contribution of these sciences while only theology can give the final answers.

BISHOP: I am asking myself if, in the popular Catholic mind we bishops are looked upon something like the Pentagon or the Board of Governors of General Motors, or something impersonal, and not at all in line with what Jesus himself said, "who hears you, hears me, and who hears me hears not me but the one who sent me". We know from our own pastoral experience that a great many people would never think of disobeying Jesus or going against His word, or refusing the opportunity to grow in relationship with Him or enter into eternal life in relationship with him. But, when it comes to listening to the bishops or the magisterium, well, that's something else. What is our responsibility in relation to that?

CARDINAL RATZINGER: Yes. We have this responsibility. I could perhaps say three things. The first, the Church is living in a determinate time and in a certain sense is always conditioned by that time. We have seen this in the past. We can say in the time of Constantine there were certain errors in the concrete behavior between Church and state, and we can say that in the Medieval Church this or that was not so good. We can say that in the last century the Church was too perhaps conservative or something.

It is not so easy for us to see our own determination from the conditions of our times, but it is clear that we are also in a certain sense the victims of our time and we must be open to reflect and to improve these problems, if possible.

One of our problems is that we live in a period of increasing anonymization. So in the Church we need more common work, more consultation, more team work, and this is very important. The word magisterium is one of the words which show how we are a little anonymized in the great bodies of consultation and realization.

I think we must do our best to find the right balance. On the one hand we have a really common work of consultation, of finding answers within the common service of the one gospel in the common responsibility of the pastors in the world. We must realize and apply all the instruments of collegiality and common finding of answers in bishops' conferences and committees.

But, on the other hand, we may not stay behind these anonymous collective realities, rather we must personalize the common word in our personal responsibility as pastors. This was one of my ideas when I spoke of better balance between conference and pastor. All the common work is really necessary, but it is also necessary to personalize our work so that people can see that this is not only an anonymous power speaking with us. This is my pastor who is personally convinced and is with his person identified with the message of the Lord in the Church of our time. He speaks with the Lord, and he speaks to me because he has spoken with the Lord and understood the word of the Lord. This is the first point.

The second point concerns your observation that people will not be disobedient to Our Lord, but disobedient and in contradiction to their pastor.

I think that obedience to Our Lord becomes concrete in our obedience to the concrete Church. Here I am thinking of Romano Guardini. For a time he lost his faith and in his conversion he found the Lord but at the same time he found also that one is in a real relation to God only if God is concrete and not just my idea. I must be obedient not to an idea of God, but to a speaking God, to a God who is real in relation to me and His own word. And so refinding God was to refind Christ. But, he came necessarily to a third step saying to the Lord, yes, speak in the gospel; but if I am only confronted with the written word, really I find just my own exposition and I can yes to the Lord, I am in agreement. But, finally, this is only myself who is in agreement with myself and I am using the Lord. And so Guardini understood that obedience to God becomes concrete only as obedience to the speaking God, but obedience to the speaking God is concrete and real only if He is speaking in present, and not just in past times.

So obedience to the speaking God, to Jesus is necessary, obedience to God here and now in His body, in the Church. I think it is clearly much more easy to be faithful to the past Jesus than to accept the body, the incarnate God here in my days. So the distinction and division between Jesus and the Church is a maneuver to avoid an obedience that could be too concrete, too difficult for me.

I think this could be and must be a moment in our education in faith to find Jesus is speaking now in the world and He continues to be incarnate and so He continues to be also a scandal as he was in his lifetime. Only if we come to an obedience to this concrete scandal of an incarnate God who has a body here and now, and has a voice here and now in the present do we arrive at Jesus Himself.

The third point is that you are right when you say we must do all that's possible to help people understand. Here, certainly, we are insufficient with the Roman magisterium alone. I think here we can see one of the reasons is because our Lord would not only have Peter and Peter's successors, but the whole collegium of the apostles and their successors sharing the common responsibility to translate the word of the Lord in all different situations. What the Roman magisterium is saying must be translated, must be concretized in many cultural situations.

A document from Rome can be good, and we hope it is good. But, it is too far from the language, from the experiences, from the concrete life, inner culture of people. It needs a concrete subject and a living voice. I think the consultations, the symphony between what the policy is saying and the concrete pastoral responsibilities of the bishops is absolutely necessary to speak an understandable word.

BISHOP: In Catholic moral theology there is that discussion concerning nutrition and hydration. There are at least two positions of moral reasoning trying to come to some sort of a reasonable conclusion concerning this issue. The theological discussion continues.

In your opinion, do you think we are beginning to approximate some maturity in that discussion that eventually will permit some sort of a conclusion?

CARDINAL RATZINGER: I hope we are moving in that direction. As you perhaps know, the Holy See three or four years ago had the intention to publish a definitive word about this problem. We studied it. It was also elaborated in a paper. But, finally, the cardinals who reviewed it found that this is not mature enough to be published as the word of the magisterium at this time.

The problem is that the basic principles are clear. We do not have sovereignty over life. We are obliged and must do all that's possible to assist and to help life from the first moment to the last moment. That principle is clear. The problem is only what will in reality be this non-sovereignty, but service to human life in given situations.

It was clear for us that we do not have sufficient evidence about the different possible and imaginable situations and that with the progress of medicine every day there can arise new and more unforeseen situations which may not find a correct answer in our text.

It was at that given moment impossible with the studies at our disposition to give a complete and sufficiently general and in the same moment sufficiently concrete answer which could embrace all the different possible situations.

So, we tabled the paper and invited the American bishops to continue their studies. I think that the Doctrinal Committee and also the Pope John Center are continuing with these studies. But, I hope we can soon publish an answer. I think the problem is approaching maturation, and I hope we can with the help, especially of the American bishops because you have the more sophisticated medicine, find in a not too distant future a synthesis which is a general view which does not go to the singular situations, but is sufficient to give illumination in the essential situations.

BISHOP: My question concerns what moral theologians call the perplexed conscience. Is it possible in the present time that there are many of our faithful people who have a perplexed conscience because of the many different opinions they are hearing. Can they simply follow the norm for a perplexed conscience and choose the lesser evil in their decisions?

CARDINAL RATZINGER: As an empirical fact I think there is really many people who find themselves in this situation. I think the *real* situation where I can only choose the lesser evil can not be so frequent. Perhaps what we heard from Father Ashley, from Professor Haas and others could help here. There are moral norms without exceptions. These norms contain moral values as the expression of the message of our being, of our likeness with God. I never can do these acts, because it's always sinful to do them, and here I can not accept the situation of *minus malum* because we must always avoid or exclude these acts.

Where we do not have such exceptionless norms, here we are in the situation of balance and of a choice. I am not a moralist so I can not give a sufficient answer for all the implicit problems of such cases. I think the essential point is the distinction between exceptionless norms which really explain our likeness to God, the message of our being and where in every situation I must say this act is impossible, I can not do it and the second level of values where choice is possible.

BISHOP: There are certain moral theologians who have questioned the level of theological certainty regarding certain things such as the intrinsic evil of abortion. Now, it was our understanding that a papal document was being prepared about moral issues. We were hoping that there would be some kind of a theological note established to help us deal with some of these moral issues. Could you let us know what's happening and what we can expect?

CARDINAL RATZINGER: As you know in 1987, the Holy Father announced in a letter to the Redemptorist Fathers his intention to prepare a moral encyclical. The first intention of the Holy Father was to publish it in the year 1987, but it was too difficult to do it. Some other priorities took precedent.

So, now by 1991, the Holy Father has worked during this time, has had consultations and much work is done. I cannot give an exact date. The first idea was really to publish it at the end of last year or at the beginning of this year, but there were two important encyclicals to be written. *"Ad Gentes"* on the missions was published twenty-five years ago. So it was necessary to publish some new encyclical about missions in this given moment. This was a priority because, as you know, the problem of the necessity of missions and the theological and anthropological foundation of missions is very urgent, with all the new theories about anonymous Christians and salvation by non-Christian religions. So it was very necessary to give answers to these problem.

If I am right, in the Spring we will have the hundred years anniversary of *Rerum Novarum*. The social problem is also urgent and important. This is a very great date: May 15, 1891. *Rerum Novarum* was the first important Catholic word on the part of the Roman magisterium about these problems. An anniversary encyclical about this problem must now be published. I would say at Easter time. Given that the Holy Father cannot publish an encyclical every month, he must give some time to read it and to meditate on it. He must make it helpful to the thinking of our Christian people, because it's not entertainment between bishops. It is for the Church.

He cannot publish the encyclical on morality right after Easter. But I would think, perhaps,—this is my hypothesis only—on the Feast of the Apostles or perhaps better in autumn.

It is true is that the Holy Father is working, is thinking and has the firm intention to publish it in this year. But, I must add, he said to me, when he was writing the encyclical about the Holy Spirit at a given time he found it too difficult and he stopped work. And two years later he made a new beginning and finally it was possible to publish it. So, it's always difficult. But I think this year could be the date of publication.

Regarding the contents, I can say it's not an encyclical about concrete issues, about concrete topics such as abortion or contraception, or some other things. It is a magisterial expression about the fundaments of how the Catholic Church can and must be a teacher in moral things. As you know, there are some quite different theories, even theories that the Holy Bible does not have concrete and obliging contents in moral things, only stimulations. Thus human reason must find the answer, and the Church could not teach concretely that such and such is wrong, but could only give advice such as, you must be good.

Over against all these theories and in all this confusion that we have, the Holy Father thought it would be important to have a clear idea in a broader sense: is the Church a moral teacher not only in a general sense, but really a concrete moral teacher? Are the teachings of the Church given especially in the last hundred years valid, even in all the centuries of the life of the Church?

The Holy Father will not be a part of the concrete academic discussions. But the fundamental problems indicated in words like consequentialism, proportionalism, and so on must be taken into account. I think the Holy Father is very anxious to respect academic freedom in the special area of theology. But, also as supreme pastor at this time he is anxious to give the essentials: fundaments of why and in what sense the Church can give moral teaching, what are the essential fundaments in scripture and tradition, and what are the obligations deriving from the certain magisterium of the Church?

In this sense, I think you can find an answer to your question about this attitude. I think the Holy Father will not give theological notes, this is a work for theologians to do. But he will give the great principles with which to distinguish and to have, as pastor, a clear conception about what obligations we can speak of.

BISHOP: All of us as bishops labor under the occupational hazard of having everything we say and do interpreted by our people, or priests, more or less accurately, but also what we do not say and what we do not do is often very much interpreted also. We are teaching by our silence, too, and the tension in us between our roles of shepherd and prophet is there. You have been most courageous in your life and your work, which we all much appreciate. Can you say just a word about the necessity to speak out or how you would look on that big problem?

CARDINAL RATZINGER: I think we heard in this conference some wonderful things about the virtue of prudence that give us the formation of our conscience as pastors and shepherds in this difficult problem of how to speak and how to be silent. As you also know, many people are saying the Holy See is speaking too much. You give answers to all things. We are indeed also educated Christians and do not need so many perceptions, they say.

On the other hand, for example, in the case of nutrition and hydration, many people are saying, why are you silent? Why do you not give some advice?

This is a very difficult decision of when to be silent, and when to have the courage also to speak in contradiction of the situation of our time, or with important groups in the Church.

I think it's impossible to give a general rule in this moment. I think the principle of personal responsibility is so important in the constitution of the Church and also a fundamental reason that Our Lord would give into the hands of persons with a responsible conscience the responsibility to decide with the prudence of a good pastor what to do in this moment for His faithful people.

Christian prudence is not to be understood in the sense of a man who always finds a way out, but prudence will give a perception of what the Lord is saying in real ecclesiastical conscience is our responsibility, in the eyes of our Lord, and so is to be found in communion with Our Lord. And as the fruit of our prayerful communion with the Lord, and our communion with the Church we discover the moment for speaking, the moment of tolerance and of silence.

So, I think we must really renew our perception of what is Christian prudence, what is Christian wisdom as the common way with Our Lord, with His present truths in the world. The truth which speaks and which can also give the space for maturation. So, our final personal responsibility, but always as a result of our deep communion with the body of Christ and with Christ, is to give an answer.

BISHOP: If we accept conscience as a memory, an anamnesis without the obligation that synderesis gives, maybe we are accepting that the commandments of conscience are not obligatory?

CARDINAL RATZINGER: It depends always upon the interpretation of the word. I think in last instance there is not a great difference between anamnesis and synderesis. I think we have a correspondence between the two expressions. Anamnesis would not say I have only ideas of information. If we would understand anamnesis or memory only in the sense of some information given in my heart, it could not be sufficient. It's an obliging anamnesis, because it is the voice of my being, no? In this sense I would understand anamnesis as the obliging voice of my being, as the presence of the truth as such with its obliging force as of the good in my being. I had no intention to diminish the obliging force but to underline it.

Another problem is the problem between this primordial original conscience and the concrete judgement of the conscience and the erroneous conscience. Here I think it's important to return to the complete doctrine of Aquinas and to see not only the article five in question nineteen of the *Prima Secundae* but also to see article six. Five speaks about the obligation of erroneous conscience. Six speaks about the deeper conscience I have. It declares that ignorance is not in every case excusing, because I must know, and I do know what God has written in my heart.

According to my information, it was Father Sertillanges who forgot to speak in his book about Thomas about article six and spoke only about article five, saying conscience only is our norm. On the one hand this seems to give new importance to conscience. But on the other hand, I must say he has reduced the importance of conscience because it's only the voice of my personal thinking and does not continue to be the voice of God really present and perceptible.

And so the important task of our moment is to recover the complete doctrine of Aquinas. Whether we apply the word synderesis or anamnesis is not so important. For me, anamnesis is clearer, but if for another the other word is clearer, I agree.

BISHOP: Would you have any thoughts you would like to share with us about the moral dimensions of the current war in the Middle East?

CARDINAL RATZINGER: I think it's too difficult for me, because on the one hand you have given your paper about peace and war. And now we must perhaps in the light of the actual events begin again to study this paper and what are the consequences. Perhaps it would be the moment to take the document in hand and to see it now not in theory, but concretely applied to a given case, and what are the consequences.